Google® Analytics

Mary E. Tyler and Jerri Ledford

WILEY

Wiley Publishing, Inc.

Google® Analytics

Published by
Wiley Publishing, Inc.
10475 Crosspoint Boulevard
Indianapolis, IN 46256

Copyright © 2006 by Wiley Publishing, Inc., Indianapolis, Indiana

ISBN-13: 978-0-470-05385-0
ISBN-10: 0-470-05385-2

Manufactured in the United States of America

10 9 8 7 6 5 4 3 2

1MA/SZ/QY/QW/IN

For general information on our other products and services or to obtain technical support, please contact our Customer Care Department within the U.S. at (800) 762-2974, outside the U.S. at (317) 572-3993 or fax (317) 572-4002.

Library of Congress Cataloging-in-Publication Data:

Tyler, Mary E., 1970-
  Google Analytics / by Mary E. Tyler and Jerri Ledford.
    p. cm.
  Includes index.
  ISBN-13: 978-0-470-05385-0 (paper/website)
  ISBN-10: 0-470-05385-2 (paper/website)
  1. Google Analytics. 2. Internet searching—Statistical services.
  3. Web usage mining—Computer programs. 4. Internet users
  —Statistics—Data processing.   I. Ledford, Jerri L. II. Title.
  TK5105.885.G66T95 2007
  658.8'7202854678
                  2006020710

From Jerri: To Beckie, who believes in me enough to take the first step herself, and for Connie, who never stopped cheering . . . ever. I love you both!

From Mary: To Jim Roberts of Carnegie Mellon University, who taught me to teach. To Lorrie Kim, who said, "This is too good to keep to yourself." To Jerri Ledford, my co-author and mentor, who said, "You can do this." Again. And again. And again. And for Mom, because there aren't enough words.

About the Authors

Mary E. Tyler is a professional technology journalist and a former software and web developer. She specializes in Open Source, enterprise software, intellectual property, motorcycles, and anything Macintosh. Tyler has three daughters, four cats, one small, fluffy lapdog, and a spouse in the career military.

Jerri Ledford has been a freelance business-technology writer for more than 10 years, with more than 700 articles, profiles, news stories, and reports online and in print. Her publishing credits include: *Intelligent Enterprise, Network World, Information Security Magazine, DCM Magazine, CRM Magazine*, and *IT Manager's Journal*. She has also written a number of books. When not writing, she divides her time between Mississippi and Tennessee, hiking, gardening, playing with electronic gadgets, and spending time with friends and family, who refer to her fondly as "tech support."

Credits

Acquisitions Editor
Katie Mohr

Development Editor
William Bridges

Technical Editor
Todd Meister

Production Editor
William A. Barton

Copy Editor
C.M. Jones

Editorial Manager
Mary Beth Wakefield

Production Manager
Tim Tate

Vice President and Executive Group Publisher
Richard Swadley

Vice President and Executive Publisher
Joseph B. Wikert

Project Coordinator
Kristie Rees

Graphics and Production Specialists
Carrie A. Foster
Stephanie D. Jumper
Jennifer Mayberry
Lynsey Osborn

Quality Control Technician
Brian H. Walls

Media Development Specialists
Angela Denny
Kit Malone
Travis Silvers

Proofreading and Indexing
Evelyn W. Still
Techbooks

Contents

Acknowledgments

From Mary: First, thanks to my stellar agent, Laura Lewin, and the staff at Studio B. They're good folks. Thanks to Bill Bridges, our developmental editor; Todd Meister, tech editor; Katie Mohr, who acquired this book for the publisher, and everyone else at Wiley who made it printable. Thanks, also, to the engineers at Google who answered our questions and to the cool staff of Browsercam.

Endless gratitude to my fellow writers online, who gave me community, advice, and various kicks in the pants as needed. There are too many to name, but they all hang out at The Writing Mother and Jay's Writers' World. For first books, there are simply too many people to thank. Apologies to anyone I forgot.

From Jerri: Mary, I really appreciate your bringing me in on this project. It's been a wild ride, girl! You're a phenomenal writer, and I've learned much along the way.

We couldn't have created the book without the help of some very dedicated "Googlites." To David Salinas, Brett Crosby, Christina Powell, Michael Mayzel, and Brandon McCormick, thanks for all your help and for pointing us in the right direction. And thanks to my very own "Google Guy," Alex Ortiz. Your passion for and belief in Google Analytics comes through, my friend. I am more appreciative than you'll ever know for your answers and your efforts in ensuring that there aregreat screenshots for our readers to see.

There's also an entire team of people at Wiley who helped make the book possible. Mary has mentioned several, and I'll add my thanks to Katie Mohr and Mary Beth Wakefield (wonderful, helpful people) and Bill Bridges, the funniest, easiest-to-work-with development editor I've encountered. And Todd Meister, who gets huge thanks for ensuring the technical accuracy of the book. His suggestions guaranteed that you, the reader, would understand exactly what we meant.

Introduction

In late 2005, Internet behemoth Google purchased leading web analytics firm Urchin and began offering the service free of charge to certain well-placed technology publications' web sites. It wasn't long before Google launched the Google Analytics service based on the Urchin software, free to the general public. Response was incredible — overwhelming — and a quarter of a million new accounts were created overnight, with an estimated half to three-quarters of a million web sites tracked.

All of this caught Google unprepared, and people had to be turned away because there weren't enough resources to support everyone who wanted an account. Google began taking e-mail addresses for interested webmasters who couldn't be accommodated at launch.

How did this happen? How did Google so grossly underestimate the demand for Google Analytics? After all, at $200/month, Urchin did only well — they had good software and a relatively low price point for the industry, but they weren't exactly inundated with clamoring customers.

Apparently, assessments based on Urchin's sales weren't exactly accurate. The demand for real analytics is huge and the price tag of "free" is exactly the price tag that draws in the masses.

But what are analytics? Most webmasters know enough to realize that they need analytics. But do they know how to read them? How to use them? Are analytics just "site stats on steroids," or can they be used by the average webmaster, who is a layman not a professional, to improve the performance of a web site?

The purpose of *Google Analytics* is to explain the concepts behind analytics and to show how to set up Google Analytics, choose goals and filters, read Google Analytics reports and graphs, and use that information to improve your web-site performance.

You'll also find numerous examples of how other companies use these reports to do business better. The authors have even included examples (though sometimes not flattering) of their own sites and usage patterns to help you understand the value of Google Analytics.

Overview of the Book and Technology

Google Analytics is a powerful tool for measuring the success of your web site, your marketing efforts, and your products and services. With that in mind, we'll strive to give you all of the tools you'll need to begin using the program immediately. You'll find an explanation of how to get started using Google Analytics, as well as chapters on how to find and use reports.

We've also tried to explain what each of the reports means, in the grand scope of your business. Where it's appropriate, we'll tell you how these reports apply to our personal web sites; and where it's not, you'll find both fictional examples and examples of real companies that use Google Analytics.

How This Book Is Organized

You'll find that the book is divided into several parts. Each part corresponds with a section on the Google Analytics user interface. Here's a quick map of what each part contains:

- Part I: Introduction — In this first part, you'll find three chapters. Chapter 1 introduces you to the concept of analytics and the reasons why you should use Google Analytics. And then, in Chapters 2 and 3, we compare Google Analytics to a program with which you may already be familiar — AWStats.

- Part II: Setting Up Google Analytics — Google Analytics can be a little intimidating when you first see the program. This section walks you through getting started in five quick chapters. Chapter 4 gives you the skinny on signing up for Google Analytics and navigating the user interface. Chapter 5 gets you started setting the program up. In Chapter 6 we try to demystify filters and filtering, and then we take that a step further by explaining goals and goal setting in Chapter 7. The last chapter in this section, Chapter 8, covers integrating Google Analytics with Google's AdWords.

- Part III: The Reporting Dashboards — We get into the meat of Google Analytics in the three chapters in Part III. Each of these chapters looks at a different Analytics dashboard, so Chapter 9 covers the Executive

Dashboard, Chapter 10 the Marketer Dashboard, and Chapter 11 the Webmaster Dashboard.

- Part IV: Marketing Optimization — The Dashboards are quick overviews of various views of your Analytics data. The chapters in Part IV are the first to go deep into that data. In these chapters you'll find marketing-specific metrics including Unique-Visitor Tracking in Chapter 12 and Visitor Segmenting in Chapter 13. If it's Marketing Campaign Results that you want to track, you'll find those reports in Chapter 14. And Chapter 15 shows you the value and results of Search Engine Marketing.

- Part V: Content Optimization — Content is more than just the articles that you place on a web site. It includes several other factors, all of which are covered in the five chapters in this section of the book. Chapter 16 shows you the reports that help you track which versions of your advertisements are most effective. Chapter 17 shows you the top-performing content on your site, and Chapter 18 helps you understand how the navigational structure of your site affects how visitors use it. You'll also find additional information about goals and something called Funnel Processes in Chapter 19; and in Chapter 20, we show you how to find clues about Web Design Parameters.

- Part VI: E-Commerce Analysis — If you run an e-commerce web site, you'll be happy to see this final section of the book. Each chapter focuses on some element of your e-commerce site. Chapter 21 focuses on Commerce Tracking, while Chapter 22 shows you everything you need to know about Loyalty & Latency. In Chapter 23 you'll see how you can quickly identify your most effective sources of revenues, and Chapter 24 helps you dig out everything you need to know about Product Merchandising.

We suggest that whether you're interested in Google Analytics for marketing, e-commerce, or content optimization, you should skim through the whole book first. Even if you don't want to know which of the pages on your site sell the most gadgets, there is value to be found in those reports, and we show you where to find it.

Once you've read through the book, you can flip back and forth between the pages to refresh your memory on how to use a report or where to find it.

One thing you may notice is that some reports are duplicated in these pages. In an effort to make it easier to work through and understand Google Analytics, we've left these repetitive reports in place. Each report is in a section of the book that corresponds with a section in Google Analytics. If you don't know where something is located in the program, look at the illustrations in the book. They'll show you exactly where we found it.

One more note about the illustrations you'll find here. You may notice that some of them seem to have no data. We've done this on purpose. Chances are that there will be areas of Google Analytics where data is not yet being collected. This is because you have to set up your web site and some of the reports and then give them time to collect data. We're leaving these blank figures just so that you can see what they might look like before you have data in them.

Who Should Read this Book

Do you have a web site or blog that you'd like to track? Can you control the HTML on that site? If that's you, you've got the right book. We tried to explain everything in the pages that follow in the context of how small business owners and microbusiness owners might need to use it. These concepts apply to home business owners as well.

Depending on where you are with your Google Analytics account, you might be able to skim over certain sections of the book. For example, if you've already set up a Google account and your Analytics account, you can glance at Chapter 1 without paying too much attention to detail. If you haven't completed one or both of those actions, however, you probably shouldn't skip that chapter.

We do recommend that everyone read Chapters 5-7, even if your situation doesn't fit neatly into one of the categories outlined in those chapters. The reports discussed in the chapters could apply to anyone, and it's wise to know where you can find a quick overview if you need it.

If you want, you can even skim through the whole book first and then come back and focus only on the sections that apply directly to your needs at this time. You can always pick the book up later if your needs change.

Tools You Will Need

As with any report that you create, there are a few supplies that you'll need along the way. With Google Analytics, it's fairly simple. First, you need a web site to track. It can be your own web site, your company web site, or even a blog site, so long as you have access to the code for that site. You have to have access to the code, because you need to alter the code so that Google can track your site.

In addition to your site, you'll also need access to the Google Analytics program. At the time this book was written, Google Analytics was still in beta testing, which meant that users had to sign up on a waiting list to be invited to use Google Analytics.

The wait time for that privilege can vary from a few hours to a few weeks, so if you haven't signed up for the account yet, buy the book; and when you get it home, flip over to Chapter 4 to learn how to sign up and get started.

You may also want a Google AdWords account. It's not essential to have, but the true power in Google Analytics lies in its integration with Google AdWords. If you don't have an account and haven't even considered using one, read through Chapter 8 and then go ahead and sign up for the account if you think it will be useful. It takes only a minute, and you can deactivate your AdWords campaigns at any time.

Finally, throughout the book you'll find references to books on certain topics. These are not requirements, just suggestions that you may find useful if you want to know more about that specific topic. The books recommended here can be found through Amazon.com or any local bookstore. We've tried not to include anything obscure or hard to find.

Moving On

Enough. We've covered everything you're likely to want to know about using the book, so it's time to move on. Well, everything except the blog. If you have questions while you're reading the book, or if you just want to learn what's new or changed with Google Analytics, check out our blog. You'll find all kinds of up-to-date and extra information about the program there.

Now it's time to get going. Have fun, and thanks for reading!

Basic Analytics

Having web-site statistics is one thing. Understanding what they mean and what you should do with them is another thing altogether. If what you want is to get into the nitty-gritty, there are reams of information available to you. If, however, what you're really looking for is a quick, easy-to-understand explanation of analytics and why you should care, read on.

This part of the book gives you the working knowledge you'll need to understand the importance of analytics, all in three short chapters. When you've finished reading these first three chapters, you'll understand basic web measurements, how they apply to your web site, and the difference between site statistics and analytics. Then you'll be ready to tackle Google Analytics.

CHAPTER

1

Why Analytics?

Short Answer (for underlings)

Because.

Slightly Longer Short Answer (for your boss)

Because it's there and it's free, and web-page counters are *so 1997*.

Long Answer (for you)

First there were log files and only people who bought really expensive software could figure out what the heck the half-million lines of incomprehensible gobbledygook really meant. The rest of us used web-page counters. Anyone could see how many people had come to a page. As long as the counter didn't crash, or corrupt its storage, or overflow and start again at zero, there would be a nifty little graphic of numbers that looked like roller skates (or pool balls or stadium scoreboard numbers or whatnot).

Around 1998, the Grand Arbiters of Taste on the Internet (i.e., everybody) decided that page counters were *so 1997* and that there must be a better way.

And also about that time, web-site statistics packages or "stats" came into common use — not common use by huge businesses that could afford thousands of dollars for software but common use by us peons who rent our web space from hosting companies for twenty bucks per month. Stats packages basically collect data but leave you to analyze that data. So they tell you what happens; they just don't put what happens into any type of business context.

If you have Windows-based hosting, you may have a Windows-specific stats package, or your host may use the Windows version of one of the Open Source stats packages (listed below). If you have hosting on a Linux web server running Apache (and about 60 percent of web servers run Linux and Apache), you'll most likely have Analog, Webalizer, or AWStats, and you may have all three. These software packages are Open Source under various versions of the GNU Public License (GPL). This neatly explains their ubiquity.

They're free as in freedom, but more important to this particular purpose, they're free as in beer. Free as in beer is a large attractant to bottom-line-conscious ISPs and web hosts. While a good site-stats package will provide numerous important metrics to help you measure traffic and fine-tune your web site's performance, there are a few key things that site stats just won't tell you. We'll get into that later.

Where stats packages leave off is where analytics come in. Comparing what a good analytics package does to what a good site-stats package does is like having Mark McGwire bat right before the Little League's MVP. One could be kind and say it's a Major League to Little League comparison, or like putting a man next to a boy, but the truth is that analytics are like site stats on steroids. McGwire fans, please feel free to start whining now. I'll be watching figure skating on webcast until you finish. The long answer to "Why analytics?" is almost as short as the slightly longer short answer: web analytics are site stats on steroids (and page counters are *so 1997*). Stats give you numbers. Analytics give you information.

If Analytics Are So Great, Why Don't We Have Them?

The short and simple answer to this is that medium and large companies that can afford analytics do have them. There are many analytics software packages that cost money, among them WebTrends, HitBox Professional, and Manticore Technology's Virtual Touchstone. The low-end price for web analytics is $200 per month. The high-end price? A couple grand a month is not unusual. To the microsite, the small site, the web merchant on a shoestring, the mom-and-pop site, the struggling e-zine, the blogger who aspires to be Wonkette but isn't yet — that is, to most of the sites on the web — two hundred bucks a month sounds like a lot of money!

Then, in mid-2005, Google rocked the boat, buying a small company called Urchin. Urchin was no Oliver Twist. It was, in fact, a runner-up for the 2004 ClickZ Marketing Excellence Award for Best Small Business Analytics Tool. Its product, Urchin Analytics, had a monthly cost on the low end of the market — about $200 a month — and was designed for small businesses.

Six months later, Google did something completely unprecedented. It rebranded Urchin's service as Google Analytics with the intention of releasing it as a free application. Google prelaunched it to a number of large web publications (among them NewsForge.com, where Mary is a contributing editor). And shortly after that, Google opened it to the public, apparently completely underestimating the rush of people who would sign up — a quarter of a million in two days.

Google quickly limited the number of sites that registrants could manage to three, though if you knew HTML at all, the limitation was pathetically easy to bypass. Google also initiated a sign-up list for people who were interested, which eventually morphed into an invitation system reminiscent of the controlled launch of Google's Gmail. The moral of this story is, "Don't underestimate the attraction of *free*."

Now That We Have Analytics, What Do We Do With Them?

What do you want your web site to do better?

Analytics is software that generates metrics. Metrics are measurements. There are all sorts of possible web-site metrics — measurements you can take — about how many times files are accessed, how many unique IP addresses access the site, how many pages are served, and so on. Analytics can calculate the most popular pages, how long the typical person stays on the typical page, the percentage of people who "bounce" or leave the site from a particular page, and thus the percentage of people who explore the site more deeply.

Ad nauseam.

Yes, you can look at a zillion different metrics until it makes you dizzy, sick, and hopeless. Fortunately, some metrics have more impact on your site than others. Which metrics matter? That depends on what your site is. If your site is content, there's one set of metrics that matters. If your site sells things, a whole different set of metrics matters.

The point here is that you have to figure out your web site's purpose. For content businesses, it might be how much time the visitors spend, how deep visitors dig, and how often visitors return. For a business concerned mainly with selling things, it might be average time to sale, rate of shopping-cart abandonment, and profit, profit, profit. Once you know what metrics are meaningful for your web site, you can use those metrics to improve the site's performance. What do you do with analytics?

You improve your bottom line.

Here's a scenario for you. Mark owns a small rug store. It's nothing fancy, but the store does have the best prices in a three-state area, so it stays pretty busy.

Mark's wife, Anna, is his official webmaster. Anna doesn't have any formal training in web-site design, but through trial and error she's managed to put up an attractive site. The problem is, attractive doesn't necessarily translate into effective, and Mark and Anna want to know how effective the site is.

That's where Google Analytics comes in. When Anna first activates her Google Analytics account, she just watches it for a few weeks to see how much traffic the site gets, where it comes from, and what pages visitors spend the most time on.

After a few weeks, Google Analytics has given Anna enough information that she knows that the planning pages of the web site are the ones that customers spend the most time on. She can also see that the majority of her visitors come from a link on their local Better Business Bureau site.

These facts help Anna and Mark make some decisions about their marketing budget. Being small means that marketing needs to be effective, because there's less budget for it than a larger company might have.

Based on what they've learned from Google Analytics, Anna decides to create a monthly newsletter for the company, which includes tips for planning where and how to place a rug and effective decorating tips for using rugs. They also agree to try AdWords for a few months to see how an AdWords campaign would improve the business.

To track all of this, Anna sets up filters and goals in Google Analytics. Using the metrics returned by these filters and goals, she'll be able to see if her decision to build on the strengths of the web site actually turns into more sales.

Anna and Mark aren't real. They're (unpaid) performers in this little skit, but their story illustrates how you can use Google Analytics to improve your marketing, which in turn will improve your business. Your specifics might be different. But if you use Google Analytics as a tool to monitor and build marketing efforts, you'll find there are many benefits to knowing the who, what, when, why, and where of web-site traffic.

What Analytics Is Not

The short answer is: Google Analytics is not magic. It's not some mystical force that will automatically generate traffic to your web site. Nor is it the flashing neon sign that says, "Hey, you really should be doing this instead of that." And it's most certainly not the answer to all your web-site traffic problems. No, analytics is none of those things.

What analytics *is* is a tool for you to use to understand how visitors behave when they visit your web site. What you do with that information is up to you. If you simply look at it and keep doing what you're doing, you're going to keep getting what you're getting.

You wouldn't place a screw driver on the hood of a car and expect it to fix the engine. So don't enable Google Analytics on your site and expect the application to create miracles. Use it as the tool that helps you figure out *how* to achieve those goals.

Analytics and AWStats

AWStats

AWStats (Advanced Web Statistics) is an Open Source log analyzer written in Perl that can use a variety of log formats and runs on a variety of operating systems. The official documentation of AWStats is mostly targeted to system administrators rather than to owners of web-site businesses. In short, it's not much help in figuring out what the statistics mean.

Wait a minute!

This is a book about Google Analytics, so why the heck are we talking about some Open Source stats program? Because the thing about analytics is that to make any sense, there need to be some data. It's gonna take at least a couple days to get any data into Google Analytics. It'll be months before there's enough data to make any sense. But you may already have a wealth of historical data right there in AWStats. Never looked at it, you say?

Thought so.

That data you've probably got in AWStats, which maybe you never really understood because there's no in-depth documentation on it, is still valuable. It's your past. For some things, bigger and newer isn't necessarily better. Google Analytics and AWStats have different features with different strengths and weaknesses. For some things — many things — Google Analytics blows AWStats out of the water. For other things, Google Analytics uses a different methodology, with its own limitations.

At some point, no matter how you gather data, you're going to have to plow into the nit-picky little boring stuff: log analysis vs. scripts, nobodies vs. people, pages that are pages vs. pages that really aren't. So since we work hard and play hard — and you note which comes first — we're going to dig in and go through some of the details, the basic concepts that will make what you see in Google Analytics mean something.

That is why we're here, after all.

AWStats Browser

We'll start by taking a look at the AWStats window shown in Figure 2-1.

The AWStats window has a left-hand and a right-hand frame. The right-hand frame shows the reports. The left-hand frame shows the domain name for the site statistics you're viewing followed by a text link navigation list. You can go directly to sections of the main report from any flush-left link. Secondary reports, left-indented with a tiny AWStats icon, replace the main report in the right-hand frame when you click the navigation link.

CASE STUDY: SKATEFIC.COM

SkateFic.com is Mary's web site. Mary's company, Private Ice, publishes figure-skating fiction, humor, essays, and poetry both as free online content and for sale as in paperback and e-book. The site is relatively simple in structure and execution and does not require any special intervention to force the metrics to make sense. There is content for the sake of content, content for the sake of advertising, and products for sale, without any of those things being overly complex. It makes a good overview, and we'll refer to SkateFic.com from time to time to compare and contrast both Google Analytics and other case studies.

We're starting out with AWStats for a couple of reasons. First, if you have a web site, you're very likely to have AWStats already. Rather than trying to extrapolate from our case study to your web site's likely results, you'll be able to look at your own web site's information populating the AWStats reports. AWStats is also a bit less complex a tool than Google Analytics. It's easier to explain basic concepts without having to deal with all the complexity.

Navigation list   Main report page

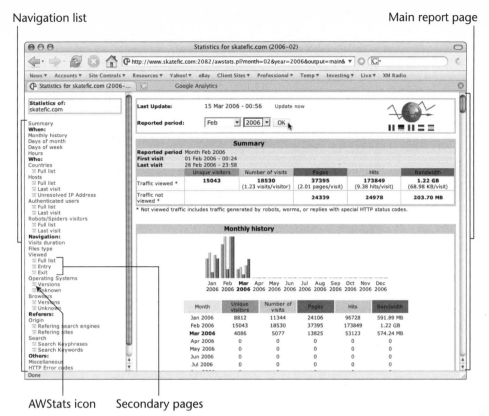

AWStats icon   Secondary pages

Figure 2-1: AWStats browser window in Firefox

AWStats Dashboard

AWStats doesn't have many controls on the dashboard (shown in Figure 2-2). Much of what can be configured is set by your web host at install time. The dashboard appears at the top of the main report. AWStats notes the time of last update. Most web hosts update in the middle of the night. The time listed is on the server's time zone and is not necessarily your time zone. You can force an update by clicking the Update Now link.

Force an update.   Go to AWStats home page.

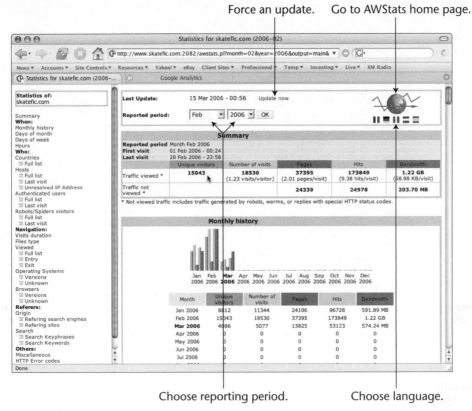

Choose reporting period.   Choose language.

Figure 2-2: AWStats dashboard at top of main report

If you need up-to-the-minute results, or if your site is very busy during a specific part of the day, it's probably smart to force an update before you look at the stats. If you're updating results for a couple days, the update can take some serious time — upwards of a half hour — depending on how busy your web site is. If your site is not very busy, or if it's only been a couple of hours since the last update, you might have the same overhead as a normal page reload.

Use the drop-down menus to change the month and year. To view a whole year, choose **Year** from the month menu and then the year from the year menu. Click the globe to go to AWStats home page at SourceForge.net. Click the flags below the globe to change the reporting language. Available languages depend on which ones your web host has installed. In this screenshot, French, German, Italian, Dutch, and Spanish are installed as well as the English default.

Summary

In Figure 2-3, the first three lines of the summary tell you what period the summary covers and the first and last visit during that period.

The rest of the summary is a two-line table. One would think the captions are pretty self-explanatory. Nope. No such luck.

Summary					
Reported period	Month Feb 2006				
First visit	01 Feb 2006 - 00:24				
Last visit	28 Feb 2006 - 23:58				
	Unique visitors	Number of visits	Pages	Hits	Bandwidth
Traffic viewed *	15043	18530 (1.23 visits/visitor)	37395 (2.01 pages/visit)	173849 (9.38 hits/visit)	1.22 GB (68.98 KB/visit)
Traffic not viewed *			24339	24978	203.70 MB

* Not viewed traffic includes traffic generated by robots, worms, or replies with special HTTP status codes.

——— Reporting period

Figure 2-3: AWStats summary showing reporting period

LIVING ON SERVER TIME

AWStats shows server time, not necessarily your time, not necessarily your time zone. For example, when reading times in AWStats reports, it's important to remember that the server might be in Central Time while you might be in Eastern Time.

Don't know *when* your server is?

There are two solutions:

1) If you have shell access to your server: open a terminal program, ssh to your web server and log in, run the date command at the prompt. The output from date lists the time zone, as shown in the figure that follows. Note that this data may not appear exactly the same on your program, because your time zone may differ. In fact, many servers outside the US will use GMT (Greenwich Mean Time).

Date command

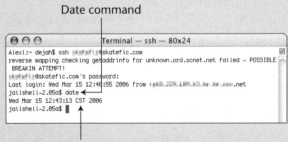

```
Alexi:~ dejah$ ssh ▓▓▓▓@skatefic.com
reverse mapping checking getaddrinfo for unknown.ord.scnet.net failed - POSSIBLE
BREAKIN ATTEMPT!
▓▓▓▓@skatefic.com's password:
Last login: Wed Mar 15 12:40:55 2006 from ▓▓▓.▓▓▓.▓▓▓.▓▓.▓▓-▓▓-▓▓▓.net
jailshell-2.05a$ date
Wed Mar 15 12:43:13 CST 2006
jailshell-2.05a$ █
```

Output includes server time zone.

Running date on your web server (usernames and IP addresses have been blacked out for security).

2) Ask your web host.

People and Not People

First off, there's the difference between Traffic Viewed and Traffic Not Viewed. In general terms, Traffic Viewed is generated by people. This isn't a completely sure thing, but it's close enough for most purposes. Traffic Not Viewed is generally generated by things that are not people. This includes robots, worms, or replies with special HTTP status codes.

Robots are software programs that access web pages for their own purposes. Search-engine crawlers (also known as spiders) are robots that index web pages for inclusion in their search results. There are other spiders with less savory purposes like harvesting e-mail addresses for use by spammers. Worms attack your web server, either to shut the server down (a denial-of-service attack) or to break into the server. Either way, worms can create a large amount of traffic that is of no interest beyond making sure it doesn't overwhelm your server completely. We'll get into "special status" HTTP requests a bit later. But in general, these are "noncontent" responses that redirect the visitor to another page or inform the user that the page cannot be found.

AWStats records only Bandwidth Used, Hits, and Pages for Traffic Not Viewed. For the most part, you can ignore those statistics. If your web site is even remotely busy, most of the Traffic Not Viewed is search engines crawling your site. This is a Good Thing(tm). Don't fret about it. In a bit, we'll discuss how to tell if you're suffering from an infestation of worms or another malady. Sit tight.

People

Now, on to Traffic Viewed. In AWStats, Traffic Viewed is, to the best AWStats can guess, traffic generated by people. Why *guess*? Because AWStats is a log analyzer. Every time your web server sends out a message to a client — any client — it logs that action. There's no real way to tell from the log if an access is really a person. It could be a person. It could be a proxy server. It could be 35 people sharing a net connection on a local area network (LAN). There could be people reloading pages from a cache (a page stored on their computer) downloaded the day before. When using any log analyzer, there's a fudge factor. That's the nature of the beast.

Bandwidth

The bandwidth measurement is a webmaster's first lesson in the importance of collecting useful metrics as opposed to useless ones. With the exception of knowing whether a site is nearing or over its bandwidth limits, there is pretty much no useful business purpose to a measurement of bandwidth. Most web sites don't benefit from knowing the size of the average download.

With one small exception. Here in the United States, we tend to think of everyone as having high-speed Internet. The fact is that broadband penetration is less than 50 percent in the U.S. According to the Organization for Economic Co-operation and Development (http://www.oecd.org) only 137 million people have high-speed access worldwide. Such figures could mean that half of the people who visit your web site are using dial-up at 56KBps or less.

At 56KBps, loading time for pages and other content like multimedia is a big issue. It used to be that you had about 10 seconds for your page to load before a user would abandon the page. Now you have about two seconds. You can use the average bandwidth per visit along with the average pages per visit to get a very rough estimate of how much data your average visitor is downloading and how much time it takes.

CASE STUDY: A VERY ROUGH ESTIMATE

Information useful in dealing with bandwidth and pages is shown below.

Summary					
Reported period	Month Feb 2006				
First visit	01 Feb 2006 - 00:24				
Last visit	28 Feb 2006 - 23:58				
	Unique visitors	Number of visits	Pages	Hits	Bandwidth
Traffic viewed *	15043	18530 (1.23 visits/visitor)	37395 (2.01 pages/visit)	173849 (9.38 hits/visit)	1.22 GB (68.98 KB/visit)
Traffic not viewed *			24339	24978	203.70 MB
* Not viewed traffic includes traffic generated by robots, worms, or replies with special HTTP status codes.					

Pages   Bandwidth

Pages and Bandwidth from February 2006

To get a rough idea of how much bandwidth each page takes, divide the bandwidth per visit by the pages per visit. Strictly speaking, this is very inaccurate, but the purpose here is not to get hard, fast numbers. The purpose here is to get a very rough idea of whether you have a problem with download times or not.

68.98 KB/visit ÷ 2.01 pages/visits = 34.31 KB/page

KBps means "kilobits/second," not kilobytes/second. There are 8 bits in a byte. So:

34.31 KByte/page x 8 bits/Byte ÷ 56KB/second = 4.9 seconds/page

As far as this analysis goes, there's not a big problem on average. Does that mean there's not a problem with specific pages? No. Does this mean you can forget about download times from here on? No.

Be aware, when you (or your designer) dream up a fantastic looking page, that if no one bothers to wait to download it, the net effect on your business will be negative, not positive. Balance your desire for bells and whistles with the reality that only a little more than two percent of world population has broadband.

Hits

For the first few years that we had web sites, we all quoted "hits." It wasn't until 1997 that we realized hits are another meaningless metric. Why? To a web server, any access of any document — a page, a script, a multimedia file, an image, and so on — is a hit. Since one page or site may have lots of images, and another may be mostly all text, hits become a particularly poor measure of a site's performance and an even worse measure of how a site performs in comparison to other sites.

HOW MANY HITS?

On the SkateFic.com home page, there are 12 images. What's more, the page is dynamic, made of five files stitched together by the server. And then there's one hit for the page itself.

12 images
5 component files
1 page
— — — — — — — — — — — — —
18 hits
Hits aren't very helpful, are they? You can see it graphically on the following figure:

Each of these 12 images is a separate hit.   Header file (1 hit)

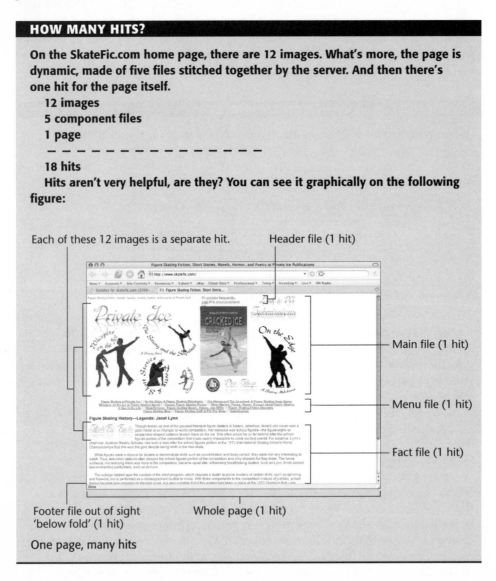

Main file (1 hit)

Menu file (1 hit)

Fact file (1 hit)

Footer file out of sight
'below fold' (1 hit)   Whole page (1 hit)

One page, many hits

Pages

Finally, we've reached a meaningful metric — pages, also known as page views or page hits, the subject of Figure 2-4.

Back in the dark ages of 1997, when we were all using page counters, page views were what we were actually trying to count. In AWStats, the Pages metric is the aggregate of page *requests*.

AWStats counts all pages, static and dynamic, plus requests for cgi scripts and a few other kinds of files. This specifically does not include requests for images or Cascading Style Sheets, though it may include files that you wouldn't think of as pages in the strictest sense, a possibility illustrated by Figure 2-5.

Pages: The aggregate of page requests.

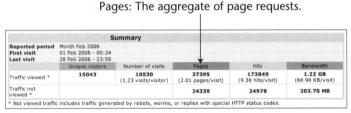

Figure 2-4: A meaningful metric

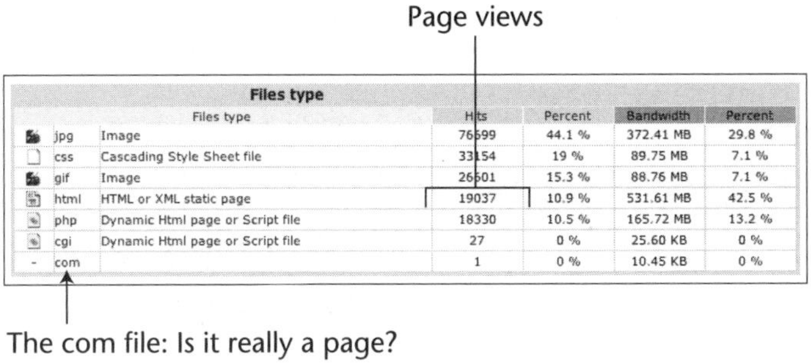

Page views

Figure 2-5: "Page" doesn't always mean what you think.

The com file: Is it really a page?

CAVEAT WEBMASTER: REQUESTS

A request means only that the web browser asked the web server for the page. It does not mean the page was actually delivered or viewed. The user may have clicked the back button because the page was loading too slowly. The user could have gotten up from the computer, allowed the page to load, and then come back later and closed the window without looking at it.

This is one of the caveats of using a log analyzer like AWStats for web metrics. You see only what the server sees. You don't see what the user actually does. It's a limitation of the software and the Internet experience. Caveat webmaster.

ASS-U-ME NOTHING

You know the old joke about assuming things. Assume makes an ass of you and me. But the truth is, every analytics package — every software package of any sort — makes assumptions. What is a page? How long is a visit? How long should the idle period between visits be? There are assumptions about any number of other aspects of data collection and processing as well. Most of these assumptions are neither right nor wrong. They're just assumptions. It's important to know what assumptions a particular analytics package is making if you want to be able to construe what your data really mean. We'll cover assumptions made by the software as we go.

Still looking at the summary on the main page, scroll down to (or click the navigation link for) **Files Type.** The Pages total, 37,395, includes 19,037 static html page views, 18,330 dynamic views for pages with a .php extension, 27 cgi script accesses, and one "com" page, which has no description. You wouldn't be a dummy if you didn't even know what that file type was. As it happens, it's a command file, a program, but exactly what it does is beyond our scope here.

Is that com file a page? Why? A program can output a page — not always, but that's one of the caveats of analytics software — assumptions. AWStats makes the assumption that a com file is a program that outputs a page, and it counts an access of that com file as a page.

Is it a page for business purposes? Unless you have a com file that you specifically know produces a viewable page, it probably isn't. And that means, for business purposes, that this portion of the Pages metric is meaningless. Only pages that are pages should count. If you have a lot of pages that are not pages counting, it's a problem. If it's only a few, a small percentage of your total, you're probably safe to ignore the pages that are not pages.

Number of Visits

The Number of Visits a web site receives should be straightforward. That would be nice and easy, wouldn't it? Of course, it would.

No such luck, as Figure 2-6 indicates.

Number of visits: It's based on assumptions.

Summary					
Reported period	Month Feb 2006				
First visit	01 Feb 2006 - 00:24				
Last visit	28 Feb 2006 - 23:58				
	Unique visitors	Number of visits	Pages	Hits	Bandwidth
Traffic viewed *	15043	18530 (1.23 visits/visitor)	37395 (2.01 pages/visit)	173849 (9.38 hits/visit)	1.22 GB (68.98 KB/visit)
Traffic not viewed *			24339	24978	203.70 MB
* Not viewed traffic includes traffic generated by robots, worms, or replies with special HTTP status codes.					

Figure 2-6: Number of Visits is almost but not quite what it seems.

Like Pages, Number of Visits has two key assumptions: How long is a visit and how much time has to pass between page loads to make one person have two visits? Fortunately, there are industry standards — after all, this isn't 1997. A visit is as long as it is. As long as the visitor keeps clicking from page to page, it's still one visit. However, when the user stops clicking for 30 minutes, the visit ends. If the user starts clicking again, it's a new visit. Thirty minutes is the industry-standard timeout for visits.

So, say a user toddles into SkateFic.com at 9:00 a.m., and between 9:00 and 9:30 she clicks from page to page, reading her favorite serial fiction. At 9:30 she gets a phone call. For the next 28 minutes, she talks on the phone. When she hangs up at 9:58, she finishes reading the page she left to answer the call and loads the next page at 9:59. That's one visit, because the break between page loads was less than 30 minutes.

Now, say the same user is having a Grand Central Terminal sort of day. The phone rings again at 10:00 a.m. This time the user talks for 31 minutes. When she goes back to reading and loads a new page, she's initiating a second visit as far as AWStats is concerned. Same person, same day — and if you asked the user, same visit — but for pretty much every stats and analytics package, it's two different visits.

The average of 1.23 visits per visitor varies in meaningfulness. For a site that gets a lot of returning visitors, it might have some meaning. For a site where 90 percent of visitors never return, the average doesn't mean much, because it is dragged down by the vast bulk of people who never return. You could have 10 people who average three visits per month and 90 people who come once and never come back. Average visits will be 1.2, but it won't be a very useful metric, except to tell you that most of your visitors don't return after the first visit.

Unique Visitors

The big problem with counting unique visitors is that it's impossible to figure out from server logs who's unique and who's a visitor. Figure 2-7 deals with this problem.

"Unique visitors" aren't always what they seem.

Summary					
Reported period	Month Feb 2006				
First visit	01 Feb 2006 - 00:24				
Last visit	28 Feb 2006 - 23:58				
	Unique visitors	Number of visits	Pages	Hits	Bandwidth
Traffic viewed *	15043	18530 (1.23 visits/visitor)	37395 (2.01 pages/visit)	173849 (9.38 hits/visit)	1.22 GB (68.98 KB/visit)
Traffic not viewed *			24339	24978	203.70 MB
* Not viewed traffic includes traffic generated by robots, worms, or replies with special HTTP status codes.					

Figure 2-7: When is a unique visitor neither unique nor a visitor?

There are caveats aplenty here, since you're counting visits from unique IP addresses, not actual people:

- Any sort of local area network connected by a single Internet gateway may have several users with the same apparent IP address.

- A proxy server owned by an ISP that caches frequently accessed pages will show up as one unique visitor even though it represents hundreds, if not thousands of users. You can put a no-cache directive on your pages, but it only works if the proxy pays attention to it. And using such a directive may slow your site for some users.

- In the home, it is very common to have more than one person using the same computer. You may have three different people visiting from one IP address.

- People visit from different places: from home, work, school, or from a laptop at the coffee shop. What looks like four unique visitors may actually be only one.

- People on dial-up change IP addresses almost every time they log in. If a person visits every day from a different IP, that person looks like 20 or 30 people, depending on how the ISP assigns IP addresses.

There isn't much you can do about these issues. It's the nature of the beast — and log analyzers. Google Analytics is script based, so it does not have many of these problems, but it has a series of issues of its own. The bottom line is that you can't measure unique visitors with complete accuracy. You measure unique visitors as well as you can and you make sure to compare apples to apples. As far as the technology goes, AWStats Unique Visitors is the number of unique IP addresses that made requests to your web server. It's the best measurement a log analyzer can provide of how many people visited.

Yearly Summary

AWStats calculates its metrics on a monthly basis. To produce yearly metrics, it adds the results from all months, with the warning shown in Figure 2-8.

Summary					
Reported period Year 2005					
First visit 01 Jan 2005 - 00:06					
Last visit 31 Dec 2005 - 23:58					
	Unique visitors	Number of visits	Pages	Hits	Bandwidth
Traffic viewed *	<= 42960 Exact value not available in 'Year' view	65382 (1.52 visits/visitor)	167257 (2.55 pages/visit)	525524 (8.03 hits/visit)	3.84 GB (61.57 KB/visit)
Traffic not viewed *			194580	197127	1.73 GB
* Not viewed traffic includes traffic generated by robots, worms, or replies with special HTTP status codes.					

AWStats methodology yields a bogus number here.

Figure 2-8:   The yearly summary warns that "unique visitors" is not an exact metric.

While this strategy doesn't affect the other metrics, it also doesn't produce an accurate number of unique visitors. If a particular IP appeared in January, March, and July, it would add three unique visitors rather than just one. It's not practical to save all the logs and run the analysis on one huge lump every time the user wants a year-to-date. Suffice it to say that the AWStats unique-visitors metric is not accurate in the aggregate.

In Summary

That wasn't so bad, now, was it?

CHAPTER 3

Oh, No! More AWStats!

Yes, There's More

So you made it through Chapter 2 okay? Good. If you want only the very basics before you jump into Google Analytics, you can probably skip this chapter. So why are we writing it? Good question. In this chapter, we're going to cover some of the caveats that make collecting and analyzing site traffic so fraught with pitfalls. We're still going to use AWStats as the prime example, and we still expect you to look at your own data if you have them. You'll also see some of the things that AWStats can do that Google Analytics can't.

Now, we think this stuff is scintillating reading, but you might find it a little less exciting than you found Chapter 2. Nothing can be done about that. Cope. And now let's go to Monthly History, as shown in Figure 3-1.

Monthly History

The Monthly History has two parts: a bar chart and a table of values. The values in the chart and the numbers in the table correspond to the Summary information for each month. Each column of the chart has a total at the bottom that appears on the earlier –Year– Summary. As with the –Year– Summary, the total of Unique Visitors is not accurate.

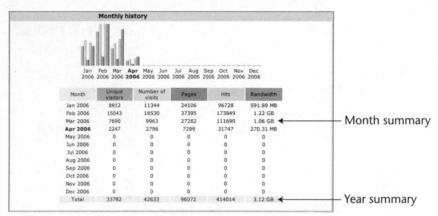

Figure 3-1:   Monthly History has values from each month's Summary.

In the bar chart, each colored bar is in proportion to other bars of that color. However, there is no correlation between different colored bars. In Figure 3-1, the tallest yellow bar and the tallest turquoise bar are the same height. But the tallest yellow bar is 18,530 visits, while the tallest turquoise bar has the value 173,849 hits.

The Monthly History has a simple purpose. It exists solely so that you can compare traffic numbers from month to month. What happened in February so that traffic doubled? Why did it drop off in March?

These questions are as much business related as site related. In the specific case at SkateFic.com, the 2006 Winter Olympics were in February, driving interest in figure skating through the roof for a short period. But then, despite TV coverage of the world championships in March, traffic fell as casual fans went back to their regularly scheduled programs. With eight years of historical data behind us, it's easy to see that the pattern of activity was the same during the 1998 and 2002 Olympics.

This is another benefit of having metrics. You can discern both short-term and long-term patterns, sometimes just by looking. Does your web site peak in August every year? Did editorial coverage in a major magazine spike traffic in January? Do you get a lot of traffic around a particular real-world event? What are the long-term and short-term trends?

Another way of looking at traffic, by days and hours, is shown in Figure 3-2.

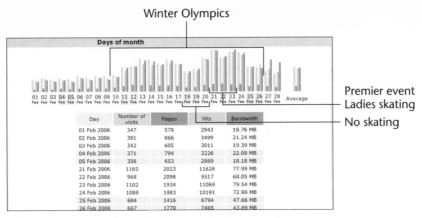

Figure 3-2: Days of Month shows traffic for each day.

Days and Hours

The Days of Month, plus Days of Week and Hours reports (see Figure 3-3), all answer the same basic questions: "Is traffic to the web site cyclical?" and "Did any special events influence traffic?" Days of Month gives you a daily break-down, lets you compare against the average, and shows how AWStats arrived at the Summary numbers.

From a business standpoint, comparing monthly reports shows that SkateFic has a much stronger showing in the winter, during the figure-skating season — duh. The 2006 Olympics also boosted traffic considerably in Febru-ary 2006. There aren't any particular intramonthly trends, even when compar-ing across months.

Too bad that the Days of Week and Hours reports aren't as useful. In the Days of Week report, averaging tends to even out both anomalous bumps and meaningful anomalies. The Hours chart, unlike the Days of Week chart, gives you aggregate numbers where averages would be more meaningful. The Hours graph is the saving grace, showing peak hours around 8:00 a.m., 2:00 p.m. to 3:00 p.m., and 9:00 p.m. (remember those are Central Time).

Averaging a few numbers can be misleading.

Day	Pages	Hits	Bandwidth
Mon	1419.25	6730.75	51.60 MB
Tue	1422	6930.25	53.13 MB
Wed	1296.25	5951	41.43 MB
Thu	1323.25	6545	45.87 MB
Fri	1274.75	6187	43.19 MB
Sat	1212.50	5263.50	38.44 MB
Sun	1400.75	5854.75	38.41 MB

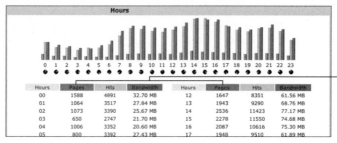

Sums are more accurate but harder to compare.

Hours	Pages	Hits	Bandwidth	Hours	Pages	Hits	Bandwidth
00	1588	4891	32.70 MB	12	1647	8351	61.56 MB
01	1064	3517	27.84 MB	13	1943	9290	68.76 MB
02	1073	3390	25.67 MB	14	2536	11423	77.17 MB
03	650	2747	21.70 MB	15	2278	11550	74.68 MB
04	1006	3352	20.60 MB	16	2087	10616	75.30 MB
05	800	3392	27.43 MB	17	1948	9510	61.89 MB

Figure 3-3:   Traffic for Days and Hours

What does it mean in a business sense? The Days of Week chart means absolutely nothing, since averaging kills any bumps that might have meant something. The Hours chart shows that SkateFic is busy before work, after school, and after the nightly news. Most visitors are probably from the continental U.S., because the site is busiest during the U.S. day. There's a significant population of night owls and people from the Eastern Hemisphere because there is a base line of traffic even while westerners are sound asleep. Which raises the geographical question in Figure 3-4.

Countries		Pages	Hits	Bandwidth
United States	us	26370	134239	935.18 MB
Unknown	ip	5152	9711	71.03 MB
Canada	ca	1928	10936	77.66 MB
Great Britain	gb	966	4306	56.65 MB
European Union	eu	633	3189	28.30 MB
Netherlands	nl	362	785	7.80 MB
Australia	au	346	2310	14.82 MB
Japan	jp	174	1113	8.58 MB
Switzerland	ch	142	203	1.33 MB
Germany	de	128	422	3.85 MB
Sweden	se	112	449	3.22 MB
China	cn	88	334	2.01 MB
Russian Federation	ru	60	355	1.68 MB
Italy	it	58	382	3.14 MB
Finland	fi	50	286	1.86 MB
Singapore	sg	49	279	1.59 MB

Countries (Top 25)   •   Full list

Figure 3-4:   Think your visitors are all American? Think again.

Countries

Americans have a terribly bad habit of being Amero-centric. AWStats uses a reverse domain name system (DNS) to figure out where site visitors are coming from. The top 25 countries of origin are listed on the main page in order from most traffic to least. Usually, there are a significant number of incoming IP addresses that cannot be resolved. These are listed as "Unknown."

By clicking the **Full List** link, you can see all the countries that showed up in the logs. Would you think that people in 96 countries — including Iran, Bermuda, Nigeria, Mongolia — would be interested in figure-skating fiction? That seems to surprise everyone who isn't still laughing over the idea that figure-skating fiction actually exists.

Your site may have a much greater reach than you realize. Knowing this can influence decisions about content and e-commerce. Would your site strategy change if you knew that 35 percent of your traffic was coming from the European Union?

We thought so.

Hosts

The hosts list (see Figure 3-5) offers several different views of the same information: the host names and IP addresses of visitors. This is the same information used to tell which country visitors hail from.

On the main page of AWStats, the first line after the title bar gives an overview of how many known and unknown/unresolved hosts there were, as well as how many unique visitors this represents. Then the main report starts with the host who requested the most pages, listing hosts in descending order from most traffic to least.

ISP proxy caches

Google spiders

Hosts (Top 25) • Full list • Last visit • Unresolved IP Address				
Hosts : 17198 Known, 2854 Unknown (unresolved ip) 15043 Unique visitors	Pages	Hits	Bandwidth	Last visit
crawl-66-249-65-48.googlebot.com	950	950	7.55 MB	15 Feb 2006 - 19:52
crawl-66-249-65-231.googlebot.com	897	897	7.40 MB	21 Feb 2006 - 15:49
crawl-66-249-66-108.googlebot.com	604	604	4.88 MB	25 Feb 2006 - 12:08
crawl-66-249-72-66.googlebot.com	551	551	6.70 MB	28 Feb 2006 - 17:44
crawl-66-249-66-241.googlebot.com	507	507	3.85 MB	09 Feb 2006 - 20:16
66-215-117-37.dhcp.mrba.ca.charter.com	493	986	399.19 KB	26 Feb 2006 - 15:52
cpe-66-1-252-195.co.sprintbbd.net	404	807	323.45 KB	12 Feb 2006 - 04:43
c-71-197-56-228.hsd1.co.comcast.net	358	358	4.67 MB	28 Feb 2006 - 17:58

Figure 3-5: All hosts welcome

In Figure 3-5, you should note two interesting points. First, unlike the other reports that show only "people," the hosts list shows both "people" and "not people." Spiders and other robots are not second-class citizens on the hosts list. Second, Google spiders have the top five wrapped up. What does this mean? Well, Google indexes the site for new content at least once a week, sometimes twice. For a small site, this is very good news. It means that the 800-pound gorilla of search engines has taken notice and indexes regularly. New content will not languish in obscurity.

In the title bar of the report are three links. Full List goes to a list of all hosts, with the highest-traffic hosts first. Last Visit loads a list of the last 1,000 hosts to visit your site, organized by the time of their last visit. Unresolved IP Address goes to a list of the top 1,000 hosts who could not be found by name, listed from highest traffic to lowest.

Robots and Spiders

In Chapter 2, we talked about visitors who are people and visitors who are not people. One particularly important kind of visitor that is not a person is an indexing spider or web crawler — ewww, it gives me the willies just thinking about spiders! The Robots/Spiders report (see Figure 3-6) lists the various named and unnamed but identified web crawlers that have run their sticky little legs all over your pages.

Named spiders are known robots from known entities: Google, Inktomi, MSN, Yahoo, and so forth. Other spiders are not known, but when they hit a special file on the top level of the web site called robots.txt, the server marks them as spiders. Robots.txt tells spiders where they are allowed to go and what they are allowed to index. For example, if you didn't want the pictures on your web site indexed, you could put a line in your robots.txt to make the whole images directory off limits to spiders. Most good spiders pay attention to these directives, but there's no money-back guarantee.

Not all spiders are "known."

Robots/Spiders visitors (Top 25) • Full list • Last visit			
15 different robots*	Hits	Bandwidth	Last visit
Inktomi Slurp	6719+1799	47.98 MB	28 Feb 2006 - 23:54
Googlebot	4799+98	52.25 MB	28 Feb 2006 - 23:58
MSNBot	3970+426	62.75 MB	28 Feb 2006 - 23:20
WISENutbot	1088+7	10.17 MB	28 Feb 2006 - 23:58
Unknown robot (identified by 'spider')	873+185	14.88 MB	28 Feb 2006 - 19:26
Unknown robot (identified by 'crawl')	598+114	9.21 MB	28 Feb 2006 - 20:12
Unknown robot (identified by hit on 'robots.txt')	0+278	89.35 KB	28 Feb 2006 - 22:31
Unknown robot (identified by 'robot')	225+9	1.75 MB	28 Feb 2006 - 01:58
AskJeeves	100+49	828.09 KB	28 Feb 2006 - 22:11
Voila	3+78	53.86 KB	28 Feb 2006 - 09:36
Voyager	69+8	1.15 MB	28 Feb 2006 - 18:05
Scooter	17+8	207.10 KB	27 Feb 2006 - 05:38
Lycos	15+9	210.00 KB	17 Feb 2006 - 12:02
Alexa (IA Archiver)	0+17	2.74 KB	28 Feb 2006 - 08:20
Fast-Webcrawler	3	263.97 KB	27 Feb 2006 - 22:42

* Robots shown here gave hits or traffic "not viewed" by visitors, so they are not included in other charts. Numbers after + are successful hits on "robots.txt" files

Figure 3-6: Get indexed. Get found.

SQUASH INVADING SPIDERS

Creating a robots.txt file isn't very difficult. Here are some resources that will help you create such a file if you don't have one:

How to Set Up a robots.txt to Control Search Engine Spiders
The how and the why of setting up a robots.txt file.

`http://www.thesitewizard.com/archive/robotstxt.shtml`

Robots.txt Validator
Make sure your robots.txt file is correct with this nifty tool.

`http://tool.motoricerca.info/robots-checker.phtml`

Robots.txt file Creator
An online tool that will create a robots.txt file for you. You still have to understand the settings, but the creator will handle the syntax.

`http://www.webtoolcentral.com/webmaster/tools/robots_txt_file_`
`generator/`

Remember, the robots.txt file goes at the top of your web-site directory structure — the same directory as your home page.

Hits from spiders are reported a little differently from hits from other entities. For each spider, the first number under Hits is the number of requests the spider made. Then there's a plus sign and the number of times the spider successfully "saw" the robots.txt file. As you can see from Figure 3-7, different spiders hit the robots.txt file in greatly varying numbers. Those numbers could mean anything from lots of spider visits to very inefficient spidering methods. In general, spiders are good. Being indexed is good. Being found is even better.

Sad truth: Most visitors bail before they read even a single page.

Visits duration		
Number of visits: 18530 - Average: 153 s	Number of visits	Percent
0s-30s	15773	85.1 %
30s-2mn	842	4.5 %
2mn-5mn	515	2.7 %
5mn-15mn	547	2.9 %
15mn-30mn	303	1.6 %
30mn-1h	306	1.6 %
1h+	244	1.3 %

On the other hand, more than 2,000 hang out.

Figure 3-7: A cringe-worthy report on the length of visits

Visits Duration

Why does this report make us cringe — okay, just Mary, it's her web site after all? The Visits Duration report shows how long visits were. The average visit is about 2.5 minutes. That's not too bad. But then, you look at the numbers that went into those 2.5 minutes. Fewer than 2,000 people stayed more than two minutes. Only 15 percent stayed more than 30 seconds! For a content site, that's enough to shake an editor to her soul.

One of the measures of a successful content web site is how "sticky" that site is. Stickiness is about whether visitors bounce in and then bounce out just as fast. Apparently, lots of people do. Either they find what they want and leave, or they don't find what they want and leave. Either way, they leave before they get deeper into the site.

This observation in itself is valuable. But where did most of these people come from? How did they encounter the site? Did they leave immediately, or did they try to load another page? Did they find what they wanted and leave? Or didn't they look? Those last two are very different things.

AWStats can't tell us. While AWStats provides the raw data of "who came, how many, where?" it can't say "who came and left immediately, how many dug in deeper, and where did they go?" For that, you need Google Analytics. This is one park where the Little Leaguer, good as he is, can't hit a homer.

Pages-URL

The Pages-URL report (see Figure 3-8) lists the top 25 URLs by the number of times that page was viewed. Links across the title bar will take you to the Full List of all URL's recorded for your site.

Same page under two different names.

Represents all chapters read, with multiple pages of content lumped as one.

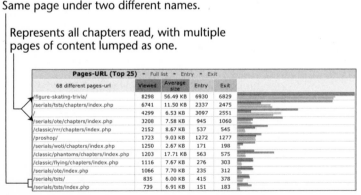

Figure 3-8: AWStats' most popular Page URL's tells you much but not everything.

The Entry and Exit links (see Figure 3-9) go to pages showing the full list of URLs sorted by the most entries and most exits, respectively.

The Entry and Exit lists, like many of the secondary pages, allow you to filter the list with Regular Expressions. A Regular Expression (abbreviated RegEx) matches patterns using a special syntax that we'll discuss in more depth in Chapter 6. Also in Figure 3-9, the RegEx `.*/serials/.*` matches all the URLs which contain the directory `/serials/`. At SkateFic.com, the serials directory contains all the currently running serial novels. From a business standpoint, knowing how to filter the Pages-URL list gives you the ability to look at different sections of your web site — that is, if your web site is structured so that different sectors of your business correspond to different structural parts of your site.

What if they don't? What if you use variables to steer people to different parts of your site? For example, in Figure 3-9, the top two URLs are for `/chapters/index.php`. While not immediately apparent, those two URLs can represent hundreds of individual chapters, because each of them comes with a variable like so: `/chapters/index.php?Chapter=23` for Chapter 23 of the serial.

A business with an online catalogue might have one catalogue page that uses an item number to pull item descriptions from a database. A site that uses a content management system (CMS) might have very few actual pages and may only differentiate pages by a series of variables in the URL. See any of those variables in the URLs that AWStats shows? Nope?

We don't either.

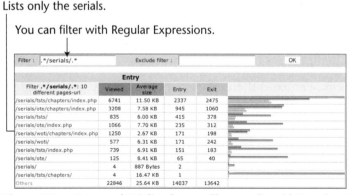

Lists only the serials.

You can filter with Regular Expressions.

| Filter : `.*/serials/.*` | | Exclude filter : | | | OK |

Entry				
Filter `.*/serials/.*`: 10 different pages-url	Viewed	Average size	Entry	Exit
/serials/tsts/chapters/index.php	6741	11.50 KB	2337	2475
/serials/ote/chapters/index.php	3208	7.58 KB	945	1060
/serials/tsts/	835	6.00 KB	415	378
/serials/ote/index.php	1066	7.70 KB	235	312
/serials/woti/chapters/index.php	1250	2.67 KB	171	198
/serials/woti/	577	6.31 KB	171	242
/serials/tsts/index.php	739	6.91 KB	151	183
/serials/ote/	125	8.41 KB	65	40
/serials/	4	887 Bytes	2	
/serials/tsts/chapters/	4	16.47 KB	1	
Others	22846	25.64 KB	14037	13642

Figure 3-9: Entry and Exit lists let you filter results with Regular Expressions.

This is another one of those things that AWStats doesn't do that you'll find you need. It's great to know how many people read chapters of one serial or another (or read articles or visit the catalogue). But it's not as helpful as knowing that 2,000 people read the newest chapter (or article) and that 337 people each read 10 other chapters or that 1,500 people looked at the week's sale item and that 1,800 people looked at a bunch of other catalogue items.

Here's another important piece of information that you both need and don't. Take a look at Figure 3-10.

The /figure-skating-trivia/ directory contains a single page with numerous short biographies of figure skaters. It has turned out to be a top search term for SkateFic.com. It's also the most visited page on a regular basis.

Look at the Entry and Exit numbers. You would think they'd have some relationship to one another, but they don't. A person could enter the site on another page, poke around a while, find the trivia page, read for a while and then leave for another site (or a cuppa joe) — no entry, one exit, one view. A person could do the reverse, enter at the trivia page, exit elsewhere — one entry, no exit, one view. A person could enter on a different page, read some, check out the trivia, and end up reading one of the poems in a different part of the site — no entry, no exit, one view. Finally, a person could enter the site on the trivia page and leave immediately — a "bounce" — one entry, one exit, one view. That's the person we want to know more about! Do we know anything about them? No.

The trivia page is only a draw insomuch as it lures people further into the site. The trivia page on SkateFic.com is like a controversial article on a content site or a sale item on an e-commerce site. It's all well and good that people look at that page, but what you really want is people to be pulled further into the site. It's that supercheap sale item at the grocery store, a loss leader. How effective your loss leader is depends on how many people get further into your site from that page.

AWStats can't tell you that. It can say how many people viewed a page. It can say how many people entered there. It can say how many people exited. What it doesn't say is how many people saw that page and only that page. That particular analytical association is a crucial one.

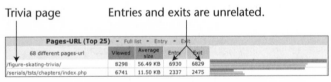

Trivia page   Entries and exits are unrelated.

Pages-URL (Top 25) · Full list · Entry · Exit				
68 different pages-url	Viewed	Average size	Entry	Exit
/figure-skating-trivia/	8298	56.49 KB	6930	6829
/serials/tsts/chapters/index.php	6741	11.50 KB	2337	2475

Figure 3-10: Is Figure Skating Trivia a good draw or not?

Operating Systems and Browsers

If you're a Mac or Linux person, how many times have you heard what amounts to "We only care about Windows users"? Certain designers and even web-site owners only want to design sites for the very newest Windows version, the very newest Internet Explorer browser. Cross-platform compatibility be damned! "So few people use Mac or Linux (or Netscape or FireFox or visit from their PDA or mobile phone) that we don't need to support it."

But is that really true?

Is it really true that all you need to support is the newest IE and the newest Windows? According to Figure 3-11, it would indeed seem that 88.9 percent of hits come from Windows machines and 78 percent from IE.

It's not as exact as it would be if AWStats gave us pages or unique visitors, but it's the best we've got. Looks like a lot of Windows users. It might lead you to decide that the right thing to do is to support the newest IE 7 and the newest Windows XP.

And you would be dead wrong.

Let's do some estimates. Fifteen thousand unique visitors, 173,000 hits among them, is about 11 hits per unique visitor. So something like 13,000 visitors are on Windows. About 1,000 have Macs and a hundred have Linux or other OSs. Maybe 12 percent doesn't seem like much, but are you willing to turn away more than 1,000 potential readers and customers? Mary doesn't happen to be, so even if she weren't a Mac-hack-from-way-back, she'd be putting the extra time and dollars into cross-platform compatibility. It's good business.

20 percent of traffic

10 percent of traffic

Operating Systems (Top 10) ◦ Full list/Versions ◦ Unknown		
Operating Systems	Hits	Percent
Windows	154709	88.9 %
Macintosh	11539	6.6 %
Unknown	6292	3.6 %
Linux	1051	0.6 %
Sun Solaris	136	0 %
WebTV	62	0 %
FreeBSD	45	0 %
HP Unix	9	0 %
CPM	5	0 %
RISC OS	1	0 %

Browsers (Top 10) ◦ Full list/Versions ◦ Unknown			
Browsers	Grabber	Hits	Percent
MS Internet Explorer	No	135654	78 %
Firefox	No	20047	11.5 %
Safari	No	7240	4.1 %
Unknown	?	5482	3.1 %
Netscape	No	2592	1.4 %
Mozilla	No	1334	0.7 %
Opera	No	1105	0.6 %
Camino	No	130	0 %
Konqueror	No	79	0 %
WebTV browser	No	62	0 %
Others		124	0 %

Figure 3-11: Why "we only care about Windows XP users" is bad business.

But say you're willing to sacrifice 10 percent of possible customers. You're sticking to the major-OS/major-browser strategy to save money. Saving money is good business. Sure, you're saving money only supporting the most recent IE version?

Take a gander at Figure 3-12 to see who's using IE 7. Almost no one.

An estimated 13,000 visitors are using IE 6, with another 400 using IE 5 and a pinch using IE 4 and IE 3, and a few thousand more are using FireFox, Safari, and "unknown." A grand total of about 14 visitors use IE 7. Supporting only the latest and greatest looks foolhardy indeed, doesn't it?

Now what exactly does "Unknown" mean? Many of those "unknown" browsers are not as unknown as you might think. Being book authors distinctly lacking in curiosity, no one here ever clicked that **Unknown** link in the title bar to find what you now see in Figure 3-13.

Lots of nonsense . . . and a gem. Those unknown browsers happen to be important if you're considering whether to support mobile technologies. Mary always avoided the subject of making SkateFic mobile-friendly, thinking, "Mobile surfers don't visit SkateFic." As it turns out, they do. Among the unidentified spiders, site-capture programs, and obvious gobbledygook promulgated by the truly paranoid are PDA browsers and the Blackberry browser. Which just goes to show that even when you know enough to write a book, there's always something to learn.

Maybe it's time to start supporting mobile surfers.

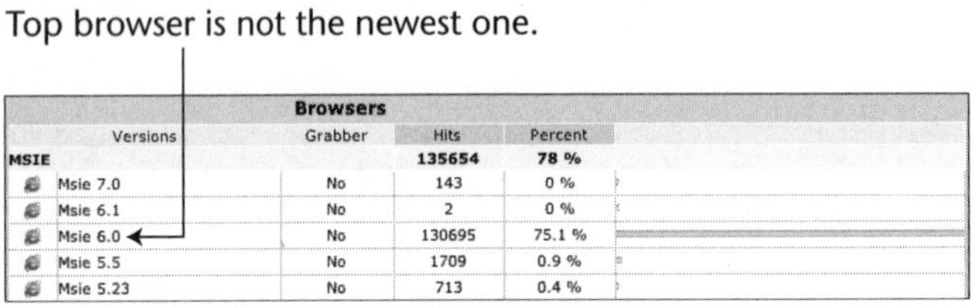

Top browser is not the newest one.

Browsers				
Versions	Grabber	Hits	Percent	
MSIE		**135654**	**78 %**	
Msie 7.0	No	143	0 %	
Msie 6.1	No	2	0 %	
Msie 6.0	No	130695	75.1 %	
Msie 5.5	No	1709	0.9 %	
Msie 5.23	No	713	0.4 %	

Figure 3-12: The Full List of browsers shows the flaw in major-browser strategy.

Unidentified spider

Blackberry browser

SBIder/0.8-dev_(SBIder;_http://www.sitesell.com/sbider.html;_http://support.sitesell.com/contact-support.html)	26 Feb 2006 - 21:25
RtpcjaorjvsgnqlRwcckR	26 Feb 2006 - 17:23
BlackBerry6280/4.0.0_Profile/MIDP-2.0_Configuration/CLDC-1.1	26 Feb 2006 - 16:39

Figure 3-13: Unknown does not always mean unknowable.

Connect to Site from . . .

The "Connect to site from" report has two sections: top and bottom. Figure 3-14 shows the upper part of the top section.

First is the traffic (pages and hits) coming from people who type your URL — direct addresses — or use a bookmark. These are your regular customers or readers, your core traffic. They know where your site is from memory or they have your site bookmarked. Chances are, they'll be back because they know you have what they want.

The second line of the upper section is for people coming in from newsgroups. Newsgroups are one of the more ancient forms of Internet communication, the killer ap of 1991. Unfortunately, newsgroups, which tend to be very uncontrolled and egalitarian, are falling by the wayside, while conduits where content can be controlled (like mailing lists and web forums) are on the rise. Boo-hoo. There was no incoming traffic from newsgroups. If there had been, it would have indicated that there was some word of mouth about your site and that people were visiting based on recommendations from other visitors.

The rest of the upper section lists search-engine activity. Google tends to rule this list with five times more traffic than everyone else put together. The first line has numbers for the aggregate of all search engines. The rest of the lines have names of individual search engines with two unlabeled numbers. Those numbers should be labeled, from left to right, Pages and Hits.

The bottom section of the table lists the external URLs that drive the most traffic. The top URL in Figure 3-15 is a Google AdWords ad. Fourteen (of 25) other URLs in the top-external-links list are either ad forms that repurpose Google results or are AdWords-for-content placements from third-party web sites using the Google AdSense program.

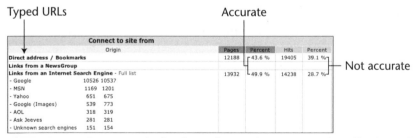

Figure 3.14: If you ever doubted Google was the 800-pound gorilla of search . . .

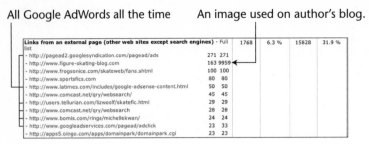

All Google AdWords all the time   An image used on author's blog.

Links from an external page (other web sites except search engines) - Full list		1768	6.3 %	15828	31.9 %
- http://pagead2.googlesyndication.com/pagead/ads	271 271				
- http://www.figure-skating-blog.com	163 9959				
- http://www.frogsonice.com/skateweb/fans.shtml	100 100				
- http://www.sportsfics.com	80 80				
- http://www.latimes.com/includes/google-adsense-content.html	50 50				
- http://www.comcast.net/qry/websearch/	45 45				
- http://users.tellurian.com/lizwoolf/skatefic.html	29 29				
- http://www.comcast.net/qry/websearch	28 28				
- http://www.bomis.com/rings/michellekwan/	24 24				
- http://www.googleadservices.com/pagead/adclick	23 33				
- http://apps5.oingo.com/apps/domainpark/domainpark.cgi	23 23				

Figure 3-15: AdWords traffic masquerading as external links

Clicking **Full List** gives you a full list of all external URLs. On SkateFic.com, the vast majority of those URLs are AdWords-for-content placements. But you have to know what to look for. You can't count on AWStats to tell the difference between a real external link and yet another AdWords placement or search-engine result.

You can, however, filter the full list results. Figure 3-16 shows only the results that explicitly come from Google (there will be others the come from Google but don't say so). It's worthwhile to note that the percentages given on a filtered full list refer to the percentage of that filtered data set, not to the over-all full list of external links. So the 63.1 percent of *all the ads that reference Google* come directly from AdWords placement on Google's own web site.

So what does this all mean? Should you be concerned with the raw numbers or only with the percentages? How should your percentages of direct-address, search-engine, and external-link traffic compare?

It's like this: You want to keep current readers and customers coming back. You also want new readers and customers to find you. A very low percentage of direct addresses may indicate that people are not returning after their first visit or that your offline promotional efforts are not effective. This means that your site is not sufficiently sticky or that people get to your site and don't find what they need. It means you're not building a core audience.

Filtering with Regular Expressions can
show who owns up to Google AdSense.

Filter : .*google.* Exclude filter :				OK	
Links from an external page (other web sites except search engines)					
Filter .*google.*: 31 different pages-url	Pages	Percent	Hits	Percent	
http://pagead2.googlesyndication.com/pagead/ads	271	63.1 %	271	61.7 %	
http://www.latimes.com/includes/google-adsense-content.html	50	11.6 %	50	11.3 %	
http://www.googleadservices.com/pagead/adclick	23	5.3 %	33	7.5 %	
http://www.charter.net/google/index.php	14	3.2 %	14	3.1 %	
http://www.chicagotribune.com/includes/google-adsense-content.ht...	13	3 %	13	2.9 %	
http://www.baltimoresun.com/includes/google-adsense-content.html	9	2 %	9	2 %	
http://www.sun-sentinel.com/includes/google-adsense-content.html	9	2 %	9	2 %	
http://www.tesco.net/google/searchresults.asp	5	1.1 %	5	1.1 %	

Figure 3-16: Filtering shows just how many "external links" come from Google.

> ### LINKS THAT DON'T ACTUALLY LINK AND OTHER ANOMALIES
>
> Occasionally, you'll find a URL in the list that has no links to your site. This is actually a form of spam. The idea is to get webmasters clicking the URLs to find out where the link is to their site. If you are finding a lot of those spam URLs, ask your web host how to block an IP or domain and then block them.
>
> For another interesting anomaly, look at the second entry in the external links list of Figure 3-15. The hits number is huge, while the pages number is comparatively small. When this happens, it's because the external site is hitting a nonpage element, such as an image. Figure-Skating-Blog.com happens to be Mary's blog, so it's not a big deal. But if a site you don't own is hitting a nonpage item hard, it is stealing your bandwidth. You should check carefully for what it is using and then block it from using that resource. Many web sites allow you to block everyone from directly linking to nonpage elements while also allowing you to make exceptions for sites like your own blog.

A low percentage of search-engine-driven traffic can mean that your site is not well optimized for search engines and people are not finding it. About two years ago, Mary overhauled SkateFic.com with search engine optimization (SEO) in mind. The percentage of traffic driven by search engines doubled, as did total traffic. Jolly good show!

If the external links aren't bringing in the traffic, you need to be concerned about word of mouth and viral marketing. This is especially so if most of your external-link traffic is coming from repurposed Google searches, small search engines, and AdWords placements. It means that you don't have a lot of sites that spontaneously link to yours.

So how is SkateFic.com doing? Search-engine traffic is about 50 percent, not too shabby. Bringing in that many new people every month is growing the core readership by hundreds of eyes every month. Direct-address traffic is about 43 percent, which means SkateFic.com has a happy and returning fan base and is a healthy content site. But with only 6.3 percent of page views coming from external links, and many of them from small search engines and AdWords, SkateFic.com isn't doing very well as far as word of mouth. Putting more effort into getting links from other sites, especially figure-skating-related sites, could pay off handsomely in the long run. Independent external links are a crucial part of an SEO strategy and would improve search-engine results, bringing in more, better-targeted traffic.

Key Words and Key Phrases

Speaking of targeted traffic, if you want to know what people are searching for in those search engines, look no further than the Keywords and Keyphrases [sic] tables in Figure 3-17.

Odd chance can bring in traffic for content that isn't.

Unless you're huge, single keywords don't mean much.

Search Keyphrases (Top 10) Full list				Search Keywords (Top 25) Full list		
8325 different keyphrases	Search	Percent		3697 different keywords	Search	Percent
figure skating facts	237	1.8 %		skating	6128	10.7 %
michelle kwan	154	1.2 %		figure	5586	9.8 %
figure skating	135	1 %		ice	2511	4.4 %
kristina cousins ice skater	113	0.8 %		skater	1355	2.3 %
figure skating history	79	0.6 %		skaters	950	1.6 %
kristina lenko	73	0.5 %		of	862	1.5 %
sandra bezic	69	0.5 %		kristina	856	1.5 %
figure skating poems	49	0.3 %		olympic	829	1.4 %
facts about figure skating	48	0.3 %		the	767	1.3 %
jef billings	46	0.3 %		facts	704	1.2 %
Other phrases	11664	92 %		history	666	1.1 %

Figure 3-17:   Why are people coming here?

These search terms are bringing visitors to your site. Unless you're an 800-pound gorilla yourself, the Keywords table won't mean a whole lot, except that having your best key words appear the most is desirable. See how "figure" appears 5,586 times and "skating" clocks in at 6,128, but "figure skating" brings in only 135? That's what we mean. SkateFic is ranked so far down in the search for "figure skating" that it seldom gets found. The traffic you do see in the table is actually brought in by AdWords.

For the most part, though, SkateFic's key-phrase performance is pretty good. There are only two anomalies (Kristina Lenko and Kristina Cousins), which bring people in but don't actually appear anywhere on the site. The rest of the key phrases are on topic and likely point to relevant content. By clicking **Full List**, one would see that "figure skating" appears in roughly half the searches, meaning people are generally interested in the subject matter SkateFic offers. This is important. Years ago, the two top searches were "Tina Wild," a porn star, and "hockey wives" — don't ask, we don't know either. Obviously, those searches did not bring in people who were interested in what SkateFic had to offer: a skating serial chapter that mentioned hockey players' wives and where the main character Tina had a wild-hair day.

Miscellaneous

At present, as shown on Figure 3-18, the only part of the Miscellaneous table that's working is the tally of bookmarks.

This measure is important for a few reasons. First, it tells you how sticky your site is — a measure of how many people feel your content has value for them. Second, the number of bookmarks helps you keep tabs on how big your core audience is — the people who intend to come back. Third, if you follow this over the months, you can see if your content is becoming more or less compelling — are more or fewer people intending to come back? SkateFic.com has run at right about 4.7 percent bookmarks for the last five years or so. It's not the greatest number in the world — we've seen blog sites where half the people who show up bookmark the site — but it works in the long run.

You can be pretty sure these people are coming back.

Miscellaneous		
Miscellaneous		
Add to favorites (estimated)	709 / 15043 Visitors	4.7 %
Javascript disabled	-	
Browsers with Java support	-	
Browsers with Macromedia Director Support	-	
Browsers with Flash Support	-	
Browsers with Real audio playing support	-	
Browsers with Quictime audio playing support	-	
Browsers with Windows Media audio playing support	-	
Browsers with PDF support	-	

Figure 3-18: Y'all come back now, y'hear?

Error Codes

We want to add a quick word about error codes and here it is, with the help of Figure 3-19.

It's worth noting that Google Analytics, by its nature, doesn't collect information on HTTP errors. Those errors are part of the log file, and Google Analytics doesn't look at logs. The only real point of interest is the 404 "not found" errors. If you click the 404 link, it'll take you to a page that lists all the URLs for the pages visitors requested that could not be found. If the URL is for a page that you've moved, you should create a redirect, so the web server will know where to send visitors looking for those pages. If the URL isn't familiar, especially if it contains funny characters like \x05, or if the URL has a long, long string of nonsense after it, or if it contains things like "admin" or .dll and you don't have stuff like that on your web site, it's likely that those are attacks on your web server. Unless those attacks are successful or overwhelming in number, you're probably safe in ignoring them.

Phew!

We made it! Now that we've tied up all the loose ends and, we hope, taught you all the basics, it's time to move on to Google Analytics. You'll see, as you go on, more of what Google Analytics can do that AWStats can't, but you'll also see that what you've learned about AWStats is valuable in itself.

Onward!

Click here for the full list of "not found" pages.

HTTP Error codes			
HTTP Error codes*	Hits	Percent	Bandwidth
301 Moved permanently (redirect)	1539	45 %	689.34 KB
404 Document Not Found	1470	43 %	938.29 KB
403 Forbidden	267	7.8 %	0
206 Partial Content	130	3.8 %	354.42 KB
302 Moved temporarily (redirect)	7	0.2 %	5.31 KB
400 Bad Request	1	0 %	372 Bytes
* Codes shown here gave hits or traffic "not viewed" by visitors, so they are not included in other charts.			

Figure 3-19: Where was that again?

Setting Up Google Analytics

The average professional analytics package is eminently flexible and powerful. It can track every detail, every goal, and every bounce on your web site. Unfortunately, that also means you have to be a propeller-head — or hire one — to set up and use the average professional analytics package. You'll spend a lot of dough getting every last detail exactly right, and it'll take more time than you have.

Google Analytics is not your average professional analytics package. Yes, it's slightly less flexible, though every bit as powerful. What sets Google Analytics apart is that it's intuitive — easy to use — even if you want to integrate Google Analytics with your AdWords campaigns. You won't even need a propeller on your hat, much less one implanted in your skull.

Still, there are some steps in the Google Analytics setup that could be a bit tricky. Part II includes everything you'll need to know about setting up in Chapters 3–7. Each chapter walks you through a different aspect of setting up Google Analytics. No propellers required.

Getting Started

When Google purchased Urchin on Demand, industry analysts predicted that the merging of Google's technology with Urchin's capabilities would be a great relationship. Chalk one up for the analysts, because it truly has turned out to be a marriage made in analytics heaven. Sure, there were some growing pains in the beginning, but combining a successful analytics program like Urchin with the power and simplicity of Google's technology has created an application that anyone can use.

It's not all roses and champagne, though. Even paradise has bugs, and Google Analytics isn't immune to them. Fortunately, the bugs have been pretty minor. You should have a minimum of frustration setting up Google Analytics. You could encounter a few issues, but we're going to walk you through those to make this as painless as possible.

Signing up for Google Analytics

When you're ready to get started with Google Analytics, the first thing you need is a Google account. If you're a Gmail or AdWords user, you've probably already got an account with Google.

If you already have such an account, all you need to do is request an invitation to Google Analytics and then wait. You can request an invitation by going to `http://www.google.com/analytics`. Figure 4-1 shows what the invitation request screen looks like. Simply enter your name and e-mail address and click **Submit.**

If you don't have an account with Google, signing up for one is easy. The amount of information required is minimal, just your e-mail address and physical location. In Figure 4-2, you can see the information required to create an account with Google.

You can sign up for a Google account through the main Google web page. Go to `http://www.google.com` and click the **Sign In** link in the top right-hand corner of the page.

On the page that appears, you'll see a sign-in dialog box where you can enter your username and password. You won't have that information yet. Instead, click the link below this box that says **Create an account now.**

On the next page, you'll enter your sign-up information. You'll be asked for your e-mail address, password, location, and a verification word. Once you've entered that information, read and accept the terms of service and then click **I Accept. Create my Account.**

Figure 4-1: Requesting an invitation to access Google Analytics

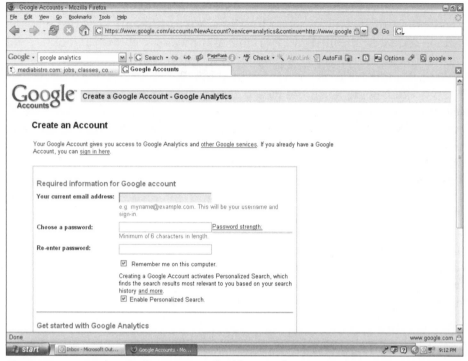

Figure 4-2: Google asks for your e-mail address and a password to create an account.

Google sends out confirmation e-mails for new accounts to prevent spambots from creating bogus e-mail accounts, so in a short while, you should receive a confirmation e-mail. When you do, click through the link in the e-mail to activate your account. Once you've clicked through the link, you'll have an active Gmail account.

The Waiting List

Once you get your Google account set up, you can just sign up for Google Analytics, right? Nope. It's not that easy.

When Google Analytics was first released, the company seriously underestimated the demand and was overwhelmed by the response. In just two days there were nearly a quarter of a million subscribers. Those users created nearly 400,000 web sites for the Google Analytics application to track and create profiles for. Google Analytics couldn't keep up with that high a demand for services in such a short time. It was gridlock, worse than the Jersey Turnpike at rush hour before the Fourth of July weekend.

For users who already had Google Analytics, there were minor frustrations. Page-loading times were a teeny bit slow. It was difficult to verify that the tracking code was installed and working on the users' web sites. It took several days for the metrics to begin appearing in the profile's reports.

For the huddled masses not yet initiated into the mysteries, the outlook was not so good. Google Analytics closed registration and started a waiting list. New users could get a Google Analytics account only after they received an invitation. As of this writing, Google Analytics is still an exclusive club — by invitation only.

But don't despair. Google will send an invitation to anyone who wants one — though it will do so in its own good time. To get on the waiting list, go to `http://www.google.com/analytics` and enter your name and e-mail address. Then, when you receive the invitation e-mail, follow the instructions in the e-mail to activate your Google Analytics account.

After you sign up to receive an invitation, it could take a few days to a few weeks to receive it. The length of time depends on the number of people in line ahead of you. Wait times are getting shorter. And it's a pretty good bet that once it comes out of Beta there won't be a wait anymore.

Activating Tracking

Your invitation will come as an e-mail with specific instructions on how to activate your Google Analytics account. When you go to the correct URL listed in the e-mail — there are different URLs for those who have AdWords accounts and those who don't — you'll need to enter your invitation code and sign in to your Google account.

From there, you'll be taken to a web page where you'll set up your first tracking profile for a web site. You'll need to provide the URL for the web site that you want to track. Then it's time for the tricky part.

Analytics uses a snippet of Javascript code to track the traffic on your web site. And you have to place that code on your site before the Analytics tracking is activated. It's not as hard to do as it sounds. All you have to do is copy the code that Google provides when you set up your account and paste it into your web site code before the `</body>` tag at the end of the page. Then save and republish the page, and Google Analytics will automatically detect the correct placement of the code.

On your Analytics Setting dashboard (which you'll learn more about in Chapter 5), you should see a message that indicates the code has been detected and data are being gathered for the analytics. The detection of the code should be immediate, but it could take a couple of days for any analytics to appear. In the meantime, if you click the **Check Status** option you'll be taken to the **Status Tracking** page, as shown in Figure 4-3.

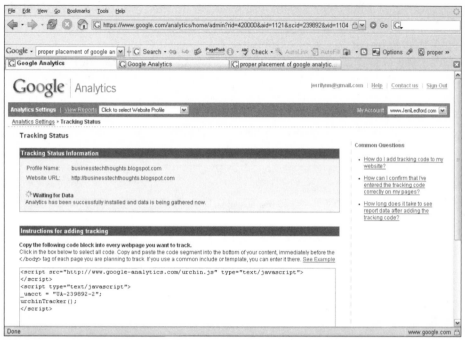

Figure 4-3: The Status Tracking page shows the status of your tracking code.

NOTE To track more than one page of your web site, you need to add the tracking code to every page you want to monitor. For example, if you have 15 pages in your web site and you want to track all of those pages, you need to place the code snippet on every one of those 15 pages. Any pages that do not contain the tracking code will not be monitored.

After a couple of days, the status message should change to Receiving Data. At that point, all of the reports and graphics for your site metrics should appear in your Google Analytics account. Google Analytics isn't real-time at this point, so the statistics that you have will be one to two days behind. It's not a perfect solution, but despite the delay, the depth of information provided is both accurate and useful.

Navigating Analytics

By now, you've had a taste of navigating through the Google Analytics site. It's an intuitive, point-and-click navigation method that lets you start at the most general of pages and takes you deeper into more specific pages as you go on.

For example, when you sign in, you're taken to the Analytics Settings dashboard. If you click one of the **View Reports** links on that page, you're taken to a page that's similar to the one in Figure 4-4.

This page is your Executive Overview, and it's just a quick look at some of the most used analytics. If you click one of the graphics, you'll find more information imbedded within them. In the Visits and Pageviews graphic, shown in Figure 4-5, clicking the round spots within the graphic will show you how many visits or pageviews were captured for a specific date.

Figure 4-4: Navigating through Google Analytics, from general to specific

Imbedded information

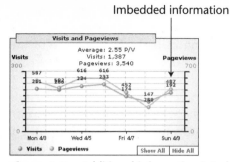

Figure 4-5:   Additional information is imbedded in the graphics.

On the left side of the page are three additional dashboards: the executive dashboard, the marketer dashboard, and the webmaster dashboard. Each of those dashboards contains additional navigational links that take you even deeper into the statistics and metrics that Google Analytics provides. Each of these dashboards will be covered in more detail in later chapters. For now, you can play around with the navigational structure of Google Analytics to get a feel for just how much information is really available once Analytics starts tracking your web-site metrics.

Integration with AdWords

Google AdWords is a pay-per-click advertising program. Customers pay to have ads appear on Google search result pages and in third-party content from advertisers who participate in the Google AdSense program. These advertisements are placed on web pages according to the keywords that users search for.

Google makes billions of dollars every year off AdWords. One of the main reasons why Google Analytics was screaming "Uncle!" on day two was that everybody and his dog who had an AdWords account signed up on the very first day to track the effectiveness of their AdWords campaigns.

Analytics, or tracking the effectiveness of AdWords campaigns, is the final piece in the pay-per-click puzzle. The metrics that Google Analytics provides answer the all-important question, "Is this ad working?" You can see if the person who clicked the ad bought something eventually, or if they dug deeper into the site. If you've purchased placement for two different ads, you can see how effective each of those AdWords has been in driving traffic to your web site.

Once AdWords has lured people to your site, you can use Google Analytics to see how users behaved while they were there. Where did they enter the site? Where did they leave? Did they buy something or bail in the middle of the checkout transaction, leaving a shopping cart full of merchandise sitting in the middle of the cyber-aisle?

The best part of the AdWords/Google Analytics integration is that it's automatic. When you create your Google Analytics account, all of your AdWords are imported into the account. The only caution is that it's best to sign up for both programs with the same Google account.

If you don't sign up for both AdWords and Google Analytics with the same account number, you can still connect the accounts. They don't just connect automatically. Here's how to connect them:

1. Log in to your AdWords account.

2. Click the **Analytics** tab at the top of the page.

3. From the bottom of the page, select the **Link to your AdWords Account** option.

4. You'll be taken to a page that shows the Existing Google Analytics Account drop-down list. Select your Google Analytics account number from the list.

5. Select **Link Account**.

Now your accounts are linked. AdWords information will be imported into your Google Analytics account. When you want to see the metrics on your AdWords campaigns, all you need to do is sign in to your AdWords account and select the Analytics tab. You'll be taken to the information that Google Analytics has gathered.

The development team at Google has a knack for making applications very usable, and Google Analytics is no exception. Getting started with the application is easy. You might experience a little delay in getting an invitation from Google once you sign up for the program, but once you do get the invitation, you're only a few steps away from a powerful — and free — analytics tool.

CHAPTER 5

The Settings Dashboard

It's one thing to collect data. Any analytics program will do that. But to go beyond gathering data like a vacuum sucking dust bunnies from under your bed and to produce usable information — that's something completely different. Most analytics programs will produce almost any kind of data your heart could desire, but they don't make it easy to use. And if you can't figure out what the data mean, what use are they?

To produce meaningful data, even with the easiest of analytics programs, you have to set up the program correctly. Set-up should be easy. The first dashboards, after all, were on horse-drawn buggies. Gee-up and away we go. Far from the horse-and-buggy days, most professional analytics programs require experienced professionals to configure them. Google Analytics is strictly DIY, with the simplest dashboards first. The more complex settings are no more than a few clicks deep.

Analytics Settings

When you log in to Google Analytics, the first page is the Analytics Settings dashboard shown in Figure 5-1. This dashboard is your gateway to creating and managing your profiles, controlling access to your profiles, and setting filters.

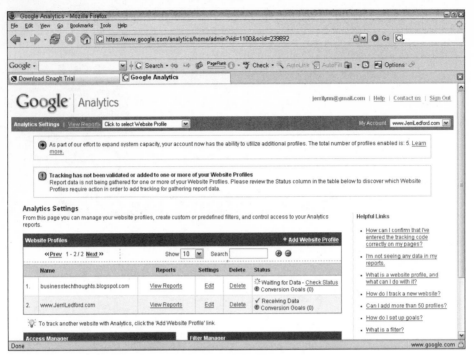

Figure 5-1:   The main Google Analytics dashboard

The main (top) menu bar of the Analytics Settings dashboard has two basic choices: Analytics Settings and View Reports. If you have more than one profile, you can select which one you'd like to view from the drop-down menu, as shown in Figure 5-2. Otherwise, the default profile (whichever one you added first) will load when you click **View Reports**. Jerri has two web-site profiles in her account: general information is at www.JerriLedford.com and there's a personal blog at www.businesstechthoughts.blogger.com.

Web site Profiles menu

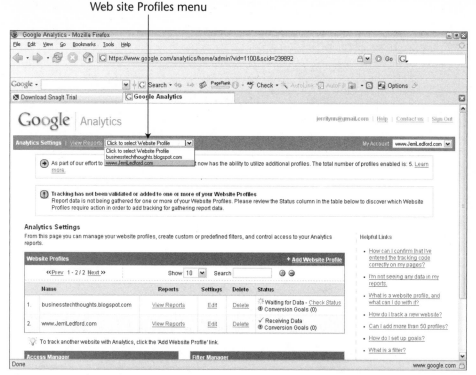

Figure 5-2: The Website Profile Menu contains up to five different profiles.

If you've been given access to profiles in another account, you will have a second drop-down menu on the far right. As Figure 5-3 shows, this is the menu that contains the different accounts connected via your Google Analytics account. For example, the www.JerriLedford.com profile is the default in Jerri's account, while the SkateFic profile is in Mary's account. Using the Access Manager, Mary gave Jerri administrative privileges to the SkateFic profile. Jerri can see all the metrics and make changes to settings in the SkateFic profile, but she doesn't have access to any of the other profiles in Mary's account.

My Account menu

Figure 5-3: You can give other people access to your Google Analytics profiles.

Website Profiles

How many web sites do you own? Do you have just one or do you collect them the way Monopoly players hoard hotels? Maybe you've got a web site and a separate blog or a personal site and an e-commerce one? If you have multiple sites to track, you know it can be a hassle if you have to track all those sites separately. It takes time to keep up with each site, and it's hard to come up with that time.

Google Analytics makes it easy for you to track the analytics and metrics for multiple sites or even subdomains by creating profiles that you can manage from one location. Below the Analytics Settings ribbon is a Web Profiles table. This table contains all the links you need to administer your various profiles, to add a profile, or to change or delete a profile. There's also a status category that gives you a quick look at the status of each profile you've created.

Adding a Profile

When you receive your invitation number from Google for the Analytics program, you'll be directed to a web site where you enter the invitation code and then set up your first profile. Once you get that first profile set up, you can add additional profiles through the Website Profiles dialog box.

Here's how to add a new profile to those you're tracking:

1. In the Website Profiles table on the Analytics Settings dashboard, click **Add Website Profile.**

2. As Figure 5-4 shows, the information page for the new web-site profile appears. Select from the options to add a new domain to track or to add an existing domain to track. The new domain is for a site that you are not currently tracking. The existing domain would be a portion, or page, of a site you're already tracking that you would like to track separately. (The way time-zone information is presented may differ slightly among users.)

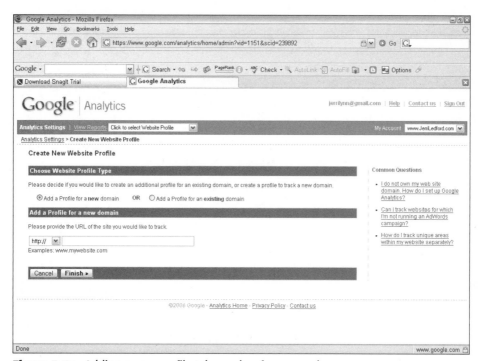

Figure 5-4: Adding a new profile takes only a few seconds.

3. After you select the Profile Type, enter the URL of the web site that you want to track in the Add a Profile for a New Domain text box.

4. Click **Finish.**

5. You'll be taken to the Tracking Status screen, as shown in Figure 5-5. The code that makes it possible for Google to track your site is located below the Instructions for Adding Tracking. Copy that code and paste it to the bottom of your Web page before the `</body>` tag, and the site will be added to your profiles for tracking.

Checking Status

Once you've added the code to your web site, it will appear in the Status category on your Analytics Settings dashboard as pending. You should see the status of the tracking on your site whether it is Pending or Receiving Data. Pending means that Analytics is still gathering information.

Figure 5-5: The Tracking Status screen shows status information and tracking code.

It could take a couple of days for Analytics to gather enough information to begin producing reports. When enough tracking information has been gathered, the message Receiving Data will be displayed in the Status category.

Editing a Profile

Once you've created your Analytics profiles, you can edit or change the profile information by clicking the **Edit** command that's on the same row as the profile name (usually the URL of the web site you're tracking) in the Website Profiles table.

You edit profiles from pages like the one shown in Figure 5-6.

Figure 5-6: You can edit profile settings for several categories from this page.

Such a page lets you change four types of profile settings:

- **Main Website Profile Information:** Change the profile name, the URL of the site you're tracking, or set a default page — the index page of the site you're tracking. Add query parameters, filter the information tracked by Analytics, or, if yours is an e-commerce site, select the reports and dashboards you want the profile to show.

- **Conversion Goals and Funnel:** A conversion goal is a target site that you want users to reach. For example, if you want to drive traffic to sign up for your corporate newsletter, your conversion goal would be the "thank-you" page for the sign-up process. The number of people who actually reach the "thank-you" page is then counted toward the conversion goal. Funnels are pages that you expect your visitors to go through to reach your conversion goal. You can specify up to 10 pages as funnel pages. Those pages are then monitored to show traffic patterns and how users navigate through your site to your conversion goal.

- **Filters Applied to Profile:** Filters help you achieve more accurate measurements of the traffic on your site. For example, you can choose to filter visitors who enter your site from a specific domain as a way to ensure more accurate reports. The most common use of this feature would be to filter traffic from your IP address. Say that your browser loads your web site's home page when you open a new window. You don't want to skew data about real visitors by counting hundreds — if not thousands — of your own visits and page loads. A filter can tell Google Analytics to ignore anything that comes from your IP address, resulting in more accurate metrics.

- **Users with Access to Profile:** In many organizations, more than one person will want or need to have access to the information that Analytics collects and the reports that it returns. There are two levels of access: View Reports and Account Administrator. View Reports allows the user to look at any reports in that profile. Administrator privileges allow the user to make changes to view reports and make changes to settings.

All these settings can be changed at any time. If you try something and it doesn't work, you can change it again until it does work. Each web site you're tracking has its own profile settings, so you can manage each profile in a way that works best for that domain.

Deleting a Profile

Change happens, and it's a good bet that your needs will change over time. You may change the name of your web site, add profiles you want to track, or delete profiles. To delete a profile, navigate to the Analytics Settings page; then find the name of the profile that you want to delete. Click the **Delete** link that's in the same row as the name of the profile. As Figure 5-7 shows, you'll be prompted to confirm that you want to delete the profile. Click **OK** and the profile will be deleted.

Make sure you really want to delete the profile from Analytics before you click **OK**. Once you confirm, there's no way to get the profile back. If you change your mind, you'll have to recreate the profile from the beginning and you'll lose all your historical data.

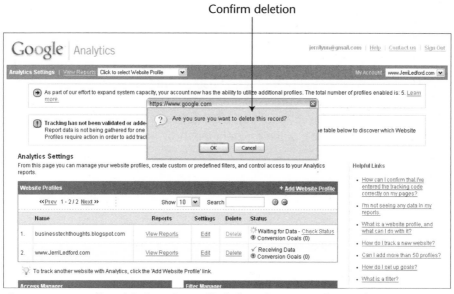

Figure 5-7: Confirm deletion of a profile before the process is complete.

Access Management

One very helpful feature of Google Analytics is the ability to give other people — your IT manager or administrator, other executives, or your partner — the ability to view and manipulate your Analytics account.

If you've ever worked with someone else and had them inadvertently change something that you didn't want changed, you may be itchy-skitchy (that means nervous) about which privileges you grant to other users. Maybe you want them to control everything. Maybe you barely trust them to look at the reports. The Access Manager lets you control who can see what and who can do what.

The Access Manager is located near the bottom of the Analytics Settings page. Click the Access Manager link and you'll be taken to the Access Manager dashboard, shown in Figure 5-8. From this dashboard you can add users and manage those users' privileges.

Adding a User

Recently there have been several studies about how executives want to be involved in the collection and reporting of business intelligence, like the information gathered by Google Analytics. According to these reports, executives want to be right in the middle of the action. They want access to the reports and to receive information about what data are being gathered, how often, and from where.

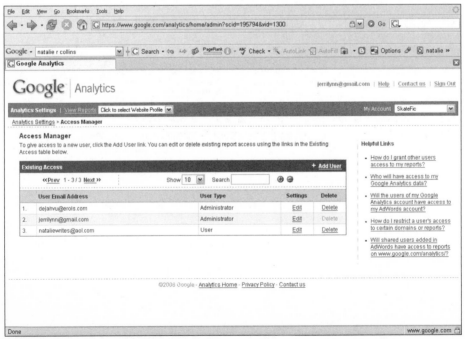

Figure 5-8:   The Access Manager lets you control who can access your account.

Google Analytics is built for multiple users. If you have an executive screaming over your shoulder every day that she wants information about the ROI (return on investment) of your web site, Analytics makes it easy to overload her with all the information she could ever desire. All you need to do is add your executive annoyance as a user on one or more profiles.

To add a user to your profile, go to **Analytics Settings > Access Manager**. In the Access Manager window is an Existing Access box that shows who your current users are and what levels of user they are. Click **+ Add User** in the upper-right corner of the box to give another person privileges.

You'll be taken to the Create New User for Access page, where you should enter the user's e-mail address, name, and set the access type, as shown in Figure 5-9. When you've entered the relevant information, click **Finish** and the user account will be created.

NOTE When creating a new user profile, the user you are adding must have a Google account, and that's the e-mail address you should use to register the user to have account access. If you use an e-mail address that isn't attached to an active Google account, the user won't be able to access the site. However, that person can use that address to set up a Google account that will then be able to access Analytics.

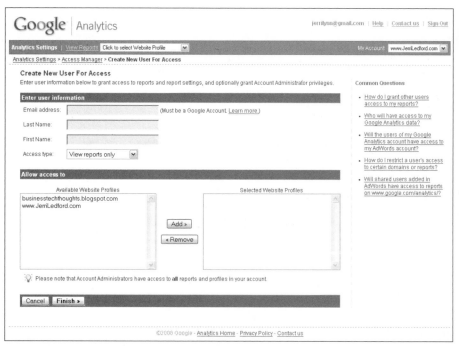

Figure 5-9: To add a new user, enter some simple information and click Finish.

Setting User Permissions

When selecting the Access type, you can set permissions so that your users have Administrator Access or authorization to View Reports Only, as shown in Figure 5-10.

Administrator Access to a profile gives the user the ability to do anything you (the owner) could do. That user can make changes to settings, add other users, and even delete the profile. Or hand out administrator privileges like black beads at Mardi Gras. An inexperienced admin can neatly sabotage a web-analytics strategy. View Reports Only allows the user to view reports but not to make any changes to the profile.

You can select and also restrict which web-site profiles the user can access. If you have multiple profiles for multiple sites, you can give users access to some and keep them out of others. For example, if you work in a bigger company, you could set up several profiles for your company's web site. One could be for the boss, which shows just the executive dashboard and associated reports. Another profile could be for marketing and another for the webmaster, each showing specific information for a specific use.

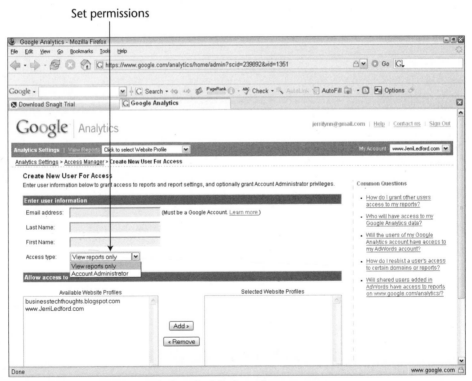

Figure 5-10: Set user permissions in this drop-down menu.

Deleting a User

People leave. They find better jobs, get downsized, move to Tahiti, or transfer to different departments. In the corporate world, it's inevitable. And you need to have the ability to delete a user from your Analytics account. Google knows this and makes deleting users easy for corporate IT geeks.

To delete a user, go to **Analytics Settings > Access Manager** and find the user you want to delete. Select the **Delete** option in the same row as the user's name. You're once again prompted to confirm that you want to delete the user, as shown in Figure 5-11. Click **OK** and the user will be immediately removed and will no longer have access to that — or any other — profile.

Be sure that you really want to delete a user, because once it's done, you can't undo it. You'll have to recreate the user.

Google Analytics makes everything point-and-click easy. It might take you a few minutes the first time you access the program to get it set up, but then adding and changing profiles and users is just a matter of clicking a few links.

Confirm deletion

Figure 5-11: You're prompted to confirm you want to delete users from your program.

Filtering Your Data

Most people look at a bolt of fabric and see nothing more than cloth. A seamstress looks at it and sees a shirt. The data collected by Google Analytics is just about the same — it's only meaningless data until you view it from the right perspective. That's when it begins to look like something useful.

In Google Analytics, a filter provides the right perspective. Filters help to separate data into two categories: the data that is used to create reports and that has no value to you. Google Analytics provides filtering capabilities that help you see through the myriad facts, numbers, and values it collects.

What's a Filter?

Suppose Google Analytics simply collected information about your web-site statistics and then dumped it in your lap without any kind of organization. It would take you longer to make sense of the statistics than it takes for a toddler to clean his room.

To help you understand what the facts that Google Analytics collects mean, data goes through filters. These filters can exclude information collected about certain domains or IP addresses (an Internet site's numerical address), or they can simplify complex sets of numbers or facts, making them easier to understand.

Because understanding data can be a real chore, Google has created a set of MadLibs-like filters that give you the ability to separate your collected metrics by plugging in key pieces of information or patterns expressed in a language called Regular Expressions, also known as RegEx. More about that later (though you'll see some RegEx wildcards in the following examples):

- **Exclude all clicks from a domain:** This filter lets you exclude visits to your site from a specific Internet site. This is especially helpful if your company web site gets a high number of visits from people on the corporate intranet looking for dirt to dish on their coworkers.

- **Exclude all clicks from an IP address:** Remember that girl who had a crush on you in the third grade and now follows you everywhere, making untoward suggestions for weekend activities? She visits your web site 150 times a day from her always-on cable modem connection 68.68.68.68. You could filter out that IP. But say she also uses her dial-up connection, which has the IP address 68.68.68.67. This filter will also exclude information about visits that match a particular kind of pattern. Filtering on `68\.68\.68\.6[78]` will match either 68.68.68.68 or 69.69.69.67 and will keep her obsession from screwing up your web-site metrics. Now, if you could only use a filter to keep her out of your favorite restaurant.

> **NOTE** Some unsavory characters have discovered several ways to mess around with your stats and analytics. One way they skew the numbers is by copying your web site's source code (which they use to create their own site) and leaving your Google Analytics code imbedded within it. Another is to copy your source code to the header on their web site. In either case, the result is screwy measurements for your site. To straighten your measurements back out, you need to use a filter that excludes the rogue's IP address from the data that Google Analytics collects.

- **Include only traffic from a specific subdirectory:** Your hot, new product finally has a page on your web site, and now you want to know how much traffic that one part of the site gets. Disappointing or not, this filter will show you how your baby is doing at the expense of all the other data on your site. "Include only" will include only the specific information that you tell it to.

In addition to these, you can create custom filters that separate out the information that you don't want or that isolate the information you do want. Custom filters allow you to:

- **Exclude a pattern:** This filter will exclude data from visits that match a certain pattern. Say you want to collect information only on your catalogue's regular products, not the sale ones. All sale products have a special E-commerce Item Code that begins with "SALE." You could filter that field to exclude any hits from those e-commerce items by filtering with SALE.* as the pattern.

- **Include a pattern:** Just as you can exclude, you can choose to include information that matches a certain pattern. Say you want to measure only the visitors who have really big screen resolution because you're going to launch a new game that requires it. You could include traffic where the Visitor Screen Resolution matches \d\d\d\d X \d\d\d\d, which would only match resolution with two four-digit numbers.

TIP The custom Exclude and Include filters are much more flexible than the predefined filters that Google has included. You can use pattern matching with any of the data fields that Google monitors, more than just the domain, subdomain, or IP address. Use these custom filters to drill deeper into the vast oil field of data that's available to you.

- **Search and replace:** Much like the search-and-replace function in your word processor, this filter lets you search for specific types of information related to user visits and replace it with other information.

- **Lookup table:** Certain specific information isn't in a format that you can understand, even if you have it in front of you. So the lookup table collects that information and translates it into a format you can understand. For example, you can use a lookup table filter to show readable names for unrecognizable or confusing URL patters. There's more to come on lookup tables, so don't fret if you don't get it just yet.

- **Advanced:** Do you wish you could exclude one pattern at the same time you're including another? You can; just use an Advanced filter that can look at multiple pieces of information at one time. Advanced filters are trickier than missing anthills in Mississippi, though, and Google documentation is literally circular, but that's why you bought this book, right?

- **Uppercase/lowercase:** Got something against capital or lowercase letters? Use this filter to change them. Why? Maybe your web developer is lazy and sometimes she used title style for tokens and sometimes she used all caps. Google Analytics doesn't know that there's no difference between "Sale" and "SALE." With the uppercase filter, you could change "Sale" to "SALE," or with the lowercase filter, you could change "Sale" and "SALE" to "sale," which would make for much more accurate metrics.

A Short Lesson in Regular Expressions

Creating many of the Google Analytics filters requires some knowledge of Regular Expressions. Don't get too excited. Regular Expressions aren't phrases like "well, bless her heart" — the Southern disclaimer for every snarky comment uttered under any circumstance. Life couldn't be that easy.

A Regular Expression is a string of text that uses characters, numbers, and wildcards to match patterns in a string of characters. RegEx has been accused of being obtuse, and that is not wholly unjustified. While basic RegEx is pretty easy, patterns can be complex and RegEx follows right along.

The characters and numbers used in a Regular Expression are the same ones you use in English every day: letters A-Z (and a-z), numbers 1-9, and certain symbols from your keyboard. The wildcards are specific symbols or combinations of symbols. Here are the wildcards used in Regular Expressions:

.   A period by itself will match any single character: letter, number, punctuation, or space but not an end-of-line character like a carriage return. To match a literal period, use \. which uses the back slash to "escape the wildcard" and make it literal.

*   An asterisk added to a character or wildcard will match zero or more of the previous items. So x* will match a string with nothing in it, x, xx, xxx, or any number of x's in a row together. More generally, .* matches nothing (empty string) or any series of characters (including numbers and punctuation but not including end-of-line characters). But take great care with the * modifier; it's greedy, meaning that it seeks the largest match possible — not always the one you mean. Say you have a paragraph with several sentences ending in periods. You would think that .*\. would match the first sentence, but it doesn't; it matches the whole paragraph!

+   A plus sign added to a character or wildcard will match one or more of the previous items. Use this modifier when you definitely know you don't want to match an empty string or when you want to require that a particular character be present. So x+ would match x, xx, xxx, and so on but would not match a blank string.

?   Match zero or one of the previous items. So x? will match x and xx but not xxx. Adding ? to * produces something interesting. Remember we talked about .* being "greedy" — that it produces the largest match possible, which is not always what you want? Well, .*? de-greed-ifies .* faster than jail time drains the avarice off a CEO. Still want to match the first sentence of that paragraph of sentences? Well .*?\. will do it.

( )   Put parenthesis around a part of a pattern when you want to store that tidbit of information for use later.

[ ]   Put square brackets around a list of characters you want to match. So when we wanted to match both 67 and 68 in your crazy crush's IP address, we used the pattern 6[78], which matched both. Don't make the mistake of putting a word in square brackets and think you'll match the word. You won't. It's strictly character by character. Use alternation with the | to match words.

-   Create a range in a list. So if you want to match any number, you can use [0-9] rather than [0123456789].

| The vertical bar or "pipe" character is used for alternation. Think of it as the word "or." Say you wanted to match "this" or "that"; you'd use a pipe this|that.

^   The carat has two possible matches depending on where it is. If it's inside square brackets, it means "not." So [^0-9] means "anything that is not a digit." But when you find ^ outside of square brackets, it means "at the beginning of the line." So ^Help will match the word Help if it appears at the beginning of a line.

$ Just as the carat is the beginning of the line, the $ is the end of the line/field. So help me$ will match only if it appears at the end of a field (or if it's followed by an end-of-line marker like a carriage return or line feed).

\   Escape any wildcard. When you escape a wildcard, it becomes a literal. When you escape certain literals, they become wildcards (for example, \d is "any digit" and comparable to using [0-9] but quicker to type). Only certain literals can become wildcards when escaped. What happens if you escape something that doesn't have a special meaning? Nothing. You're safe. You can even escape an escape, like \\, which you'll need if you want to match a literal back slash. RegEx is like Amelia Bedelia, a children's book housemaid who takes every direction completely literally unless you tell her not to.

Here are some additional tips that you'll need for working with wildcards in Regular Expressions:

- The characters ^ and $ represent the beginning or end of an expression. They're called *anchors* and can speed up the processing of your request when used properly.

- Use the | to group patterns together. For example, if you need to return graphics with these extensions: .jpg, .gif, .bmp, and .png, you don't need to escape the period in front of each extension. Instead, you can use the expression \.(jpg|gif|bmp|png) to group the pattern.

- The expression . * matches everything, so don't forget how greedy it is! Use . *? when you don't want to match everything and it's dog and cat and bird and fish and — well, you get the idea.

- Keep it simple. The more complex you make your Regular Expressions, the longer it will take them to process. With a very complex Regular Expression, you also introduce more opportunity for error. As my editors are fond of telling me, add only what you have to and leave everything else out.

You could spend months — even years — learning Regular Expressions and still not learn everything there is to know. What you need to know right now is that you will need some simple Regular Expressions, like the ones in the preceding examples, to create an advanced filter. Of course, more advanced expressions will result in more advanced filtering capabilities, so if you'd like to know more than what's here, check out the sidebar for some additional resources on Regular Expressions.

LEARN MORE ABOUT REGULAR EXPRESSIONS

If you're interested in learning more about Regular Expressions, these resources will give you something to chew on:

Beginning

◆ *Beginning Regular Expressions,* by Andrew Watt. ISBN: 0-7645-7489-2.

Intermediate

◆ *Regular Expressions: The Complete Tutorial,* by Jan Goyvaerts. ISBN: 1411677609.

Advanced

◆ *Mastering Regular Expressions,* by Jeffery Friedl, ISBN: 0596002890.

ARTICLES ON THE 'NET:

◆ **Regular Expressions Wikipedia Entry**

   http://en.wikipedia.org/wiki/Regular_Expressions

◆ **Common Applications of Regular Expressions, by Richard Lowe at 4GuysFromRolla.com**

   http://www.4guysfromrolla.com/webtech/120400-1.shtml

◆ **Understanding Basic Regular Expressions Patterns, by Tom Archer at Developer.com**

   http://www.developer.com/net/cplus/article.php/3485636

More resources can be found by Googling "understanding Regular Expressions."

Managing Filters

Setting up filters begins with the Filter Manager, which is located near the bottom of the Analytics Settings dashboard. Click the **Filter Manager** link and you'll be taken to the dashboard shown in Figure 6-1.

Creating New Filters

To set up a new filter, click the **Add Filter** link in the upper-right corner of the Existing Filters box. This opens the Create New Filter page shown in Figure 6-2.

Enter the filter name, filter type, and domain name, if necessary. Then select a web-site profile to apply the filter to and click **Finish**. You'll be returned to the Filter Manager dashboard, and as Figure 6-3 shows, your new filter will appear in the Existing Filters box.

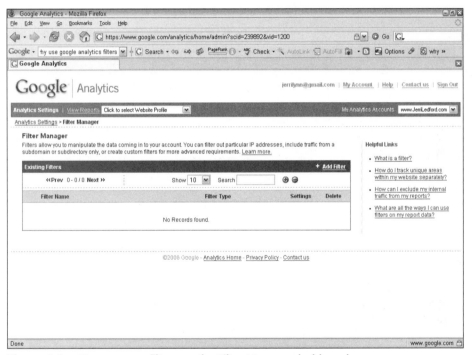

Figure 6-1:   Manage your filters on the Filter Manager dashboard.

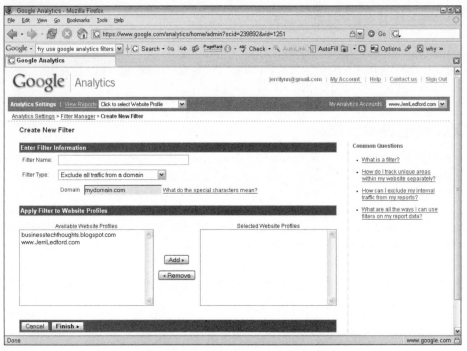

Figure 6-2:   Create a new filter by entering the requested information.

New filter added

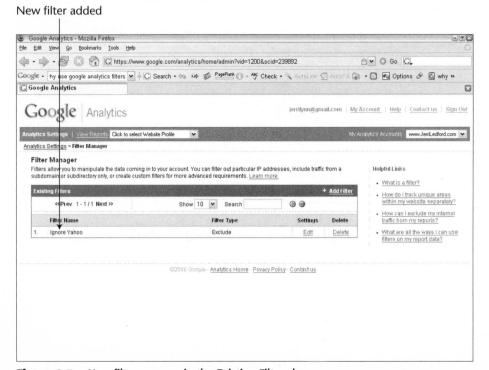

Figure 6-3:   New filters appear in the Existing Filters box.

NOTE If you have multiple domain profiles on your Google Analytics account, you can apply the same filter to all of the domains (or any number of the domains) at one time. For each domain you want the filter applied to, highlight the domain name in the Available Website Profiles menu and click Add. The domain will be moved to the Selected Website Profiles menu. Complete the filter setup, and the filter will be applied to all selected domains.

For example, if you want to create a filter to exclude the internal traffic from your network because your home page is set to the front page of your web site, from the Filter Manager you would select **Add Filter.** Now, enter a filter name; for the purpose of this example, we'll use the name *Exclude Internal Example.*

FILTER VALUES IN PREDEFINED FILTERS

If you're using the filters that Google Analytics already has predefined, there are a few fields that you might want to know a little more about. Here's a quick list of the fields you might encounter and how you can use them:

◆ **Domain:** This allows you to determine the complete domain or a portion of a domain that you want to filter. So if you want to keep your brother-in-law's traffic out of your stats (because you share a domain) you could set up your filter to exclude his subdomain (sub.domain.com) by using the expression `sub\.`.

◆ **IP Address:** You can filter an IP address or a range of IP addresses using Regular Expressions to tell Google what to look for. To filter a single IP address, enter the IP address like this: `192\.125\.1\.1`

To filter a range of addresses like 192.125.1.1 to 192.125.1.25, you would use the expression: `192\.125\.1\.[1-9]|1[0-9]|2[0-5]`

To filter an additional range such as 10.0.0.1 and 10.0.014, use a | symbol between the ranges.

◆ **Subdirectory:** Again, you can use Regular Expressions to include (or exclude) the subdirectory of a site. So, if you wanted to include a specific subdirectory, the expression that you would use is: `subdirectory/` where you replace the word subdirectory with the name of the subdirectory you want to include.

RegEx can be pretty confusing, even for experienced users. When you understand the expressions more, they will make more sense. Until you're more comfortable with them, you may need to refer to the portion of this chapter titled "A Short Lesson in Regular Expressions" to help you figure out how to write the Regular Expressions you'll use in your filters.

Next, go to **Filter Type** and select **Exclude All Traffic from an IP Address.** When you select this option, the IP Address field will automatically show a default IP address. *This is an example address and should be changed.* Replace the address with your own IP address using the exact same format as the example that is filled in for you. This is a Regular Expression — a piece of code that tells Google Analytics exactly what to look for.

Finally, select the web-site profile to which you want to apply the filter and click **Add** and then **Finish.**

Now you have set up your first filter to exclude any internal traffic to the web site that you're measuring.

There's one more thing you need to understand about filters, and that's the order in which they are applied. Many people have trouble with Google Analytic's filters because they don't realize that all of the filters that you apply to a web-site profile are applied in the order in which they are set.

When you're looking at your list of filters for a specific web site, the order in which you see those sites is the order in which they are applied to your analytics. If you happen to have an exclude filter set for the very first filter, only what remains after the filter action will be affected by the next filter in the list.

But don't despair. Changing the order of the filters is easy enough. All you have to do is log in to your Analytics Setting and then click **Edit** in the same row as the web-site profile that you want to change.

On the Profile Settings page, navigate down to the Filters Applied to Profile box and click the **Assign Filter Order** link. You'll be taken to a page like the one in Figure 6-4. Highlight the filter that you want to move and then click the **Move up** or **Move down** buttons to rearrange your filters into the order that you want them to be accessed.

Custom Filters

When you're creating a new filter, one option you have is to create a custom filter. When you select the **Custom filter** option as shown in Figure 6-5, the menu for custom filters expands to show you additional options for that filter.

These custom filters can be used to dig deeper into the statistics that Google Analytics collects. Use them to filter for specific activities like including only a subset of traffic or excluding a type of visitor. You can also perform search-and-replace functions and rely on a table function to clarify the data that is returned. Let's look closer at each of those types of filters.

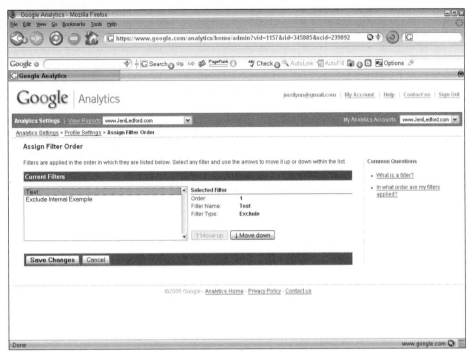

Figure 6-4: Rearrange the order in which filters are accessed.

Include and Exclude Filters

Include and exclude filters are just what they appear to be — filters that include or exclude specific data. But the custom include and exclude filters go beyond simply filtering web-site domains and IP addresses. With these filters you can choose to include or exclude specific fields or capabilities. If you don't want to know about any of the users hitting your site who have Java capabilities installed, you can choose to exclude them. Or maybe you want to include only the users who have Java capabilities. In that case, all of the visits from users who don't have Java capabilities will be discarded, and you'll see information only from those who do.

Figure 6-5:   Additional options on the custom filter menu

Here's what you need to remember:

> Include filters discard visits that don't match the inclusion pattern.

> Exclude filters eliminate visits that you want to exclude.

The reason it matters? Multiple include and exclude filters can result in no traffic at all. Say you set up an include filter specifying that you want only traffic from users with Java enabled. Then you set up an exclude filter that says you don't want any users who aren't using Internet Explorer. You end up with *only* people who use Java and Internet Explorer.

Think of it this way. When you decide to buy a car, you go to the lot and first choose a model that you like. That choice (which you could call an include filter, because you want to include only cars that are that specific model) cuts your choices down by at least half and probably more.

Then you decide that you want this specific model only in blue. You've added another include filter that reduces your number of choices again.

Your last decision is that you don't want a standard transmission. Now you've added an exclude filter and the result is that there might be three cars on the lot that you can choose from. Include and exclude patterns work the same way to narrow your results.

Search-and-Replace Filters

Ever look at something and have no clue why you're looking at it? Chances are, if you were looking at it from a different perspective, you'd understand it immediately. Let's say you're selling jet skis, snowboards, and surfboards through your web site. And on the site, each item is assigned a different numerical value for classification purposes.

When you look at reports, you have to remember what each numerical category represents (for instance, 1000=jet skis, 2000=snowboards, and 3000=surfboards). Unless you have a photographic memory, or those are the only three items that you sell, memorizing all of the classification numbers could take forever.

If those numbers were converted to readable, easy-to-understand text on your reports, your hair might not go gray for another month or so.

That's what a search-and-replace filter does. This nifty tool lets you turn mundane, hard-to-recognize results into something that's immediately understandable by replacing a matched expression with a different string or group of numbers or text.

If you have a web site with several different categories of pages, this is an easy way to understand what the category IDs for each page represent.

That means that your pages will appear in your reports as something unexciting like `/docs/product.cgi?id=1000` (or =2000, or =3000, depending on the category). It's especially troublesome if you have dozens of category IDs to keep up with. You can use the search-and-replace filter to change those mundane category IDs to something that has meaning. Like this:

Go to **Analytics Settings > Filter Manager > Add Filter** and then enter a filter name. For this example, we're using *Search & Replace Example*. From the drop-down menu, select **Custom Filter** and then click the radio button beside **Search and Replace**.

A new information section that has to this point remained hidden (Google doesn't want to scare you off with confusing stuff before it's necessary) will appear. In the Filter Field, select **Request URI.**

Now for Search String, type `/docs/document.cgi?id=1000`. (This is just for the example, not for your actual site. For your site, you would replace this information with your actual search string.) Then for Replace String you would type the information you want to replace it with. Let's use "Surfboards."

Now you can select whether you want to make this filter case-sensitive. In most cases, you'll want to leave that alone because it won't matter whether your entries are capitalized or lowercased. However, you may have an instance where the search string is case-sensitive, and you may need to specify the correct case. For now, leave it alone.

At this point, your filter should look like the one pictured in Figure 6-6. All that's left is to select the web site you want the filter to apply to and click **Finish.**

Now you're seeing meaningful labels "surfboards" or "jet skis" instead of ID=1000 or ID = 2000, which really only means something to your web server. You won't have to wonder if you're selling more surfboards or jet skis. The answer will be right in front of you in an easy-to-read format.

Figure 6-6: An example search-and-replace filter

Lookup Table Filters

As with search-and-replace filters, lookup table filters substitute something understandable for the incomprehensible. But there are some differences. Let's look at our surfboards again. Say your page IDs are set up to look like this: `www.example.com/page.html?id=691` (where the number represents a specific product ID).

A lookup table filter gives you the ability to return the page ID, SurfTech, which tells you that's the page that displays your SurfTech surfboard line.

What a lookup table does is to work in conjunction with advanced filtering to substitute readable text for request parameters used with dynamic URLs (unlike search-and-replace filters, which are used with static URLs). And this requires Google's help.

To begin using a lookup table, the first thing you need to do is create a spreadsheet saved as a *tab delimited plain text file* that maps query parameters to the readable code.

Confused yet?

For this to work properly, the spreadsheet has to have a specific setup. Name, column 1, row 1 must have the heading # Fields, and column 2, row 1, must have this heading: request_stem. In each of the rows below row 1, you'll enter first the ID that you want replaced and then the ID that you want to replace it with. For example, your spreadsheet might look something like what's shown in Figure 6-7.

Once your spreadsheet is complete, save it as a tab-delimited, plain-text file with the extension .lt for lookup table. If you're using Excel, you'll probably receive a program prompt that tells you that you can only save the active sheet rather than the whole workbook. This is exactly what you want to happen, so click **OK**.

	A	B	C	D
1	# Field	request_stem		
2	691	/help/software/overview		
3	790	/help/installation_guide		
4	1555	documents/white_papers		
5				
6				
7				
8				
9				

Figure 6-7: The basis of a lookup table filter

Now you have to send the sheet to the folks over at Google for processing. Attach the file to an e-mail to `analytics-support@google.com`. And since a human will be reading your message, make sure you specify which web-site profile you want the table applied to. Then wait. It could take a few days for the team at Google to get you fixed up, so be patient. When they do get you ready to roll, you need to create an advanced filter to put that file to use. That information is in the next section.

Advanced Filters

Advanced filters are where things get even more hinky because creating one isn't as easy as picking two options from a list and then clicking okay. You actually have to work a little to put an advanced filter into place. The pay-off is that you can create filters that meet your specific needs, including customized tracking for advertising campaigns and tracking specific measurements.

Creating Advanced Filters

Now that you understand just enough about the other types of filters to be dangerous, it's time to learn how to create advanced filters. Buckle in. It's going to be an interesting ride.

Step back just a bit and remember where we were with the lookup table filters. We're going to continue that example by using the surfboard information to create an advanced filter.

You start creating an advanced filter just as you would start any other type of filter. Go to **Analytics Settings > Filter Manager > Add Filter.** The Create New Filter page appears. Enter a name for your filter (for the example, I'm using Advanced Filter Example as a filter name); then, from the **Filter Type** drop-down menu, select **Custom filter** as shown in Figure 6-8.

The custom filter menu will expand to show several options. Select the radio button next to the **Advanced** option, as shown in Figure 6-9, and the advanced filter fields will appear on the page.

Select custom filter

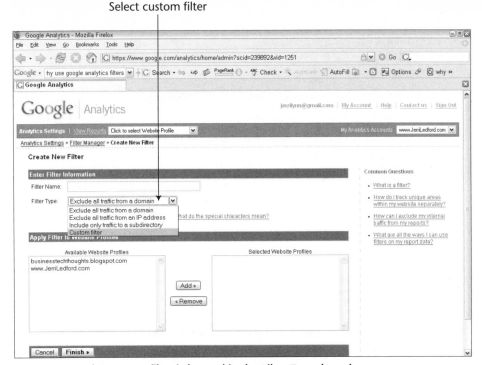

Figure 6-8:   The custom filter is located in the Filter Type drop-down menu.

Here's where things get pretty complicated, so pay close attention to this part. Advanced filters contain two fields: Field A and Field B. These fields work together to produce a new field called Output. It's not enough just to select the functions that you want to combine in Fields A and B, however. You also need to enter a Regular Expression for each field to narrow the results further.

For both Field A and Field B, the text box you see after the drop-down menu is the Extract field, and this is where you'll need to enter a Regular Expression. You can use complete or partial text matches and wildcards in these fields. For the example that we're working, select **Request URI** from the drop-down menu in Field A; then type **690=([^&]*)** into the Extract A text box. In this expression, id should be replaced with one of the ID numbers in the table that you created for the lookup table filter.

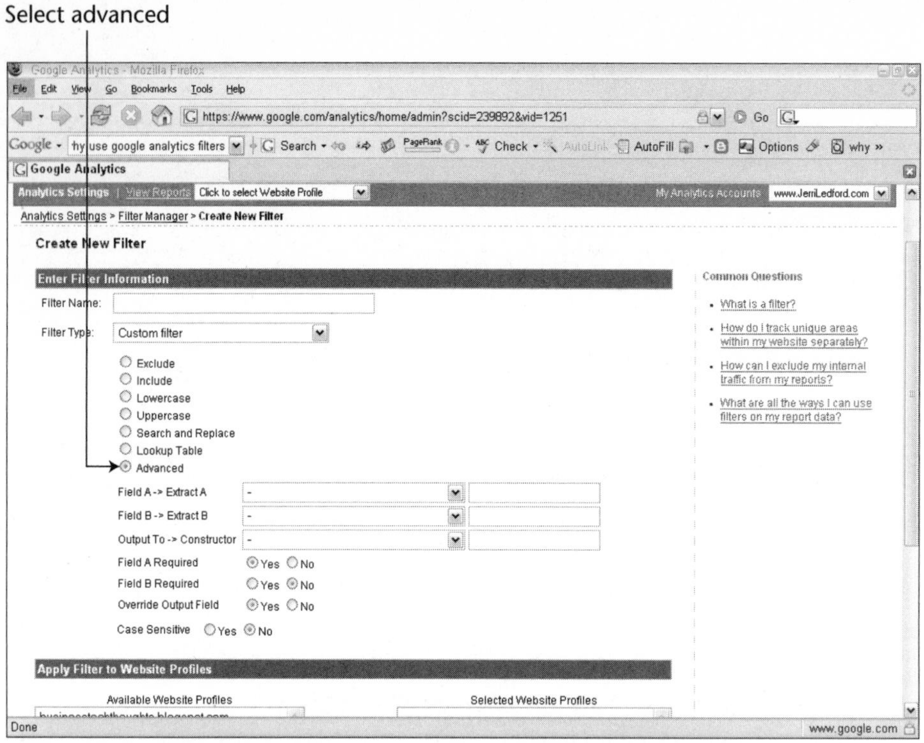

Select advanced

Figure 6-9: Each option brings you closer to creating the advanced filter.

For Field B, select "-" from the drop-down menu. This is the equivalent of leaving the Extract B field blank.

Next, in the Output to drop-down menu, select request_stem (Auto) and then enter $A1 for the Constructor field.

> **NOTE** When selecting the Output, you won't see the request_stem (Auto) option unless Google has finished processing the spreadsheet that you sent to them. For that reason, the request_stem (Auto) isn't shown in Figure 6-10.

Now, for the Override Output field, be sure the radio button beside **Yes** is selected; for Required Fields, be sure that the radio button beside **A required only** is selected. Set your Case Sensitive field, and select the web site you want to filter. Your filter should look similar to Figure 6-10. Click **Finish** and you've created your first advanced filter.

It could take up to two days before your filter starts working on your data. The filter will be applied to all your new data but will not apply to any historical data that has already been collected.

Select fields to combine   Enter regular expressions

Figure 6-10: How the example advanced filter should appear on your screen

There are many other ways that you can use advanced filters, but there's not room to include all those examples in this book. Play with it to see what it does and how it can help you. Check out our blog for more information and examples — or send us yours and we'll make you famous!

Editing and Deleting Filters

Filters don't run off to Tahiti to hang out under palm trees and slurp umbrella drinks. But you may find now and then that they need a vacation — maybe a permanent one. So you need to know how to change or delete them. (And Tahiti could still be a problem if the boss spent a week there and came home with some grand ideas that require different analytics.)

Before the tropical high wears off, change your filters and then ask for a big raise. We can't help with the raise, but we can tell you that you change or delete filters by clicking the **Edit** or **Delete** links in the Existing Filters box.

Editing will take you to the same page you saw when you set up the filter, and then you can change anything about the filter that you want (or need) to change. Just make the changes and click the **Finish** button and the updated filter will be changed and will automatically take effect.

When you select the option to delete a filter, you'll be prompted to confirm that you truly do want to delete it, as shown in Figure 6-11. By now you should be familiar with this routine. The confirmation is there for your protection, so double-check everything and then click **OK** and the record will be deleted.

The Power of Filters

What you can do with filters is limited only by your ability to create them. If you're not familiar with Regular Expressions, it is well worth your time to learn more. As with any computer language, RegEx is confusing in the beginning, but as you become familiar with how the wildcards work, it will get easier to create a Regular Expression for your advanced filters. Before you know it, you'll be filtering out all of the useless tracking information that Google Analytics collects by default. Don't worry; those monkeys in the back room banging away at keyboards won't care that you're filtering them out as long as you keep them supplied with bananas.

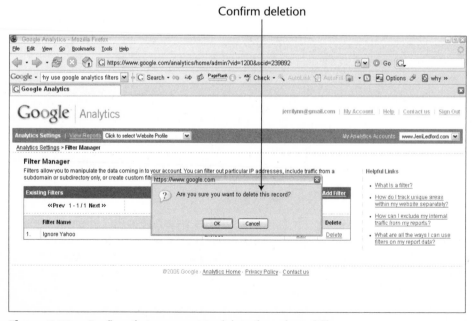

Figure 6-11: Confirm that you want to delete the selected filter.

CHAPTER 7

Using Analytics Goals

What's the point of tracking web-site metrics if you don't have some reason for tracking them? It's like jumping on the interstate in your brand-new Mustang with no particular destination in mind. You've got the vehicle to get somewhere, and the road to follow, but without a destination, how will you know if you're headed in the right direction?

That's where goals come in. Like having a destination in mind when you set out on a journey, goals provide the "why" of collecting user data. Why do you want to know how many users dropped off your e-commerce web site during the checkout process? Because knowing will help you decide if you've reached your goal of providing an easy, effective means for users to purchase your products through your online channel.

Google Analytics actually has a capability that allows you to decide what you want the program to do for you. Then you can add a goal to your web site profile so you can track the goal and your progress toward reaching it.

Before we get any further into the specifics of Google Analytics' goal capabilities, let's run through some of the management-speak you'll encounter in this chapter. The keywords are objectives, goals, and specifics.

- **Objectives:** An objective is your big picture or what you want the big picture to look like when you're finished. An objective for a company that imports and sells Russian nesting dolls might be to sell more dolls and make piles of money. It's a long-term outlook.

- **Goals:** If objectives are long-term aims, goals are shorter-term aims. What has to happen for you to sell more nesting dolls? And specifically, what do you want to accomplish with Google Analytics? Your goal could be to increase sales by 20 percent and to do it using Google Analytics.

- **Specifics:** Now you're getting to the heart of what you want to accomplish, both in the short term and the long term. Specifics are the "how" — the action steps — of goal setting. A good set of specifics for the nesting doll goal would be to use Google Analytics to find the most efficient way to funnel traffic to my sales confirmation page (the "thank you for placing your order" page that appears after an order has been approved). Reach sales goal within six months. And generate proof of my efforts and successes in the form of reports to get the boss off my back.

Now, back to an important question: Why should you have analytics if you don't have goals? The answer is that you shouldn't. If you aren't tracking specific actions with specific results — if all you're looking for is who visits your site — then all you need is a stats program. And it doesn't have to be particularly advanced.

Understanding Goal Setting

Pop quiz: What's a frequent response to the question, "Why do we need this or that technology, application, or program?"

Give up? Try: "Because it's the best." To which the typical reaction is to scratch your head and keep your mouth shut because you don't want to look like a complete idiot to the obvious genius trying to explain that "having the best" means the tech gods smile on you, revenues flow from the heavens, and the door on the corner office automatically opens.

Yeah, right.

Every technology, application, or program should have a purpose to fill: a goal to reach that leads to the big-picture objective. If you're putting a firewall in place, the purpose (or goal) of that firewall is to keep the wrong sort of people off your network. And if you want to track analytics, what you track will be determined by the business problem that you're trying to solve with your web site.

Of course, this whole theory assumes that you have taken the time to develop a web site for a purpose. Are you selling a product, collecting customer information for marketing purposes, or trying to recruit the next downline star for your network marketing group? If you just threw the site up for the fun of it, you can skip this part.

For all other business problems, you need a goal. Simply saying the business problem is the goal isn't enough. Yes, you want to sell more of your Russian nesting dolls. But that's your objective, and alone it isn't enough to drive business or increase sales. And trying to track that goal will have you pulling your hair out by the roots.

What you need is a goal or set of goals that specifically track the behavior that leads to the sale of the nesting dolls. So the goal we mentioned earlier — to increase sales by 20 percent and do it using Google Analytics — is more measurable than a goal of simply selling more nesting dolls.

That's an important point: To be effective, you need a goal you can measure or track.

Using the second goal, you can develop a set of metrics, or specifics, that show how visitors navigate through the site to complete the sale. The information returned by these metrics will illustrate what works — and what doesn't — making it easier for you to alter your marketing campaign or customer approach to achieve your goal.

For the real-estate franchise RE/MAX, an ineffective goal may have been to drive traffic to the RE/MAX web site. It would seem to be an effective goal because a study conducted by the National Association of Realtors in 2004 found that nearly three-quarters of all home buyers begin their search for a new home online.

But simply driving traffic online isn't enough. It's like herding cattle in the direction they're already going. You sit in the saddle and let the horse follow the cows while you watch the scenery.

RE/MAX needed to do more than just drive traffic to its web site; it needed to turn online traffic into sales. Kristi Graning, senior vice-president of IT and e-business for RE/MAX, said that instead of just pushing users to the web and tracking how many visitors the site had, the company created a goal to help people find a house and select an agent, which follows the general objective of increasing sales.

To reach the goal, RE/MAX used Google Analytics to learn more about why people were visiting the RE/MAX web site, where they were coming from when the visited the site, and how they behaved while on the site.

Those analytics were then turned into a strategy — the specifics — to make it easier for people to find houses and select agents. The web site was redesigned to better suit visitors' property-search behaviors, to capture lead information that's passed to agents, and to track the lead-to-sale-conversion rate.

RE/MAX set a goal it could act on and then went to work using Google Analytics to create strategies to reach that goal.

Why Set Goals?

There's some consensus in the business world that those who set goals tend to go farther than those who do not. It's a truth to be heeded. Look around your organization, circle of friends, or family group. How many of the people there have solid goals and can voice those goals in a clear, understandable way?

Now consider where those people are in comparison to Uncle Danny, who really doesn't seem to have a goal, or Colleague Jenny, who's very happy with her position in your company. How much more have the people with goals accomplished than those who don't seem to have them?

There's probably a pretty sizable difference in accomplishments there.

Setting analytics goals works the same way. If you have a clear, reachable goal that is in alignment with your overall objective, there's a better chance that some action will be taken to achieve that goal. What is it that they (who-ever "they" are) say about some action being better than none at all?

It's the difference between passive and active. If you're passive, the world happens to you. If you're active, you make the world happen.

So setting goals is the precursor to action. You set a goal with an overall objective in mind, and then you can choose specifics that will make things happen to reach that goal.

Choosing Which Goals to Set

Here's where the waters start to muddy just a bit. How do you know what goals to set? No worries. It's easy. There's this glass jar with the word GOALS painted on the front. Someone in the office has it. Just reach in and pull one out.

Okay, maybe that won't work. But it still seems to be some people's approach. They grab at thin air and hope that something will magically appear for them to latch onto. Instead, try asking yourself this question: What business am I really in?

It's not fate, magic, or divine intervention that makes a goal great. It takes a solid understanding of your business — or your objective — and how your web presence fits into that larger picture. If your business is management training, how will your web site improve that business? Maybe you want to expand training beyond your local area by offering online classes to management wannabes still living in their parents' basements. You could also use your web site to gather sales leads by enticing potential management trainees (or even corporations that might need your services) to sign up for a monthly newsletter.

What you need to accomplish with your web site is what should drive your analytical goals. A good goal for your management training business could be to increase sales by providing training services that are more accessible to individuals and companies in the region (or U.S. or world).

That goal could apply to either of the actions that your management training company might take with your web site.

Ultimately, the analytics goals that you choose are determined by your specific situation and needs. A goal that puts you on a path toward fabulous results might put a similar company on a path toward certain doom or at the very least back to the drawing board. So examine your business. Determine what *your* needs are. And then create goals that help you fill those needs.

One company that truly understands the business it's in is the Warren Featherbone company. Back in the 1800s, Warren Featherbone made corset stays — those horrid, rigid pieces of hard material that ensured a woman couldn't slouch or bend over at the waist. Obviously, corset stays went out of style. So, in the 1920s, Warren Featherbone got into bias tape. It's a sewing accoutrement that makes creating even hemlines a little easier.

Over time, however, customers' needs changed again. No longer did customers have time to sew all the garments their families wore. There were even — gasp — women who couldn't sew!

Because the Warren Featherbone company knows what business it's in — the fabric and clothing business — it shifted gears yet again to meet the needs of the customer. Today, Warren Featherbone sells kids' clothing under the Alexis label.

Warren Featherbone completely understood its business, which led to a clear understanding of its objectives, and so the company can create, achieve, and recreate effective goals.

Now, let's see if we can help you do the same thing.

Setting up Goals

When you first set up a web site for tracking on Google Analytics, you're given the option to create goals for the site. Most people don't set those goals up at the very beginning, because they're not sure what they're doing. That's okay. You can set the goals up anytime you're comfortable with the process.

It'll be easy. We'll give you all the steps you need. All you have to provide is the goal.

To set up a goal after you've created your web-site profile, go to Analytics Settings. Under the Website Profiles menu, find the profile to which you want to add the goal. Click the **Edit** link in the same line as the web-site name, and you'll be taken to a page like the one in Figure 7-1.

Figure 7-1: Create goals in the Conversion Goals and Funnel menu.

The Conversion Goals and Funnel menu is the second box on the page. There you'll find the name of any goals you've created, the URL of those goals, and a status area that shows whether the goal is active or not. Click the **Edit** link in the line of the goal number that you want to change or set up.

NOTE Google allows only four goals for each web-site profile that you set up. Should you need to track more than four goals for your web site, you should set up another web-site profile for a section of your site. That allows you to have four goals for that section and four goals for any other sections of the web site that have their own profiles.

After you click the **Edit** link, you'll be taken to the Goal Settings page shown in Figure 7-2.

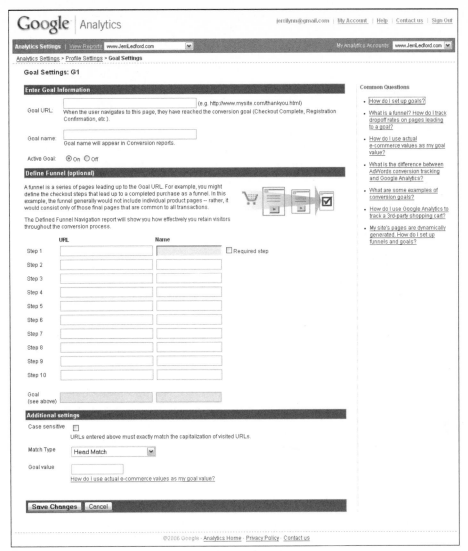

Figure 7-2: Create a goal to track on the Goal Settings page.

Here's the information you need to enter to create a new goal:

- **Goal URL:** The Goal URL is the web page within your site that you want your customers to reach. If yours is an e-commerce site, the Goal URL might be the purchase confirmation page after the transaction has been submitted. It could also be a confirmation page on a site where the goal is for users to sign up for a newsletter.

- **Goal Name:** Choose the name you want your goal to have. In the preceding example, the name Purchase Complete would be a good choice.

- **Active Goal:** Select the **On** or **Off** radio button to activate or deactivate your goal.

- **Define Funnel:** For every Goal URL, there is a logical way that consumers reach that goal. In the case of the e-commerce site, a funnel might include the index page, the products page, the shopping-cart page, the checkout page, and then the Goal URL, which is the confirmation page.

  A funnel is used to measure how often users take the logical path to your Goal URL. If they deviate from that path frequently, you know that what you think is the logical path may not be for the consumer. This allows you to redefine the funnel and creates additional opportunities for you to reach your customers.

  Enter the URLs for the funnel in this section.

- **Additional Settings:** Select additional settings, like the capitalization of the Goal URL, the Match Type, and the Goal Value of your goal. The Goal Value can be an exact value or a dynamic value, based on your needs.

When you finish entering all the information requested, click the **Save Changes** button and your new goal will be created. Then you'll be able to see it in your goals list, as shown in Figure 7-3.

TIP To quickly determine how many goals you have set for a particular website profile, all you need to do is look in the status column on the Analytics Settings page. The number of goals for each web-site profile is displayed there, but you can't see the actual goals.

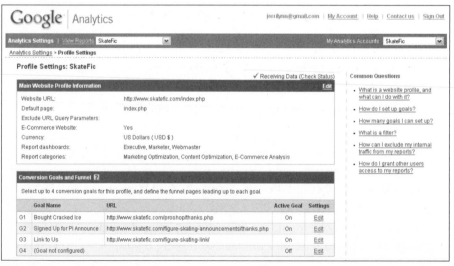

Figure 7-3:   Once created, goals appear on your Profile Settings page.

Editing and Inactivating Goals

Like the other functions of Google Analytics, editing goals is easy to do. To edit your goals, enter the Goals Settings screen by going to **Analytics Settings > Profile Settings** and then click **Edit** in the same line as the goal number that you want to edit or delete.

If you're editing the goal, your prepopulated Goal Settings screen will appear, as shown in Figure 7-4. All you have to do is edit the information that you want to change and click **Save Changes.**

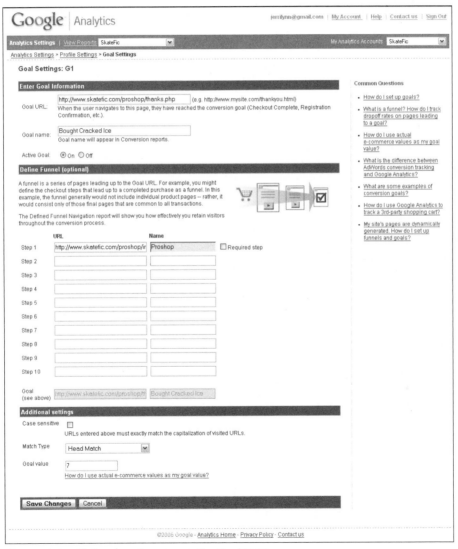

Figure 7-4: Make your changes on the Goal Settings screen.

The one failing here is that you can't actually delete a goal once you set it up. You can change it or turn it off, but you can't remove it entirely. It's not a problem unless you happen to be the minimalist type who can't stand clutter. In that case, having an unused goal just floating around in your web-site profile might drive you a little crazy, but it won't hurt anything at all.

CHAPTER 8

AdWords Integration

Whatever else Google Analytics is, it's a power tool for Google's AdWords program. Like the radial arm saw that you use to create the perfect shelf for your entertainment hutch, Google Analytics is the tool you use to build the perfect AdWords campaign.

So which came first, the chicken or the egg? Does it really matter if you have both? AdWords and Analytics have the same concept. It doesn't matter which you have first, since the two are (or can be) connected to form a single entity that helps you do more, better.

Why Google Analytics with AdWords?

If you're already using AdWords, you might be wondering why you would want to put the two together. Even without Google Analytics, AdWords has decent reporting capabilities. But when you add Google Analytics, what you get is a picture of your campaign performance worth a thousand (Ad)Words.

Using the tools of Analytics, you can measure the ROI (return on investment) of your ad campaign by tracking not just your AdWords campaigns but also any banner ads, referral links, e-mail newsletters, or offline advertising campaigns you run.

Once you link the two accounts, Analytics will automatically track any active campaigns in your AdWords account. You get a single view with all the information you need. It saves you a ton of flipping back and forth between programs, trying to figure out what's working and what's not. Not to mention all of the work that you save in trying to tag ads so that Analytics tracks them.

Linking Analytics and AdWords

Not much is different between a lone Google Analytics account and one linked to AdWords. First step: Get an invitation to Google Analytics. Once Google Analytics is out of beta (we'll announce it in our blog), you won't have to wait for an invitation. Until then, remember what you learned in kindergarten: Wait patiently (but you don't have to hold hands with your line partner).

To get an invitation to Google Analytics, log in to your AdWords account and click the Analytics tab. Enter your name and e-mail address, as shown in Figure 8-1, and click the submit button. Then wait.

Once you do receive the invitation to use Google Analytics, the setup wizard will automagically walk you through everything you need to do.

Figure 8-1:   Enter your name and address to receive an invitation.

Linking Separate AdWords and Analytics Accounts

If you weren't sure when you set the accounts up that you wanted to link AdWords and Analytics, you might have kept the accounts separate. When you change your mind, you can link two existing accounts by clicking the **Link to Your AdWords Account** link at the bottom of the sign-up page. If both AdWords and Analytics are associated with the same user name, you'll get confirmation of the link. If you signed on to AdWords and Analytics with different user names or if you don't have an AdWords account, you'll get an error similar to the one in Figure 8-2.

If you did register your accounts under two different user names, simply give the other user name access to your AdWords account. It's also good to add your AdWords user name to your Analytics account just to be safe.

Once you've connected the two accounts, you can create profiles, add users, set up filters, set goals and funnels, and much more. Much more? Read on, intrepid explorer. The wonders of AdWords integration await.

AdWords and Analytics need same account.

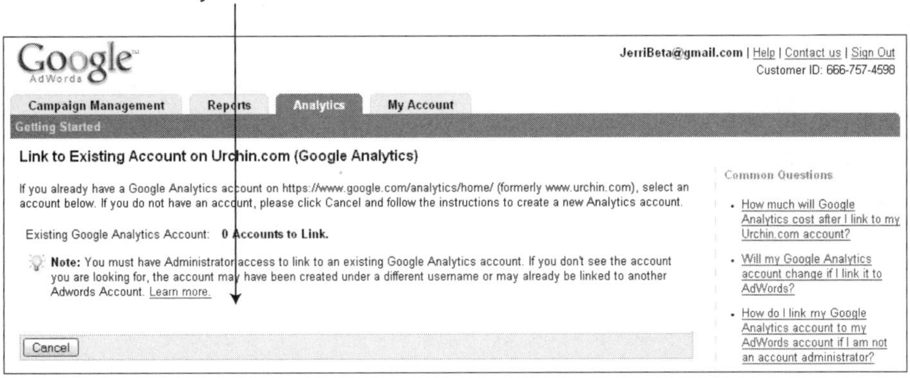

Figure 8-2: AdWords and Analytics can't connect if they're under different accounts.

Tag, Your Link Is It!

How does Google AdWords know that a certain visit is the result of clicking an ad? Very simple. Whether it's a banner image on a web page, a text link in an e-mail, or any other advertising vehicle, the link is tagged with a variable that says, "Ooo! Ooo! Me! Me!" There are two ways of doing this. You can let AdWords auto-link the incoming links — auto-link is on by default. To turn it off, go to **My Account > Account Preferences**.

Auto-linking takes the work out of tagging your links by using a special parameter, called "gclid," which adds an extension to your URL containing the information Google needs to track the details about how a user behaves when they click the link. The URL is then referred to as an arbitrary URL.

An auto-tagged link will look something like this:

```
http://www.yourwebsite.com/?gclid=hit475
```

That's the good news. The bad news is that some sites won't display arbitrary URLs properly. So, instead of seeing the page displayed, users will see a server error. To be on the safe side, you should test your site's reaction to the tags before you call it done.

For more control, tag links on your own. Each tag has a name and a value in the following format `name=value`. If you want more than one tag, you separate name/value pairs with an ampersand, like this `tag1=value1&tag2=value2`.

Say SkateFic advertises on SkateWeb `<www.frogsonice.com/skateweb/>`. Mary might set the link underlying the banner ad to:

```
<http://www.skatefic.com/?utm_source=skateweb&utm_medium=banner&utm_
campaign=rebate>.
```

See the part of the URL after the question mark? Those are tags. You can use your own variable names to tag your links. Search the Google AdWords help files for "existing campaign variables" to see how. But even if you do your own, AdWords requires three particular variable tags. They are:

- **Campaign:** If you're running more than one advertising effort, the campaign variable uniquely identifies each one. The default variable name is `utm_campaign`. In the preceding SkateFic example, "rebate" is the value of the campaign variable.

- **Source:** This is where the advertising actually appears. The default name of this tag is `utm_source`. In the preceding SkateFic example, "skateweb" is the value of the source variable, since that is the web site where this link will appear.

LEARN MORE ABOUT GOOGLE ADWORDS

Google's AdWords program is a great tool for advertising. But it can get a little complicated. We don't want to distract you from Google Analytics too much, but if you're interested in learning more about AdWords, there are several really good books on the subject. Here's a sample of books that you might find useful:

Beginner:

◆ *Winning Results with Google AdWords,* by Andrew Goodman. McGraw-Hill, ISBN: 0072257024.

◆ *Google Advertising Gorilla Tactics: Google Advertising A-Z Plus 150 Killer AdWords Tips & Tricks,* by Bottletree Books, LLC. ISBN: 1933747013

Advanced:

◆ *Google Advertising: Cashing in with AdSense, AdWords, and the Google APIs,* by Harold Davis. O'Reilly Media, Inc. ISBN: 0596101082

And if you just happen to want to know more about key-word marketing in general, there's also this great book:

◆ *Pay Per Click Search Engine Marketing For Dummies,* by Peter Kent. Wiley, ISBN: 0471754943.

■ **Medium:** This is the type of advertising you're placing. The default name is `utm_medium`. In the preceding SkateFic example, "banner" is the value of the medium variable, since it's a banner ad we're tracking.

If you're still not sure about all of the various aspects of AdWords, there's a pretty thorough training section in the AdWords Learning Center.

Tracking AdWords Campaigns

The reason people stampeded Google Analytics like bulls charging a red cape was its capability to track AdWords campaigns. There are hundreds of thousands of AdWords subscribers. And all of them want to know more about how their AdWords campaigns are performing.

AdWords does provide a tracking and reporting mechanism. But Figure 8-3 shows what an AdWords tracking page might look like — not very descriptive is it?

Figure 8-3: A typical tracking page from Google AdWords

And then there's the reporting. Figure 8-4 shows what a simple report might look like.

Rather than a dry listing, Analytics graphs the effectiveness of your AdWords campaigns as in Figure 8-5. See the difference? In this Analytics report, you can quickly see how AdWords (google[cpc]) drives traffic relative to other source/medium combinations.

Connecting AdWords to Analytics gives you access to all of the reporting power in Google Analytics — all of it. You'll find the AdWords specific reports in the Marketing Dashboard. The details of that dashboard are located in Chapter 9.

Figure 8-4: AdWords' reports contain only essential information.

Figure 8-5: Google Analytics gives you a clearer picture of your AdWords results.

The Reporting Dashboards

Irina, Johnny, and Evan are the employees Mary wishes she had in the IT department at SkateFic.com, her skating-fiction business. All three have access to Google Analytics, but that's where their similarities end.

Irina, in this story, is the company's webmaster. She designs all the web pages — the look and feel of the company's presence online — and she heads the IT team that makes her visions (and the boss's demands) come alive.

Johnny is in charge of the IT component of marketing. He's responsible for creating banner ads (which he hands off to Irina), executing the company's AdWords campaign, overseeing other pay-per-click programs, and all of the other online marketing ventures the company takes on.

Evan is the ringmaster. He monitors all of Irina's and Johnny's efforts and reports to The Man (who in this case happens to be The Woman).

When these people come to Google Analytics, they want different metrics. Irina needs web-site metrics, Johnny needs marketing metrics, and Evan needs a good overview of all those metrics. Google Analytics makes it easy for them to get what they need. Maybe not *everything*, but everything in the context of analytics, and Google provides it in the form of a window on the soul of analytics.

In this next section, we'll show you each of the three main Google Analytics views: the Executive Dashboard, the Marketing Dashboard, and the Webmaster Dashboard. We'll give you some tips on how to use each dashboard to quickly find the metrics you need, too, but we're saving the explanation of why you should use each report for future chapters. We urge you to read through the Executive Summary, even if you're an Irina or Johnny. There are explanations in it that apply to dashboard elements you'll find in all the sections.

The Executive Dashboard

Evan has to answer for all of the efforts in the IT department. He's responsible for all of the web metrics at SkateFic.com, and it's his responsibility to "prove" to the boss that all of the efforts in his department are working. And if they're not working, he'd best have something he can use to illustrate why they aren't.

That's why Google Analytics is Evan's best friend.

Who Should Use This View

The Executive Dashboard is for people just like Evan. Maybe your situation is a lot different — *you* are the boss and the head of marketing and the webmaster. Maybe you do only some of those jobs. It doesn't matter.

If you need a quick overview of your web-site analytics, the Executive Dashboard is where you'll find it.

To reach this dashboard, go to Analytics Settings and click **View Reports.**

TIP Analytics Settings is the page you're taken to when you first log on to your Google Analytics account. This is the "front page" of your Analytics account.

Sometimes Google Analytics seems to have a mind of its own. (Don't worry; computers aren't taking over the world just yet. It's supposed to happen this way with Analytics.) If you select the **View Reports** link at the top of your Analytics Settings page, you'll automatically be taken to the Executive Dashboard for the first web-site profile in your list.

It won't save you clicks, but to go directly to the Executive Dashboard in a specific web-site profile, click the **View Reports** link on the same row as the profile name in the Website Profiles box.

No matter how you get there, the default report view is the Executive Dashboard, shown in Figure 9-1.

All three of the dashboards are arranged in the same way. On the main page of the dashboard (and aren't we thrilled it doesn't actually resemble the dashboard in your car?), the report links and date ranges are in the navigation bar on the left. Your graphics appear in the center and on the right side of your page.

Figure 9-1: The Executive Dashboard is the default report view.

Date Ranges

We'll come back to the navigation links shortly, but right now let's focus on the Date Range. This control allows you to view reports by hour, a single day, a week, a month, or a custom range.

By default, the date range is set to show weekly reports. The week usually runs from today to seven days ago. For example, if you're viewing your reports on Saturday, your week will run from Saturday to Friday.

You can change your date range by clicking the **View By** drop-down menu shown in Figure 9-2.

This drop-down menu will change date ranges only in increments set by default (for instance, weeks according to the most recent seven-day period or months that are the most recent 30-day period). But, as in many companies, our guy Evan runs campaigns Wednesday through Tuesday.

If you want a custom date range — maybe you need to view reports for the 3rd through the 15th because that's when there was a sale running — you can change your report coverage by clicking the small calendar in the upper-right corner of the Date Range box.

As Figure 9-3 shows, the Custom Date Range dialogue box appears when you click this calendar. Select the beginning date for the report in the left-hand box and the ending date for the report in the right-hand box. Then click **Apply Range.**

Your reports and your current report page will refresh automatically to reflect the new date range.

TIP The Date Range tool is available in all of your dashboards and all of your reports. You can make changes to it at any time, so if you need a monthly overview for one report and a weekly overview for another, you can have it Burger King-style — your way.

Figure 9-2: Change your default date range to hour, day, week, or month.

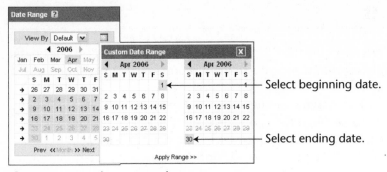

Figure 9-3: Apply a custom date range to your reports.

Executive Overview

Evan has his date ranges squared away, and now he's back to looking at his Executive Overview. Four graphs give you a quick overview of some of the most frequently consulted metrics. They are:

- Visits and Page Views: If you want a quick graph of how many visits and page views there have been on your site, this is where you'll find it. The visits and page views for the date range you've selected appear in this graph, similar to the one shown in Figure 9-4. The Show All and Hide All links on this graph will show or hide the *exact* number of visits and page views.

- Visits by New and Returning: The number of new and returning visitors to your web site are shown in the pie graph in Figure 9-5. You can view or hide the exact percentages by clicking the segments of the pie graph.

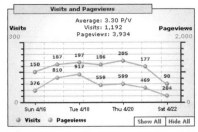

Figure 9-4: The Visits and Page Views graph

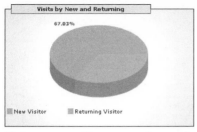

Figure 9-5: View new and returning visitors to your site in this graphic.

■ Geo Map Overlay: For some companies, advertising is about reaching people from a certain area or region. The Geo Map Overlay, shown in Figure 9-6, gives you a quick view of your visitors' physical location. For Evan, this means he can tell at a glance if the company's latest advertising campaign is bringing visitors from the intended region to the company web site. And for even more specific information about the cities in which your visitors are located, you can mouse over each dot on the map to view the city and the number of visitors from that city.

CAVEAT What you're actually getting is the location of the visitor's IP address. It may not be the visitor's location within 10 feet. For rural residents, it's likely the nearest town where the dial-up is. It could also be the location of the proxy or of a server that intends to hide the actual location of the visitor. Close enough but not exactly exact.

■ Visits by Source: Because his company runs banner ads on partner web sites, Evan also wants to be able to tell where visitors come from. The Visits by Source graphic gives him a quick summary of what the referring source is for his web-site visitors. Figure 9-7 shows the pie chart that details the referring sources. To view the exact percentage of visitors from any source, click that segment in the chart.

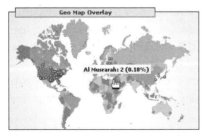

Figure 9-6: The Geo Map Overlay

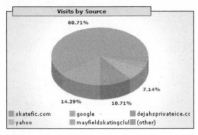

Figure 9-7:   The pie chart shows Visits by Source.

One more useful function of the Executive Overview is the Export and Print buttons that you'll find in the right corner of the Executive Overview title bar. The boss is always after Evan, looking for something that shows where marketing efforts are working or not working and what portions of the web site are most frequently visited. These export and print buttons give Evan some options for the type of file or even an exact print out he can pass on to the boss. Exporting options include:

- Tab Separated (Text)
- XML
- Excel (CSV)

The **Print** button takes you to a printer-friendly page that should result in a nice, pretty picture.

E-Commerce Summary

SkateFic.com is mostly a fans web site; however, a few products are sold through the site, so Evan needs some kind of e-commerce overview to show him (and the boss) what's happening with e-commerce sales at the site.

For Evan and his employer, there's an e-commerce summary page off the Executive Dashboard. However, not every site has e-commerce capabilities, so it's possible that you won't see this option on your Executive Dashboard. You can turn on e-commerce functions by going to **Analytics Settings** and clicking the **Edit** link next to the web site you want to enable e-commerce setting for. This takes you to your Profile Settings. Click **Edit** in the Main Website Profile information bar, and then you can change your e-commerce settings.

If you have turned on the e-commerce capabilities, the E-Commerce Summary page, shown in Figure 9-8, is very similar to the Executive Summary page covered previously.

Figure 9-8: The E-Commerce Summary page

The graphics on the E-Commerce Summary page are slightly modified versions of the graphics you've already seen. Rather than being general traffic stats, these graphics represent the different breakdowns for revenues. The graphics that you see are:

- Revenue and Transactions
- Revenue by New and Returning
- Geo Map Overview (representing revenue)
- Revenue by Source

Each of the graphics is similar to the graphic that you've already seen in the Executive Summary graphics. The data populating the graphs are different.

Conversion Summary

A simple (and appropriate) definition of conversion is the number of web-site visitors who meet a goal you set. SkateFic.com has a goal that site visitors reach a "Thank you for subscribing" page after they sign up for the company newsletter. The conversion, then, is the number of people who actually reach that page.

As you can see in Figure 9-9, the Conversion Summary looks a little different from the summaries you have encountered so far.

The Conversion Summary is based on a range of dates. On the left side of the Conversion Summary screen are two calendars. The range you select on the first calendar will be compared to the range you select on the second calendar.

The Conversion Summary table has three columns. Goal Conversion is a list of the goals for your web site. This column is indicated in Figure 9-10.

The second column, Visits, is the number of total visits for each goal. There's also a red or green arrow and a percentage number. An up arrow (green) is an increase and a down one (red) a decrease from the first period to the second. The percentage is how much conversions have increased (or decreased) from the first date range to the second. This column is also shown in Figure 9-10.

Figure 9-9: The Conversion Summary page

CALCULATING CONVERSION RATES AND PERCENTAGE CHANGE

Throughout the rest of the chapter, you'll see a rate and then a percentage change up and down. All these numbers are calculated the same way. A conversion rate is always: Visitors who met the goal ÷ visitors who began the process = Conversion rate.

The percentage change over time, whether it's in the raw numbers or the conversion rates, is figured the same way: Current figure ÷ previous figure (with figures converted to decimals) minus 1 and then times 100 = percentage rate of change over time.

So if the current period has nine conversions and the comparison period has six, the percentage increase is 50 percent. If the current period has a conversion rate of 5 percent (0.05) and the comparison period has a conversion rate of 10 percent (0.10), there is a decrease of 50 percent in the rate over the period.

Conversion rates in the third column of Figure 9-10 show how well you're doing at getting visitors to meet your goals. In the same figure, the arrows show an increase or decrease in conversions, and the percentage shows how much the increase or decrease was.

The purpose behind tracking conversions is to monitor the effectiveness of marketing campaigns, web-site changes, and other events that affect the way people reach your conversion goals. Over time, SkateFic.com decided that its company newsletter wasn't getting enough subscribers, so it changed the pages that funnel visitors to the newsletter. Evan watched the Conversion Summary for a few weeks after the change to see what the results where.

The Conversion Summary gives you a quick (though not detailed) glance at how certain factors — including time — affect your conversions and goals.

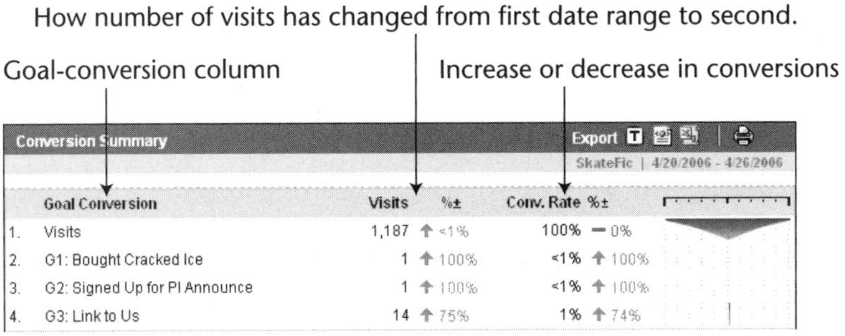

How number of visits has changed from first date range to second.

Goal-conversion column   Increase or decrease in conversions

Figure 9-10: Each column on the Conversion Summary has a different meaning.

Marketing Summary

Evan's next problem is marketing. The boss wants to know what marketing efforts are working and which are not. The Marketing Summary page is going to save Evan's bacon with its lean and mean look at the increases or decreases in web-site visits and conversion rates for the top five sources, the top five key words (which also happen to be the AdWords he's buying), and the top five campaigns. Your marketing summary might look something like what's shown in Figure 9-11.

Figure 9-11:   The Marketing Summary page

The Date Range on the Marketing Summary Page works the same way as it does on the Conversion Summary. The top calendar is for your starting date range, and the lower calendar is for your comparison date range.

There are several more columns in the Marketing Summary graphic. Here's what each of these columns represents:

- **Column 1:** The first column is the "Top 5" column. This is a listing of the Top 5 Sources, Top 5 Keywords, and Top 5 Campaigns. The listings in this column will change according to the current effectiveness of these factors in your marketing campaigns. This column is shown in larger form on Figure 9-12.

- **Column 2:** The "Visits" column shows the total number of visits referred by particular source, key word, or campaign during the current date range. Little red or green arrows and percentage numbers illustrate the increase or decrease in number of visits in comparison with the comparison date range. This column also is indicated in Figure 9-12.

- **Columns 3+:** Each goal gets a column showing conversion rates for that goal for the current date range — the one you've selected in the top Date Range calendar. Red or green arrows and percentage numbers indicate the increase or decrease in the conversion rate from the comparison date range. You'll have one column for each goal. SkateFic has three goals. These are columns 3, 4, and 5 in Figure 9-12.

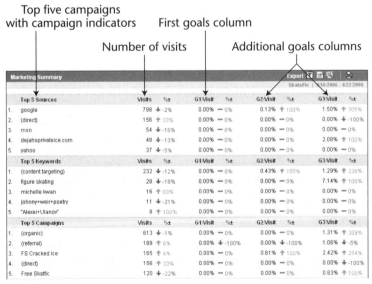

Figure 9-12: The Marketing Summary shows how well traffic becomes conversions.

You may see campaign indicators in parenthesis. These represent prede-fined headings for your marketing campaigns. So, a campaign in parenthesis represents one of the following special cases:

- **(organic)** This indicates that visitors came from an unpaid search engine listing, meaning the visitor typed a search string into a search engine, and your web site was one of the results returned. These are not paid search engine listings (as AdWords *is* a paid listing), so they are counted separately.

- **(referral)** A referral is a referral — a link to your site from some other site or listing. However, this indicator means that visitors were referred to your site by links that were not tagged with any type of campaign variables. That means they could be part of a marketing campaign that you have going but were missed when it came time to tag that campaign, or it could mean that someone else is linking to your site and pushing visitors over outside of any campaign that you have running.

- **(not set)** It's possible to get traffic to your web site that is the result of an advertising campaign for which you have not yet established campaign variables. This indicator will show you the number of visitors referred by links that were tagged with campaign variables that you have not set Google Analytics to recognize.

- **(direct)** As mentioned previously, this indicates visitors who typed the URL directly into the browser rather than clicking through some other link to reach your page. It can include people who have bookmarked your page and click the bookmark link to get to your site.

- **(content targeting)** In AdWords, you can set your ads to appear only for certain kinds of content. For example, SkateFic is a winter sports site — at least as far as Google is concerned — but Mary felt it was pointless to pay for skating-fiction ads on sites related to hockey. Just because both skating and hockey are winter sports doesn't mean they share a fan base.

- **(site targeting)** In AdWords, you can choose the exact sites where you want your ads to appear. Those clicks get tallied separately.

Content Summary

One of the most important facets of SkateFic.com that Evan needs to keep track of is how effective the content on the web site actually is. He needs to know what pages get the most visitors, where visitors come into the web site, and where visitors fall off (or leave) the site. It's especially important for Evan to keep up with where people leave the site if they leave without completing one of the conversion goals set for the site, because the boss is most certainly going to want to know why people aren't signing up for the company newsletter or completing a purchase. If Evan can show her exactly what parts of the site are working or not working toward the goals, he's probably going to keep his job a little longer.

The Content Summary page, shown in Figure 9-13, is where you'll find all of this information.

Figure 9-13: The Content Summary page summarizes your site-visit stats.

The Content Summary page is slightly different from the last two sections that we've looked at. It is still divided into columns, but different information is included in each column, so let's look at each section of the table.

- **Top 5 Entrances:** This section of the page, noted in Figure 9-14, shows you the five pages where visitors arrive most frequently. In Evan's case, SkateFic.com has a campaign running that includes a link directly to a newsletter signup page. The URL for the page is `http://www.SkateFic.com/campaign/home/nl?rid=4569`. This URL indicates the exact campaign that's running, and Evan wants to know how often people enter the company web site through that page. If it's one of the five most frequent entrances, this is where he'll find it.

  There are also other columns in the Top 5 Entrances categories. The second column in Figure 9-14 shows entrances and the third shows the number of immediate exits — called bounces — from your top five entrance pages during the date range you specified. The red and green arrows and percentage numbers indicate the percentage increase or decrease from the previous date range, as they have for other measurements in the Executive Dashboard.

  The fourth column in Figure 9-14 illustrates the bounce rate — the exit rate — for the pages listed in the Top 5 Entrances section. Again, the red and green arrows and percentage rate let you know the percentage of increase or decrease from the previous date range.

- **Top 5 Exits:** The Top 5 Exits title, shown in Figure 9-15, is exactly what it says it is — the top five web pages where people exited your site. They may be exiting by closing out their browser window or by clicking a link that takes them away from your site, but one way or another, they're leaving.

  The second column in Figure 9-15 is the number of exits during the specified range. You'll also find (what should be pretty standard to you now) the red and green arrows and the percentage that indicates the difference from the date range you've specified for comparison.

  Next in Figure 9-15 is the column that indicates the number of Page Views. This is your comparison (accompanied, of course, by the red and green arrows and the percentage numbers) of the number of page visits for this date range in comparison to the second date range that you've selected.

  Finally on this figure, you have a percentage of Exits. This indicates, using the red and green arrows and percentage numbers, the number of users who have exited on the page shown, in comparison with exits on the same page from the previous dates you've selected.

Five pages where visitors enter most
frequently and number of entrances

Number of 'bounces' (quick exits)

Bounce rate

Top 5 Entrances	Entrances	%±	Bounces	%±	Bounce Rate	%±
1. /index.php	339 ↓ -5%		180 ↓ -12%		53.10% ↓ -7%	
2. /figure-skating-trivia/index.php	221 ↓ -11%		195 ↓ -11%		88.24% ↓ 0%	
3. /proshop/index.php	120 ↓ -4%		101 ↓ -7%		84.17% ↓ -3%	
4. /serials/ote/index.php	67 ↑ 18%		8 ↑ 80%		11.94% ↑ 36%	
5. /serials/tsts/index.php	26 ↑ 24%		10 ↑ 67%		38.46% ↑ 35%	

Figure 9-14: The Top 5 Entrances section of the Content Summary Page

Five pages from which visitors exit
most frequently and number of exits

Number of page views (pages visited)

Percentage of exits

Top 5 Exits	Exits	%±	Pageviews	%±	% Exit	%±
1. /index.php	247 ↓ -14%		579 ↓ -5%		42.66% ↓ -9%	
2. /figure-skating-trivia/index.php	218 ↓ -12%		253 ↓ -11%		86.17% ↓ -1%	
3. /proshop/index.php	119 ↓ -3%		178 ↑ 5%		66.85% ↓ -8%	
4. /serials/ote/index.php?Book=2	52 ↑ 68%		213 ↑ 49%		24.41% ↑ 13%	
5. /serials/woti/index.php	28 ↑ 22%		95 ↓ -17%		29.47% ↑ 47%	

Figure 9-15: The Top 5 Exits portion of the Content Summary graphic

■ **Top 5 Content:** This section is similar to the other two, except that it shows the top five pages that were viewed by your site visitors, as shown in the first column of Figure 9-16.

The second column in the same figure shows the number of visits (and those red and green arrows and percentage signs again) as compared to the visits to those pages in your previous date range.

The third column shows the number of page views and the percentage of change. This section is identical in feel and function to the same segment of the Top 5 Exits section.

The last column in Figure 9-16 is a little different. This column shows the average amount of time (with arrows and percentages) spent by visitors on each of the top five pages.

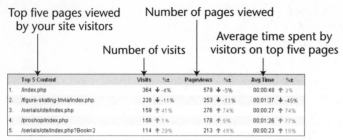

Figure 9-16: The Top 5 Content section shows your most visited pages.

Site Overlay

The last report in the Executive Dashboard is the Site Overlay. This neat little report, shown in Figure 9-17, allows you to navigate your site while viewing traffic and conversion data for each link.

In the upper-right corner of the Site Overlay in Figure 9-17, you'll find the exit range for the page shown.

In the same figure, you'll also find blue and green bars that are graphic indicators of clicks and quality, respectively, for each link on the page. You can click any set of blue and green bars to view metrics for that link, like the ones also shown in Figure 9-17. These metrics include:

- The number of clicks
- The conversion rates for each goal you have defined
- The $ Index

TIP Links with the highest $ Index are those links most commonly visited before high-value conversions during a visit. Click any link to navigate to that page.

You can view all of these metrics for any page of your site that's being monitored by Google Analytics by surfing through the site within the Site Overlay box.

Graphic indicators for clicks and quality

Additional metrics linked from graphic indicators   Exit range

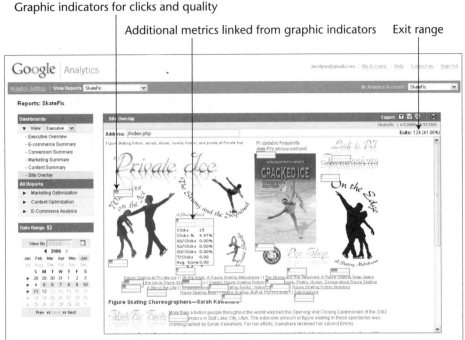

Figure 9-17:   The Site Overlay lets you see where users click through your site.

NOTE   One thing you should know about the Site Overlay: It doesn't work properly with all web browsers. For example, if you're using Firefox (which the authors are) you can see the Site Overlay, but you won't be able to navigate through the site within the Site Overlay. You may also find that the coding of the web site creates errors in the Site Overlay. If you experience issues with this (or other) reports, check the site requirements for Google Analytics and consider temporarily using a different web browser or check the code for you site, because there could be a rogue command creating havoc.

The Executive Overview gives you all the tools you need for a quick snapshot of the health and well-being of your web site in the context of the various jobs that affect the site. If you're like Evan, and your boss is constantly on you to provide more information, these quick, one-off-type reports should give you all the ammunition you need.

The Marketer Dashboard

Evan, the IT manager Mary wishes she had for SkateFic.com, has all the reports he needs, so let's focus on Johnny for a little while. Johnny is the online marketing manager Mary also wishes she had.

Poor Johnny.

He has his work cut out for him. SkateFic.com runs every online marketing campaign known to the virtual world, at least in this story. He has to keep up with AdWords campaigns and other pay-per-click (PPC) advertising, paid search advertising, banner ads, affiliate links, and even newsletter marketing.

All those marketing efforts make it difficult for Johnny to keep up with everything, so when he pulls up Google Analytics, he wants to see all his metrics without having to sift through mountains of data. He needs answers, and he usually needs them fast.

Google Analytics has a special dashboard just for Johnny. It's the Marketer Dashboard. From this central location, Johnny can get what he needs. And if he needs to export or print those reports to share them with Evan or other members of the marketing department, he can print graphics or export the reports in several different formats.

NOTE If you've just started using Google Analytics, some of the reports covered through this book will appear different. Either the graphics will be empty, there will be no graphics, or some of the features covered in these pages will be unavailable to you. As you configure Google Analytics and the program begins collecting data, this should change. You can always come back to these reports when you do have data to compare what you have with what's covered here.

Who Should Use This View

If you're like Johnny, the Marketer Dashboard is for you, too. Do you need to know which key words are really drawing more traffic to your web site? Maybe what you really need is an analysis of your cost-per-click (CPC) or key-word conversions. These reports and nine others, most of them targeted specifically at marketing campaigns, are the substance of the Marketer Dashboard.

To get the Marketer Dashboard, go to Analytics Settings and click the **View Reports** link. Remember that you'll automatically be taken to the Executive Dashboard. To reach the Marketer Dashboard, select Marketer from the drop-down menu shown in Figure 10-1.

Three dashboards to choose from

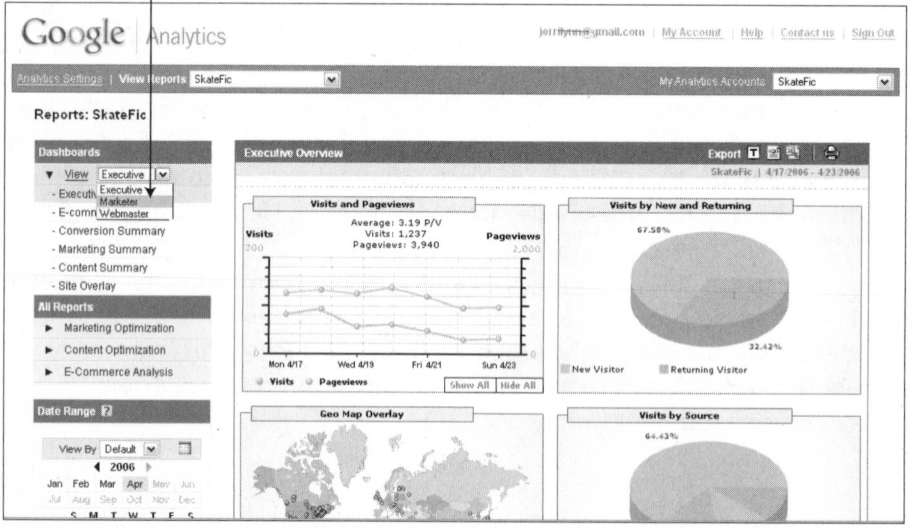

Figure 10-1: The View drop-down menu gives you three dashboards to choose from.

Marketer Overview

When you first come into the Marketer Dashboard, shown in Figure 10-2, you should immediately recognize the four graphics in the Marketer Overview. These four graphics — Visits and Pageviews, Visits by New and Returning, Geo Map Overlay, and Visits by Source — are the same four graphics you saw in the Executive Overview.

These graphics are a quick overview of the status of your web site. We're not going into a lot of detail about them here, since we've already covered them. But if you need a quick refresher, it's in the beginning of Chapter 9.

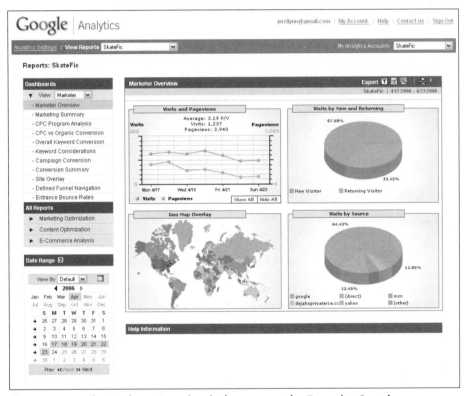

Figure 10-2:   The Marketer Overview is the same as the Executive Overview.

Marketing Summary

Johnny's real interest isn't in the Marketer Overview. He'll usually glance at it, but he's more interested in the other marketing reports, and his first stop is usually the Marketing Summary.

The Marketing Summary, shown in Figure 10-3, gives Johnny a quick look at some of the metrics that tell him whether his marketing efforts have been a smashing success, a complete failure, or somewhere in between.

Figure 10-3: The Marketing Summary shows the effectiveness of marketing efforts.

If the Marketing Summary looks a lot like the Marketing Summary from the Executive Dashboard, that's because it's the same darn summary. If you haven't read Chapter 9, we encourage you to backtrack and read the full coverage of this report. Here's what the graphics on the Marketing Summary tell Johnny (and you):

- Top 5 Sources: This section of the Marketing Summary, shown in Figure 10-4, shows your web site's top five referring sources. The source listed as (direct) means those visitors came directly to your site either by clicking a bookmark for your site or by typing your web address into the address bar on their web browsers.

  Also in this section are two columns labeled Visits and G1/Visits. The Visits column shows the number of visitors to your site and the increase or decrease in those measurements according to the date ranges you've selected. Those infamous red and green arrows and percentages are also back, just to help you get a clear understanding of the changes.

  The other columns — G1/Visits, G2/Visits, G3/Visits — indicate the conversion rate of those visitors for each goal you've set.

- Top 5 Keywords: Johnny wants to monitor the key words used to find the SkateFic.com web site for two reasons. First, he wants to know how effective the key words he's chosen for his AdWords marketing campaign are. And second, he wants to see what the most frequently used search terms are. The Top 5 Keywords section of the Marketing Summary, shown in Figure 10-5, shows him that he does just as well with content-targeted ads that he buys for $0.10 per click as he does with the $0.30 ads that run on "figure skating" and "Michelle Kwan."

Top 5 Sources	Visits	%±	G1/Visit	%±	G2/Visit	%±	G3/Visit	%±
1. google	797	↓ 0%	0.00%	— 0%	0.13%	↑ 100%	1.51%	↑ 297%
2. (direct)	154	↑ 35%	0.00%	— 0%	0.00%	— 0%	0.00%	↓ -100%
3. msn	57	↓ -3%	0.00%	— 0%	0.00%	— 0%	0.00%	— 0%
4. dejahsprivateice.com	46	↓ -2%	0.00%	— 0%	0.00%	— 0%	2.17%	↑ 100%
5. yahoo	34	↓ -11%	0.00%	— 0%	0.00%	— 0%	0.00%	— 0%

Figure 10-4: The Top 5 Referring Sources for visitors to your web site

Top 5 Keywords	Visits	%±	G1/Visit	%±	G2/Visit	%±	G3/Visit	%±
1. (content targeting)	220	↓ -16%	0.00%	— 0%	0.45%	↑ 100%	1.36%	↑ 258%
2. figure skating	30	↓ -9%	0.00%	— 0%	0.00%	— 0%	6.67%	↑ 100%
3. michelle kwan	15	↑ 50%	0.00%	— 0%	0.00%	— 0%	0.00%	— 0%
4. johnny+weir+poetry	11	↓ -15%	0.00%	— 0%	0.00%	— 0%	0.00%	— 0%
5. "Alexei+Ulanov"	7	↑ 250%	0.00%	— 0%	0.00%	— 0%	0.00%	— 0%

Figure 10-5: The Top 5 Keywords used to find your site are listed in this section.

The Visits and G1/Visits column are also in this segment of the Marketing Summary to show you the number of visits and goal conversions for the comparative period you've selected.

■ Top 5 Campaigns: This section of the Marketing Summary in Figure 10-6 shows you which five campaigns are performing the best. FS Cracked Ice and Free Skatefic are AdWords campaigns. The others in parentheses are default categories managed by Google Analytics. If you have fewer than five campaigns of your own, you'll probably see them.

If you don't have at least five marketing campaigns running, the campaigns you are running will be displayed from most successful to least successful.

You'll also be able to tell with a glance at the Visits and G1/Visits how many visits have resulted from the campaigns, the conversion rate of those visits, and the percentage of increase or decrease based on the date range you've selected.

All CPC Analysis

The cost-per-click (CPC) marketing revolution has hit full throttle. CPC programs, like Google's AdWords, continue to gain in popularity because they are a relatively inexpensive way to put your name in front of a large number of potential customers. But keeping up with the effectiveness of key words that you select can be a full-time job.

You're constantly looking at which key words drive the most traffic and experimenting to find the right mix. The All CPC Analysis report, shown in Figure 10-7, is your way to quickly analyze the value of your chosen key words.

Top 5 Campaigns	Visits	%±	G1/Visit	%±	G2/Visit	%±	G3/Visit	%±
1. (organic)	622	↑ 4%	0.00%	— 0%	0.00%	— 0%	1.29%	↑ 291%
2. (referral)	185	↑ 14%	0.00%	↓ -100%	0.00%	↓ -100%	1.08%	↑ 74%
3. FS Cracked Ice	161	↑ <1%	0.00%	— 0%	0.62%	↑ 100%	2.48%	↑ 294%
4. (direct)	154	↑ 35%	0.00%	— 0%	0.00%	— 0%	0.00%	↓ -100%
5. Free Skatefic	115	↓ -23%	0.00%	— 0%	0.00%	— 0%	0.87%	↑ 100%

Figure 10-6: The Top 5 Campaigns graphic shows you which perform best.

Clicking here produces view shown in Figure 10-10.

Clicking here on plus (+) sign produces view shown in Figure 10-11.

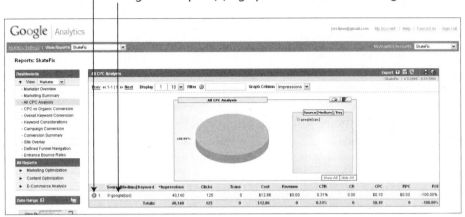

Figure 10-7:   Monitor key-word marketing with the CPC Program Analysis report.

The CPC Analysis illustrates a number of key-word measurements, including these categories, stretched across the bottom of the bar in Figure 10-7:

- Source: Which search engine your site visitor used
- Impressions: The number of times a page was shown
- Clicks: The number of times visitors clicked an ad
- Transaction: The number of e-commerce transactions resulting from ads
- Cost: The cost-per-click figure
- Revenue: The revenue generated by the ad
- CTR: The click-through rate for the ad
- CR: The conversion rate for the ad
- CPC: The average cost-per-click paid on key words
- RPC: The revenue per click for key words
- ROI: The return on investment calculated by subtracting cost from revenue and then dividing what remains by the cost ([Revenue-Cost]/Cost)

A few tools in the menu bar of this graph make using it a little more intuitive for your situation as it changes. The first tool, shown in Figure 10-8, is the display drop-down menu. This menu lets you change the number of CPC programs for which you view information. The default is set to 10, but you can view as many as 500 per page if that's what you need to see.

Also in the menu bar of Figure 10-8 is a text box with a small green plus sign or red minus sign next to it. This feature allows you to add or remove the various filters you have set for the information in the graph.

There's one other control in the menu bar that you should be aware of. The Graph Column drop-down menu gives you the ability to view various metrics related to your CPC programs, as shown in Figure 10-9. The graphic will automatically shift to the bar-graph display when necessary.

Other graphics in the CPS Program Analysis area (first shown in Figure 10-7) also let you see a few elements that will be available to you in a number of other Google Analytics graphics. These elements help you dig down even further into your site's data.

First (still in Figure 10-7) there is a double red arrow button next to entries in the columns below the graph. Clicking the arrow produces the display shown in Figure 10-10. It allows you to view Data Over Time or by Cross Segment Performance if that data is available.

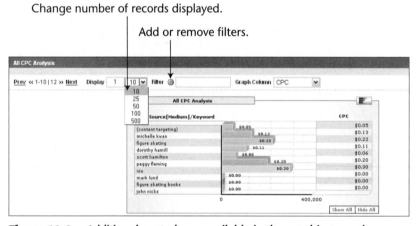

Figure 10-8: Additional controls are available in the graphic menu bar.

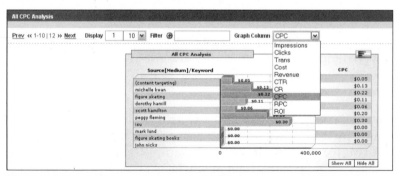

Figure 10-9: Switch to a bar-graph display for even more information.

Select additional data views.

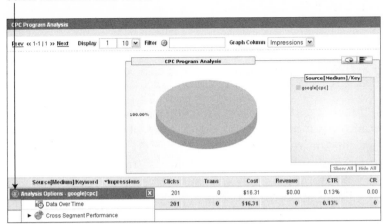

Figure 10-10: Select the double arrow for additional data views.

Data Over Time simply expands your view to show you exact numbers for each day within the selected period. Cross Segment Performance allows you to select from the list of 18 cross-segment options that include entries such as source, campaign, network location, platform, and visitor type, to view additional data specific to that selection.

Also in Figure 10-7, there's a small plus (+) sign next to each entry in the Sources column. Clicking the sign brings you to the display shown in Figure 10-11 and lets you expand the Source (or Keyword) listings so that you can examine which is performing better.

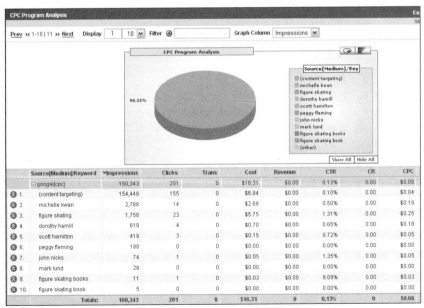

Figure 10-11: Additional information displays after clicking the plus (+) sign.

These last two elements will appear frequently in your Analytics reports, so familiarize yourself with how they work. In future reports, we may mention them, but we won't go into detail about how they work.

CPC vs. Organic Conversion

If you're curious about the number of visits to your site that are driven by your key-word marketing in comparison with the number of organic — or naturally occurring — visits, this report will tell you. The CPC vs. Organic Conversion report, shown in Figure 10-12, compares paid referrals to the number of visits from people who stumbled upon your site. (This view was reached by clicking the CPC vs. Organic Conversion link at the left of the screen.)

Figure 10-12: The CPC vs. Organic Conversion report compares types of visitors.

This report also contains comparisons for several additional factors, including:

- Source: The search engine the referral comes from. Here you'll see, in brackets, whether the referral was organic or paid.
- Visits: The number of visits referred by each source
- P/Visit: Average page views per visit
- G1/Visit: The percentage of people who arrived via that source/ medium who completed Goal 1. There are similar columns for other goals.
- T/Visits: The average number of e-commerce transactions per visit
- $/Visits: The average e-commerce revenues or goal value per visit

For additional information, you can also click the plus (+) sign next to any source entry in Figure 10-12 to drill down into the key-words searchers used. Click the double arrow beside any key word for access to more reports. As Figure 10-13 shows, clicking any of the double arrows next to the sources will produce a graphic in this menu that you haven't seen before — To-date Lifetime. This is in addition to the Data Over Time and Cross Segment Performance graphics.

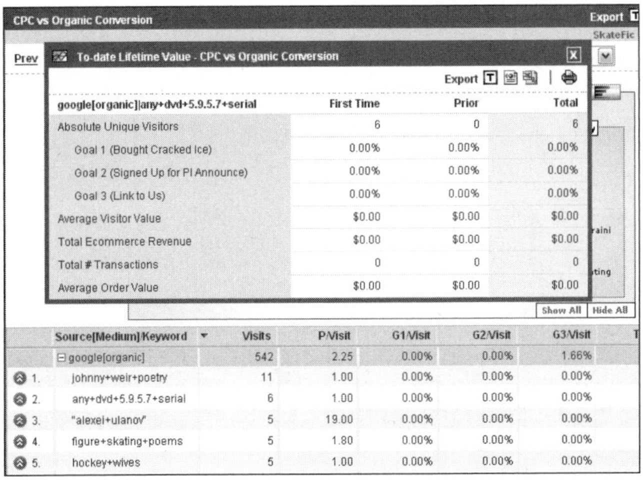

Figure 10-13: The To-date Lifetime graphic shows additional key-word information.

Overall Keyword Conversion

Key-word conversion shows which key words drive the most traffic to your site, as shown in the Overall Keyword Conversion report in Figure 10-14.

In this report, clicking the plus (+) sign next to each key word allows you to examine search engines and paid vs. organic visits within a key word. The report also contains some columns of information that you've seen before:

- Keyword/Source
- Visits
- P/Visits
- G1-G4/Visits
- T/Visit
- $/Visit

Figure 10-14: Analyze which key words perform better.

Key-Word Considerations

Have you ever wondered what key words that you're not taking advantage of that people are using to find your site? The Keyword Consideration report, shown in Figure 10-15, shows you exactly that — how effective other key words are at driving traffic to your site.

As with the other reports in this chapter, you can click the double arrow button to change the data view of your report, and there are additional data controls in the menu bar above the graphic. This report also contains the same reporting columns you've seen in previous reports.

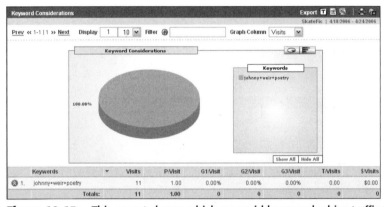

Figure 10-15: This report shows which nonpaid key words drive traffic to your site.

Campaign Conversion

Are you tired of trying to figure out which of your online marketing campaigns are working and which are not? As long as you have tagged your various campaigns, the Campaign Conversion report, shown in Figure 10-16, lists all of your tagged marketing campaigns by visits.

In this report, the plus (+) sign beside each campaign allows you to compare the sources within a campaign, as shown in Figure 10-17.

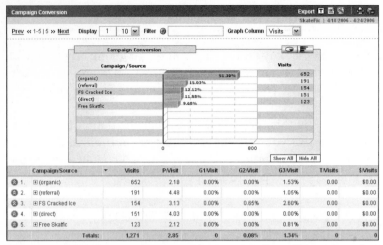

Figure 10-16: The Campaign Conversion report lists all tagged marketing campaigns.

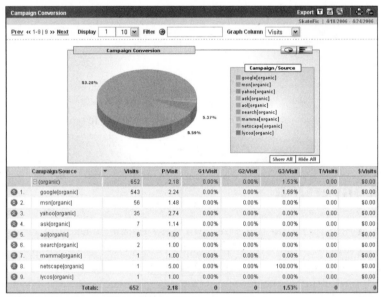

Figure 10-17: Additional Campaign Source information appears after you click the plus (+) sign next to a Campaign/Source entry.

Conversion Summary

The Conversion Summary, shown in Figure 10-18, is a report you've seen before — in the Executive Dashboard. This report shows whether the total number of visits, the number of goal conversions, and the number of conversions for each goal have increased or decreased.

Our old friends the red and green arrows and the percentage that quantifies the amount of gain or loss also return in this report. Visit Chapter 9 for more in-depth information.

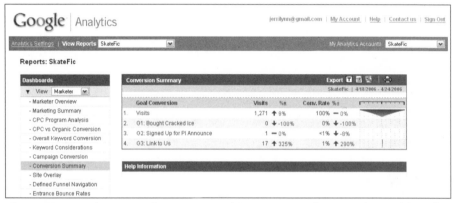

Figure 10-18: The Conversion Summary also appears on the Executive Dashboard.

Site Overlay

The Site Overlay report that we saw on the Executive Dashboard in Chapter 9 is also back. You may remember that this report, shown in Figure 10-19, shows your web site with navigational links tagged with additional information about the number and types of clicks for each link.

You can actually navigate through your web site in the Site Overlay window to see how each different link on all of your pages measures up.

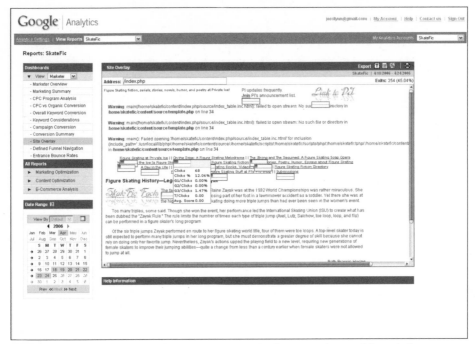

Figure 10-19: The Site Overlay report appears in the Executive Dashboard also.

Defined Funnel Navigation

Here's an interesting report that you haven't seen before. Remember the goals and funnel navigation that we covered way back in Chapter 7? This is your graphical representation of that information.

The Defined Funnel Navigation report, shown in Figure 10-20, shows you where, along a defined funnel process, you lose visitors.

Remember that funnel navigation is a set of pages that you have defined as leading a visitor to a specific goal. For example, if you have established the goal that users will sign up for your company newsletter, your goal page would be the page with a "Thank you" message. How the user gets to that page is the funnel.

The Defined Funnel Navigation graphic shows you how site visitors navigated through the pages you defined as a funnel and where in that process your visitors dropped off.

By default, this report appears with your first goal as the tracking initiative. To change which goal you're seeing, click the **Select Goal** drop-down menu, shown in Figure 10-21. You can then select any goal you have listed.

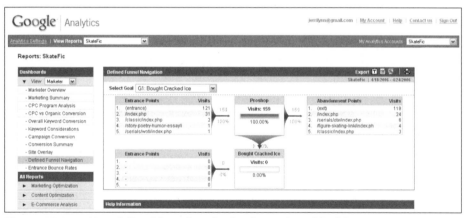

Figure 10-20:   Your defined funnel navigation is monitored in this report.

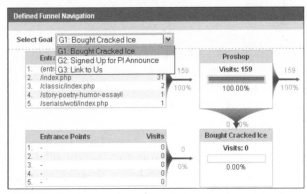

Figure 10-21:   Change the goal view for the Defined Funnel Navigation report.

Entrance Bounce Rates

Where do visitors come into your web site, and where do they leave? If that's the burning question in your mind (or in Johnny's or Evan's), the Entrance Bounce Rates report, shown in Figure 10-22, should give you all the information you need.

When you first pull up this report, it defaults to the Entrances pie chart that shows the top pages where visitors come onto your web site. To change that view, select an alternative view — Entrances, Bounces, or Bounce Rate — from the Graph Column drop-down menu, shown in Figure 10-23.

Bounces are defined as the number of times visitors leave your site immediately from the same page where they entered. The bounce rate, then, is the number of bounces divided by the number of entrances. This shows you how often your visitors fall off your site as soon as they land, meaning that they didn't find what they wanted, or what they wanted was on that page and they didn't bother to go any deeper — a compelling content problem, pun intended.

There is so much information in these reports that you might want to take time to play with the different options and tools available on each page. At first glance, all of the most essential information is right on the screen. But as cream rises to the top of fresh milk, if you dig a little deeper, what's underneath shouldn't be discounted. There's plenty of value to be found in all of this buried information. Now that you know how to get to it, all you have to do is put it to use.

Figure 10-22:   This report shows where visitors enter and leave your web site.

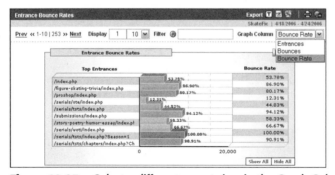

Figure 10-23:   Select a different report view in the Graph Column drop-down menu.

CHAPTER 11

The Webmaster Dashboard

Mary is the only Google Analytics person over at SkateFic.com that we haven't followed yet. You may remember that she's the company webmaster. She's in charge of everything from design to content — even traffic statistics.

When Mary pulls up Google Analytics, she's already got 50-gazillion things sitting on her plate to complete in the next 10 minutes and the last thing she wants to do is wade through reports that have no bearing on her problems.

That's why the Webmaster Dashboard was designed — for Mary and people just like her who need stats and information specifically related to their jobs as webmasters.

Using the Webmaster Dashboard, you can learn how your content is performing, track any goals you have set for the web site, and — most important — have access to something called Web Design Parameters that will help you develop a web-site design that is truly targeted at your users.

Who Should Use This View?

Mary. And anyone like Mary. If you're a webmaster, you need stats and information to help you keep track of what works and what doesn't on your site. You need to know how, when, and why users access your web site. Most of all, you need to know what they do (or don't do) while they're on your site.

If you can find out how much time they spend in a specific area, where they leave your site, or how they travel through your site, that's even better. The Webmaster Dashboard will give you all of that information. It's all contained in more than a dozen reports that will have you "in the know" in no time.

Webmaster Overview

Here's a page you've seen before. The Webmaster Overview, shown in Figure 11-1, is the same overview page that you saw in the Executive Dashboard and in the Marketer Dashboard.

This Overview just gives you a quick look at some of the top metrics. We've already covered those in Chapter 9, so we'll skip over them here. You can flip back before continuing if you need a refresher.

Figure 11-1: The Overview is the same in all of the Dashboard views.

Content Summary

Throughout the dashboards, you'll notice that there is some overlap in reports. This is because what Evan needs, Johnny and Mary may also need — just like real life. The Content Summary, shown in Figure 11-2, is one of those overlappers.

Figure 11-2: The Content Summary also appears on the Executive Dashboard.

Again, we're not going to torture you by going through the whole report another time. Just remember that this report summarizes the top five entrance pages, exit pages, and content pages on your site, and you'll be good to go.

If you don't remember everything we covered on the Content Summary, you can flip back to Chapter 9 to review it.

Defined Funnel Navigation

Defined Funnel Navigation was covered in Chapter 10. This report, shown in Figure 11-3, illustrates where users enter the funnel process that you defined when you defined your goals and then shows how many reached the goal you set and where those who didn't fell out of the process.

This report hasn't changed from the last time we covered it, so there's more information about the report in Chapter 10 if you need to refer to it.

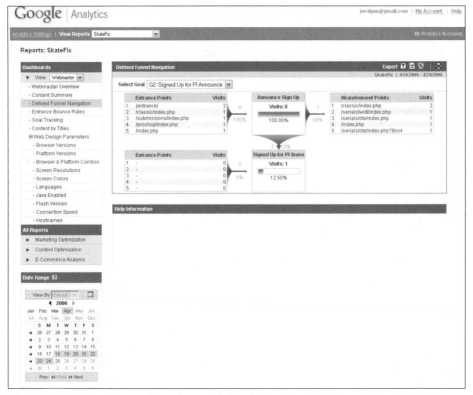

Figure 11-3: Track users through your defined funnel navigation on this report.

Entrance Bounce Rates

If you have kids, you know that their favorite game is Copy-Cat. It's a mocking game where you say something and they say it back to you, with as close to the same tone, inflection, and expression as they can manage. It's also a favorite way for siblings to torture each other.

Google has no intention of torturing you, but this is another of those Copy-Cat reports that we've seen so much of. The Entrance Bounce Rates report, shown in Figure 11-4, was covered in depth in Chapter 10, so we won't go through it all again here.

In case you really don't want to flip back, just remember that this report shows you the top entrances, bounces, and bounce rates for your web site. If you need to know more than that, it's all in Chapter 10.

Figure 11-4: The Entrance Bounce Rates report also appears in the Marketing Dashboard.

One aspect of these reports that you'll see often and that should be mentioned are the additional reports that you have access to when you click the small double arrow next to any entry. When you click the double arrow, you'll see there are three reports to choose from: Data Over Time, To-date Lifetime Value, and Cross Segment Performance.

Each of these reports gives you a different view of the information presented here. Additionally, if you want to compare the information in the report with some other aspect of analytics, the Cross Segment Performance report lets you choose from numerous options to compare.

- Source[Medium]
- Campaign
- Keyword
- Content
- Country
- Region
- City
- Network Location
- Language
- User Defined
- Browser
- Platform
- Connection Speed
- Screen Resolution
- Colors
- Java
- Flash
- Visitor Type

This report is especially useful if you want to see how a specific factor affects the metrics for any given report, including the Entrance Bounce Rates.

Goal Tracking

Like a breath of fresh air, we finally get to something new — kinda. Remember when we went through all of that mumbo jumbo about setting goals, way back in Chapter 7? Seems like eons ago, doesn't it?

Now is when you see the payoff. Or not. The Goal Tracking report, shown in Figure 11-5, gives you a graph of the goals you've set for your web site.

This report is pretty self-explanatory. There's a bar for the number of goal conversions in a time period for each of your site's goals. Remember that you can only set up four goals for each profile, so at the most you'll have four different graphics in this view.

The most interesting feature of this report is the ability to compare goal conversions over a period of time by selecting different date ranges in the Date Range options, as shown in Figure 11-6. For Mary, that means she can track goal conversions for SkateFic.com by hour, day, week, or month to learn when the highest traffic patterns happen at the site. She can then use that information to determine what factors are having the most influence on web-site traffic.

Figure 11-5: Goal Tracking lets you visually track the progress of your goals.

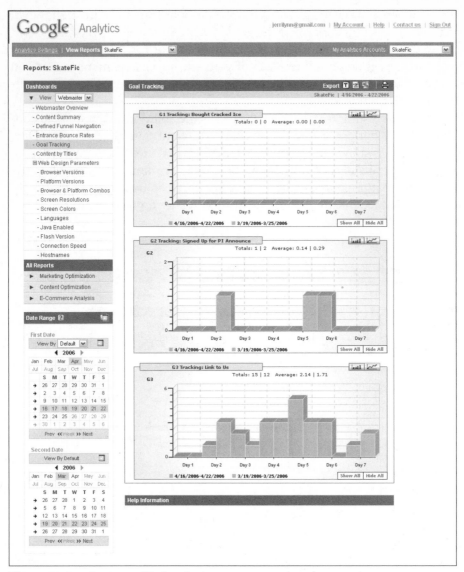

Figure 11-6:   Compare differing date ranges to reveal goal-conversion patterns.

To achieve the results shown in Figure 11-6, open the Goal Tracking report, and then click the double calendar on the Date Range title bar on the left side of the page. The default comparison graphics appear, which show a comparison based on the View By time frame that you have selected. For example, if your View By time frame is set to default, you're viewing your reports by week. When you click the double calendar, the graphic view changes to show you the current week (in yellow) compared to the previous week (in blue).

A second calendar appears — labeled Second Date — beneath the first one, and you can change the date range you are comparing by changing the dates highlighted in the calendar.

Content by Titles

"Content is king!" How many times have you heard that phrase or some variation of it? Maybe you even hear it quoted to you by the boss every other day (or what seems like every other day). Even if the phrase is more tired than a one-legged frog after a jumping contest, it still holds true — content will make or break your web site.

To help you figure out what content on your site works best, Google Analytics has the Content by Titles report, shown in Figure 11-7.

Figure 11-7: Learn what content performs best with the Content by Titles report.

When this report, which is based on the HTML tags on your content pages, first appears, it is set as a default to show you which page — by title — gets the most unique traffic.

NOTE If you have multiple pages that have the same HTML title tags, all of those pages will be grouped together and will appear in this report as a single page. For the best (and most accurate) results, make sure that each page in your web site has a different HTML title tag. On the other hand, if you have pages that really do belong grouped, this is one way to do it.

You can change this view by, as shown in Figure 11-8, to view Pageviews, Average Time, % Exit, or $ Index. Just select an option from the Graph Column drop-down menu.

Below the graphic (regardless of which view you're looking at) are several columns:

- Page Titles: The page title column is pretty self-explanatory. Just remember that page titles could actually represent a group of pages if those pages all contain the same HTML title tag.

- Unique Views: Unique Views is the number of unique visits that viewed this page. The column is automagically sorted from greatest number of views to least number of views. You can change the sorting by clicking the arrow in the cell that contains the Unique View title.

- Page Views: Page views is a different measurement than unique views, because it counts every time the page was viewed, rather than just counting once for multiple views.

- Average Time: How long, on average, did visitors spend on each of your pages? Which page did users spend the most time on? Did visitors actually read the content on your site? Anything longer than about 10 seconds shows that they at least perused the page. Longer than a minute and you have it made in the shade, or it's possible there was a phone call or some other distraction that took the user away from the page for a while.

- % Exit: Your most popular page may not be the one that serves you best if the people who read it leave right from there. Which is better, the Pro Shop seen by 1,427 people where 71.93 percent leave or the skating soap seen by 1,135 people where only 26.13 percent of visitors bail? The Pro Shop looks better at first glance, but only 400 people stay compared to 838 for the soap.

- $ Index: How much money did you make off those page views? Your busiest pages may not be your most profitable ones.

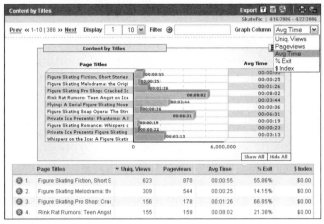

Figure 11-8: Change the content view on the Content by Titles report.

In this report, you'll also have double arrows that drill down into the data. You can also change the date ranges to a time frame that suits your needs.

Web Design Parameters

Web-design parameters are the different factors that affect the way users see your web site. When you click the link for Web Design Parameters in the Dashboards menu, shown in Figure 11-9, it expands to show you additional report options.

You won't see any changes in the graphical display until you select one of the suboptions listed in the menu.

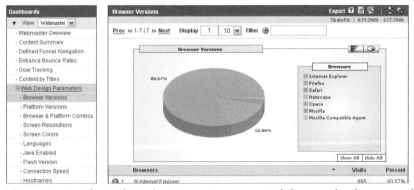

Figure 11-9: The Web Design Parameters menu at left expands when you select it.

Browser Versions

Web-site design affects how the site renders in different browsers. Jerri's site is a good example. It's designed for viewing in Internet Explorer. Unfortunately, in some cases this means the site won't look so hot in other browsers. In Firefox, the graphics on her page don't show up at all.

To prevent this issue early on, Jerri could have used the Web Browser report to see what browsers most frequently accessed her web site. Instead, she's still trying to figure out how to make the site compatible with other browsers.

So the Web Browser report, shown in Figure 11-10, shows you the top web browsers that access your web site.

The usual tools are also there to help. You'll find the double arrow that lets you dig down into the results to view Data Over Time, To-date Lifetime Value, and Cross Segment Performance. You can also use the calendar to compare date ranges by hour, month, day, or week. But the really interesting part of this report? You can see the version of the browser that your site visitors are using.

As Figure 11-11 shows, you can click the small plus sign next to each browser listed in Figure 11-10, and you'll be taken to a report that shows the browser versions and the number of users for each version.

Within the versions, there's yet another double arrow that lets you dig even deeper into the version data that's collected by Google Analytics. If you click the double arrow, you'll be taken to the option for Data Over Time, To-date Lifetime Value, and Cross Segment Performance, as shown in Figure 11-12.

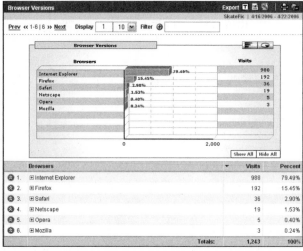

Figure 11-10: This report shows the top web browsers used to access your site.

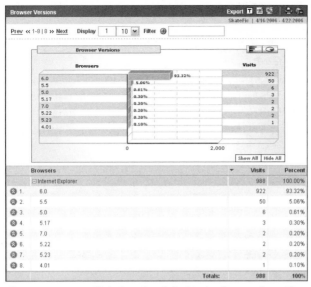

Figure 11-11:   Click the plus (+) sign in the previous Figure 11-10 beside a browser name to see this display about the version used.

Figure 11-12:   Click the double arrow for even more information.

Platform Versions

More often than not, web sites support only the dominant operating system. As we discussed in Chapter 3, that may not be good business. But if you don't have AWStats, or if the boss doesn't believe anything that doesn't come from the lips of corporate America, here's Google Analytics to the rescue. The report dashboard in Figure 11-9 lists "Platform Versions." Clicking this gets you to the view in Figure 11-13, showing you which operating systems are most frequently used by your visitors.

As with the Browser Version report, you can click next to any listed platform to drill down deeper into what version of that operating system visitors use. The double arrow and the ability to compare date ranges are also available on this report.

Browser & Platform Combos

Visitors don't come to your site using a browser that is independent of an operating system. Nor do they come to your site using a platform that's independent of a browser. And very often, the platform that a browser is running on affects the way the browser behaves. So Google Analytics makes it easy for you to figure out what combination of platforms and browsers are used most often to access your web site.

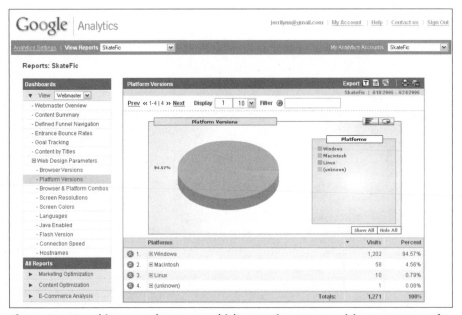

Figure 11-13: This report shows you which operating systems visitors use most often.

The Browser & Platform Combos report, shown in Figure 11-14, shows you the combination of web browser and operating system used most often to access your web site.

All of the information available in this report is also available in other reports, just not in such a user-friendly version. This graphical representation makes it easy for you to see who is using what without flipping back and forth between reports.

Screen Resolutions

How Jerri views a web site from her Windows-based laptop might be different from the way she views it on the 19-inch monitor of her desktop computer, and that's certain to be different from what Mary sees on her iBook. The screen and screen resolution that visitors use to (actually) view your site will make all the difference in the world in what they see.

To help you determine whether your site is displaying as well as it can for the majority of users, the Screen Resolutions report, shown in Figure 11-15, ranks visits according to screen resolution.

Figure 11-14:   The browser and platform combination affects how users see your site.

Figure 11-15: Screen resolution affects how visitors see your site. Literally.

Users are ranked according to the resolution of the screen that they are using, and you can click the double arrow or use the calendar functions to dig deeper into the information to view different time representation.

Screen Colors

Anyone who has ever printed a color picture or ordered a colored garment over the Internet knows that colors on a screen are vastly different from colors in real life. What you might not realize, though, is how different colors look on different types of monitors.

Because SkateFic.com has a very specific color scheme for certain parts of the site, Mary needs to ensure that all of the colors in the site are distinguishable. To do that, she refers to the Screen Colors report to see what color-rendering standard most of the site's visitors are using.

The Screen Colors report, shown in Figure 11-16, breaks down the graphic viewing capabilities of your site visitors so that you can be certain they're actually seeing what you intend for them to.

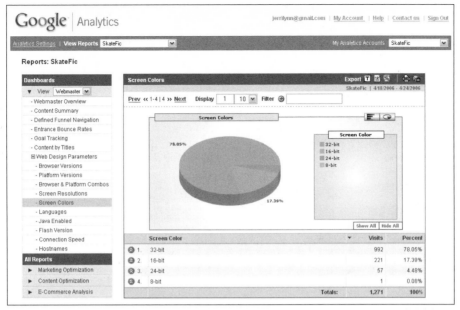

Figure 11-16: The Screen Colors report breaks your visitors up by graphic capabilities.

If you're not targeting the right graphics capabilities with your web site, users could be seeing red when you want them to see fuchsia.

Languages

There's nothing more frustrating than locating a web site that you think is exactly what you're looking for, only to learn that it's in a language that you can't understand, even with your propeller hat on. That's why monitoring the language of the majority of your site visitors is important.

The Languages report, shown in Figure 11-17, gives you a graphical illustration of what language preferences the majority of your users are. Typically, this is going to be the language for the country that you live in, but in some cases, your site will draw more users from other countries than it does from your own.

As with the other reports in this section, you can use the double arrows or the calendar function to dig deeper into the data.

Figure 11-17: Use this graphic to understand what language is used most by visitors.

Java Enabled

To Java or not to Java? That is the question. . . . Okay, so maybe it's corny, but if you're considering putting a Java-enabled application on your web site, it's a question you could be asking yourself, no matter how corny it might sound.

Web-site visitors are a fickle bunch. Scores of studies have been done to show what users want and don't want from a web site. Among those reports are some that focus solely on Java, and the findings generally point to the fact that users who don't have a capability installed don't usually want to install it. So, if you're putting Java on your site, you should probably make sure the majority of your users have Java-enabled browsers, unless you have a very good reason for doing otherwise.

The Java Enabled report is your way to tell. The report, shown in Figure 11-18, tells you exactly how many visitors have Java capabilities and how many do not.

The remaining controls on this report (like the double arrow) are the same as previous reports.

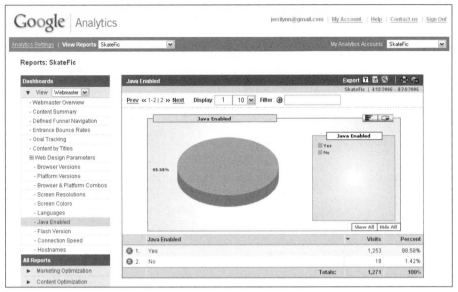

Figure 11-18:   How important is that two percent?

Flash Version

Here's a news flash: Most web-site visitors hate Flash (not because it's a bad technology but because it's very often used in advertising). That means when visitors see a Flash graphic coming up on their page, they're a little reluctant to download a new version of Flash, just to be hit with an advertisement.

On the other hand, Flash openers are more acceptable (to Jerri at least; Mary hates them even more than she does — well, she's trying to think of someone she hates that much who doesn't have a lawyer or a fan club).

If you absolutely must have one of those exceptionally cool Flash splashes on your site (we know *you* would never use Flash advertisements), the Flash Version report, shown in Figure 11-19, will show you what version of Flash the majority of your users has installed.

Figure 11-19: The Flash Version report shows you what version of Flash visitors use.

Connection Speed

Back in the late 1990s and early 2000s, there were scores of reports put together about web-site usability. The concept behind such usability was to provide web sites that were easy for visitors to navigate. At the time, the studies looked at a variety of factors, including how long it took for a web page to load.

What was discovered was that Internet users are an impatient lot. We like to have our pages served up to us in less time than it takes to nuke a cup of coffee. Remember the days of going out for Chinese while a page loaded? These days, if a page takes more than a few seconds to appear, we're ready, willing, and able to move on.

Today, more and more users are connecting to the web via high-speed, broadband connections, but there are still some users who have dial-up connections, including the vast majority of non-American users (except in Korea). And those users don't want to deal with pages that take forever (in Internet time) to load. The Connection Speed report, shown in Figure 11-20, illustrates what speed your users connect to your site with.

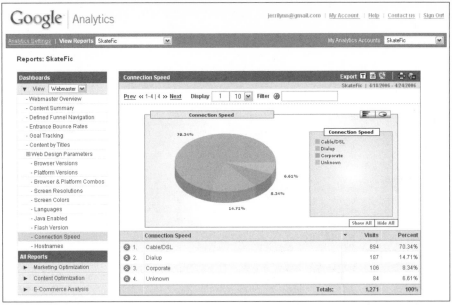

Figure 11-20:   This report shows what connection speed your visitors use.

Hostnames

Some web site owners, like Mary, have multiple domains pointing to the same physical web space (some black hats have the same content on multiple sites). If you park an old domain on your current site, separating old traffic from new could be difficult. Could be. With Google Analytics, it's not. Analytics provides the Hostnames report, shown in Figure 11-21, to help you see which site got what traffic.

NOTE This report is one way to see if someone else is copying your web site's source code to build their own or to create a spoofed copy of your site. If a web site appears in this list that doesn't belong to you, it's possible that the site owner has copied your source code (and even your content) to use as his or her own.

Before you get all up in arms, make sure that it's not an ISP's proxy or cache, which, by law, is allowed to maintain copies of your pages. This is a place where it's worthwhile to note that because the proxy copies the whole page, including the Google Analytics code, page views that might escape a log-based analyzer like AWStats don't get lost in the shuffle. To Google Analytics, they look no different from page views served directly from your site.

Figure 11-21:   This report separates traffic for domains with the same content.

Even for a webmaster, making sense of web metrics is a tedious chore. The Webmaster Dashboard provides all of the metrics that a webmaster needs to build and improve a web site. It may be hard work reading, learning to understand, and learning to use all the reports, but it's well worth it. Sometimes, even small changes can make a big difference in traffic.

Marketing Optimization

Marketing optimization — it's a term you've heard so often that it seems to have little meaning. Or worse, the meaning of the term is so broad that it's hard to get a handle on exactly what marketing optimization is. For our purposes in this part of the book, marketing optimization is a set of tools that you can use with Google Analytics to improve your online marketing campaigns.

Specifically, there are chapters in this section that cover visitor tracking, visitor segment performance, marketing campaign results, and search-engine marketing — such as AdWords. These chapters all look at the different reports for that area of marketing optimization, and you'll find tips and graphics that help you quickly navigate through all the reports as well as help you use them.

You've already seen a few of the reports in this section, but there are also some new reports and new information, so if you want to improve your marketing efforts, this is a chapter you'll want to read. Of course, if marketing isn't your gig, there are plenty of other offerings in the book, so there's no need for you to read through something that's of no use to you. Feel free to skip forward to a section that has more meaning and purpose for you.

CHAPTER 12

Unique-Visitor Tracking

Unique visitors to your web site are people who have never been to the site before, right? Not exactly. There are certain qualifications that make visitors unique. For example, did you know that a person can visit your site this month as a unique visitor and then return to the site next month and also be a unique visitor? It can happen.

It's one of those situations where things may not always be as they seem. Like stepping on the scale first thing in the morning. It seems that you weigh about two pounds less first thing in the morning than you do by lunchtime. Surely you're not putting on two pounds in four hours, right? Don't worry. You're not. But first thing in the morning, your body is deprived of liquid and may be slightly dehydrated. So, naturally, you're going to weigh less when you first get out of bed than you will at lunchtime after you've had several drinks and probably even some food, too.

That's the problem with measurements of any kind. The only time you can be absolutely certain that a measurement is accurate from one time to another is to completely understand and recreate the circumstances under which you take the measurement the second time. Fortunately, Google Analytics makes it possible for you to recreate those measurements easily.

Unique-Visitor Tracking

There are several categories of visitors to your web site. There are unique visitors, absolute unique visitors, and return (or prior) visitors. Each of these categories differs slightly from the others and so is measured a little differently.

A unique visitor is a person who visits your web site for the first time during a stipulated period of time. What this means is that people can visit your site once this month and be counted as unique visitors, but when they return other times during the month, they are counted as visitors, not unique visitors.

However — and here's where it gets hinky — when these same visitors return to your site for the first time the next month, they are counted as unique visitors again but only one time for that month.

The one-month time frame isn't anchored in concrete. In fact, it may be a week or every hour, depending on how you set the date ranges for your reports. The time frame that you determine will designate how often your returning visitors are counted as unique visitors.

Absolute unique visitors are a little different. The number of absolute unique visitors to your site is the count of people who come to your site for the very first time, ever. It's like the first time you step into a new school or get your first raise. It's something that can never be duplicated. That's an absolute unique visit — it can never be duplicated.

Then there are return visitors, who form a pretty self-explanatory category of visitors. They've been here before and decided it was worth coming back.

You may be wondering how Google Analytics knows the frequency with which a visitor comes to your site. Google uses two small pieces of technology to determine this. The first is your IP address. Every computer has an IP address; it's like your street address on the web. Just as a street address designates your house, your IP address designates your computer — the physical "where" of your location.

Another tool that Google (and every other company on the web) uses to keep up with visitor comings and goings on your site is called a cookie. A cookie is a small piece of information placed on a visitor's computer and that contains information about the visitor relevant to the site that places the cookie.

Think about the last time you logged on to Amazon.com. If you've ever used Amazon, you were probably prompted to create an account that included a user name and password. The next time you returned to Amazon, did you happen to notice that near the top of the page, as shown in Figure 12-1, you were greeted by name and even directed to a store designed specifically to recommend items similar to those you've purchased in the past? That's what cookies do for you. They make it possible for companies to know that you've visited before and even to know some information about those past visits to help them serve you with better, more targeted content.

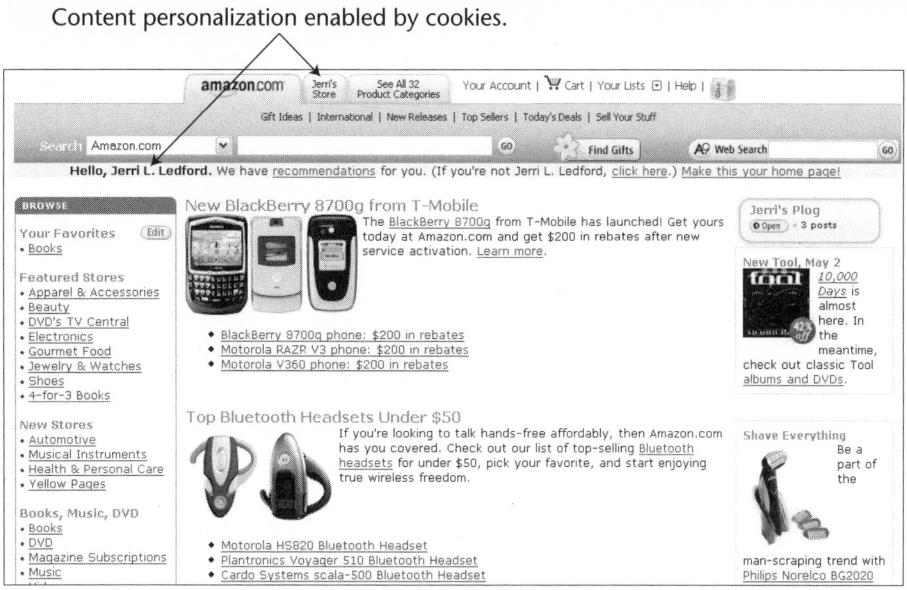

Content personalization enabled by cookies.

Figure 12-1: Amazon uses cookies to personalize the content it serves to visitors.

All of this is to say that a cookie makes it possible for Google Analytics to know whether a visitor is an absolute unique visitor, a unique visitor, or a returning visitor. And that information helps you understand how many and how often visitors return to your site. This information in turn can be used to optimize your site content for those categories (or to achieve those categories) of visitors.

Daily Visitors

The first report in the Unique Visitor Tracking segment of the Marketing Optimization menu is the Daily Visitors report, shown in Figure 12-2.

The Daily Visitors report shows you two bar graphs. The first is an overview of the number of visitors to your site in the defined time frame. It includes all of the visitors to your site, whether they are absolute unique, unique, or returning visitors. Right above the graph, you see the total number of visitors for the time frame and an average daily number of visitors. Exact numbers for each day are represented in the graph.

The second graph represents the percent of new visitors to your site. In Figure 12-2, each bar represents a day of the week, so the percentage of visitors for each day is represented by a bar.

Figure 12-2: Daily Visitors shows you a breakdown of daily web-site visitors.

These two graphs are designed to give you a quick overview of the traffic on your site for the defined time period. If bar graphs aren't your thing, you can switch them to line graphs by clicking the line graph button in the top-right corner of the graphic.

Visits & Page View Tracking

There is a distinct difference between the number of visitors to your site and the number of page views on your site. A visit is counted when a person first navigates onto your site, whether it's by clicking a link that leads there or by typing your URL directly into the address bar of a web browser.

The number of page views on your site is how many pages a visitor actually clicked when visiting your site. For example, if one person visits your web site, that counts as one visit. However, while visiting, that person might look at five different pages on your site. Those are page views.

The Visits & Pageviews report is shown in Figure 12-3.

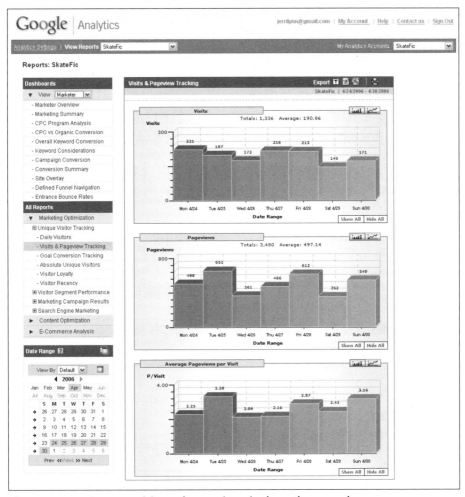

Figure 12-3: Compare visits and page views in these three graphs.

Each of the three graphs in this report illustrates a different aspect of visits and page views. The first graph, Visits, is only the number of visits to your page. Each time a person comes to your web site, he or she is logged as a visitor. Visitors are counted and shown here.

The second graph illustrates the number of page views — pages shown to visitors. In Figure 12-3, you can see that the number of visitors to this site was 1,336, but that the number of page views was considerably higher at 3,480.

The last graph shows you what the average page views per visit was by day, hour, or month, according to the date view you've selected — the graphs in Figure 12-3 are shown by day.

Again, you can change your view from a bar graph to a line graph if it suits you better, but there's no way to dig down into this report to find out more information about the visits to your site. That information is included in later reports. This report is designed just to give you an overview of the traffic to your site.

Goal Conversion Tracking

At first glance, this report looks just like the Goal Tracking report from Chapter 11 (the Webmaster Dashboard), but it's not exactly the same. The same information is used, but as you can see in Figure 12-4, it's presented to you in a slightly different format.

Click to compare date ranges.

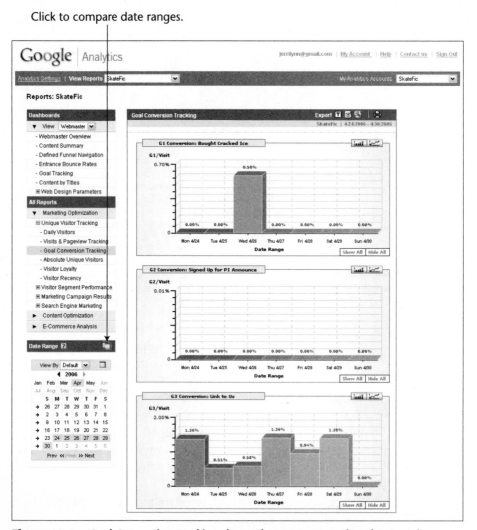

Figure 12-4: Goal Conversion Tracking shows the percentage of goal conversions.

In this report, each of your goal conversions — remember that you can have up to four goals per web-site profile — is shown as a percentage. You can quickly see what percentage of your visitors is reaching the page that you've established for each goal.

This report also has a feature that allows you to compare date ranges. Click the small double calendar in the Date Range menu bar to select the date ranges you want to compare. Figure 12-5 shows a section of the page, with the comparisons in place.

When you've finished comparing date ranges, you can click the double calendar again, and the page will return to the view that you saw when you first entered the report page.

TIP Google chose to keep the buttons on any given page to as few as possible. More often than not, a button that leads you to a different view with one click (like the double calendar) will lead you right back to your original view if you click it again when you're finished. This is true with the calendar buttons, the plus signs (which become minus signs), and the double arrows that you see in many of the reports.

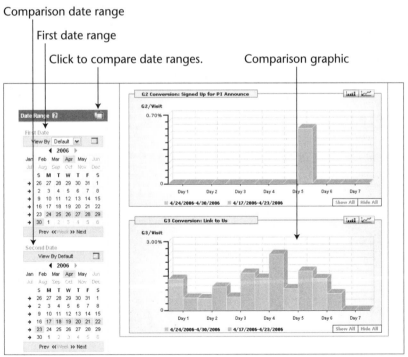

Figure 12-5: Compare date ranges for goal conversions.

Absolute Unique Visitors

Earlier in this chapter, you learned about the difference between unique visitors and absolute unique visitors. Now it's time to look a little closer at the concept. The Absolute Unique Visitors report, shown in Figure 12-6, shows additional information about these unique site visitors.

In the graphic there are two designations for unique visitors. The First Time (Absolute Unique) Visitors designation represents visitors who have come to your site, during this particular date range, for the very first time. Prior Visitors (returning ones of any kind) represent both simple return visitors and ones who have visited in the past but are "unique" (first-timers) for this period.

You can use this information to view how effective your marketing efforts are at driving absolute unique visitors to your web site — the true first-time folks. If you were tweaking an existing marketing campaign to drive more of these visitors to your site, this information would help you decide how future iterations of that marketing campaign could be changed or enhanced to get more of them, as well as more returning visitors.

One thing you should note about these graphics is that each visitor is counted only one time. What that means to you is that visitors who appear in the First Time Visitors (the absolute unique) section of the graphic are not the same visitors who appear in the Prior Visitors section. These counts don't overlap at all.

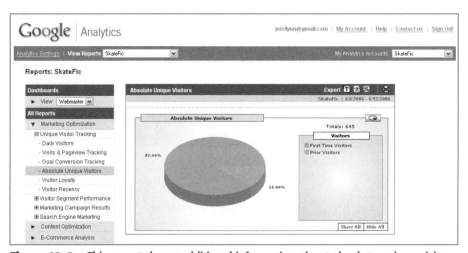

Figure 12-6: This report shows additional information about absolute unique visitors.

Visitor Loyalty

How often do visitors return to your site? Is it once? Two hundred times? You can't know without some kind of indicator, and that's what you get with the Visitor Loyalty report, shown in Figure 12-7.

"What's it all mean?" the reader wails in frustration. The histogram — bar graph — shows you, from 1 to 200+ visits, how often visitors return to your site. If the histogram isn't your style or doesn't show you clearly enough what you want to know, you can change the graphic to a line graph, as shown in Figure 12-8.

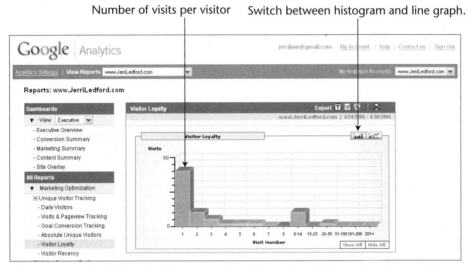

Figure 12-7:   The Visitor Loyalty report shows how often visitors return to your site.

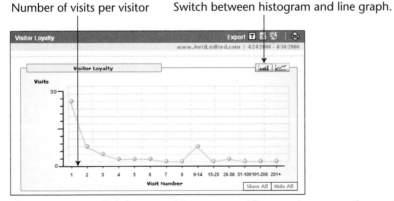

Figure 12-8:   Switch between histogram and line graph to get a clearer view of visits.

The information contained here is used to gauge how loyal your site visitors are. If you find that you have a low number of returning visitors, it could indicate that you need to add something more to your web site to draw visitors back on a regular basis. Using time-shifted content, like newsletters, blogs, and podcasts, is a great way to increase visitor loyalty.

Visitor Recency

A number that goes hand in hand with visitors' return visits to your site is how often they return — the recency of their visits. Do visitors come back every two days? Once a year? Knowing when visitors return to your site helps you understand what's driving them to return.

If you're using a weekly newsletter to drive return traffic to your site, the Visitor Recency report, shown in Figure 12-9, indicates whether that newsletter is successful in bringing people back to your site every week.

The graph shows the visitor from zero days through more than 366 — over a year. So at a glance you can tell if visitors come one time each year for your annual sale or if they return for your daily podcast review.

Visitor behavior reveals a lot about the effectiveness of your web site. Graphics such as visitor loyalty and visit recency show you when (or if) your site visitors return and give you cues as to what works to drive traffic or returning traffic to your site. What you do with that information will determine how successful your site is in the long term.

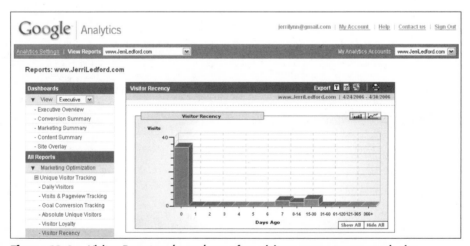

Figure 12-9: Visitor Recency shows how often visitors return to your web site.

CHAPTER 13

Visitor Segmenting

Dump a box of multicolored, different-shaped blocks on a table, and at some point someone will come along and separate them by color, shape, or both. It's human nature. We want to make sense of things, so we place everything in its own compartment.

This tendency to compartmentalize things serves other purposes, too. Think about working in your yard. If you reach down to pull a weed out of the yard and spot something long and rounded, it's a pretty good bet you'll yank your hand back before you're even certain what you see.

That's the result of compartmentalization — also called segmentation. We give objects general classifications, like long, rounded, hairy, green, or fat, because that helps us know quickly where that object belongs. And it's not just objects. Basically everything can be classified as one thing or another.

Visitor segmentation works the same way, except it applies to your web-site visitors. By segmenting visitors, first generally and then more specifically, you can determine how effective portions of your site are, what groups of visitors are the most valuable (or spend the most money), and which group of visitors provides the best return on investment.

Visitor Segment Performance is a group of reports that helps you drill down into the various segments of site visitors to find ways to target better, provide more customization, and reap more rewards from your efforts.

New vs. Returning

When you first click into your Google Analytics reporting sections, you're shown four overview-type graphics that give you a quick snapshot of your web site's performance. One of the graphics — in the top-right corner — is the Visits by New and Returning graphic. It shows you a quick snapshot of how many visitors have come to your web site and how many of them are new.

The New vs. Returning report, shown in Figure 13-1, takes that quick-glance graphic to the next reporting level.

This report shows you how the number of new and returning visitors to your site compares to the number of goal conversions by those visitors. You've already seen all of the columns on this report, but here's a quick recap in case it's been a while.

- Visitor type: Defines whether a visitor is new or returning
- Visits: The number of visits for that Visitor Type
- P/Visit: Average page views per visit
- G1-G4/Visit: Average goal conversions for that goal, per visit
- T/Visits: Average number of transactions per visit
- $/Visits: Average goal value or revenue per visit

Date range title bar

Click to compare date ranges.

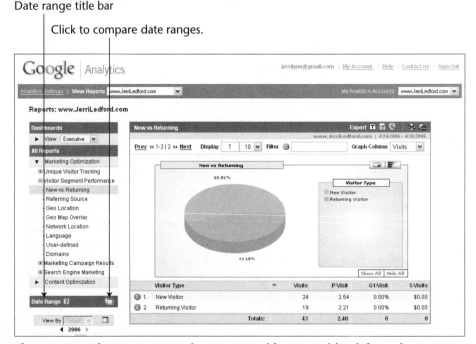

Figure 13-1: The New vs. Returning report provides more visitor information.

You can also perform a date-range comparison on this report by clicking the double calendar icon. As shown in Figure 13-2, information for the comparison date range is displayed below the information for the original date range.

So why do you need this information? Simply put, you need it to see how often your new and returning visitors reach your goal pages. If you offer a free report from your web site and have the download of that paper as one of your goals, you can track how often that happens. And if you find that only first-time visitors download that report, what does it tell you? Maybe that the report is drawing traffic to the site. But also that something else is pulling returning visitors back to the site. It could be another of the goals that you have established for the site, but it could be something entirely different. This report is the first stop along the way to finding those answers.

Referring Source

One of the big questions about web sites is, "Where do users come from?" Who refers them? Knowing where your traffic comes from makes it easier to target marketing efforts. It also lets you know if your current marketing efforts are working.

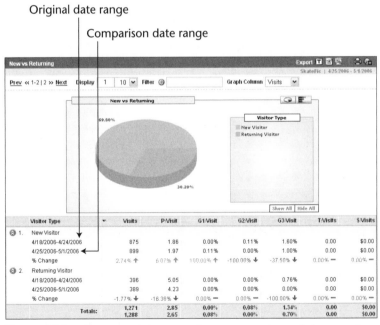

Figure 13-2: Compare date ranges to see percentage of change.

So, where does traffic come from? There's always the direct route — typing the URL for your web site directly into the address bar on the browser. But then there are links that you've paid to have placed on other sites, links from banners, newsletters, and other marketing efforts. And then you have the people who stumble onto your site because they find it through a web search.

People come to your site from all manner of sources. To see what those sources are, there's the Referring Source report, shown in Figure 13-3.

This report lays out the referral sites for your visitors and then illustrates how those visits translate into goal conversions. Do the visitors who come from your newsletter buy more than the visitors who come from your AdWords campaigns? Or maybe the visitors who come from a high-end referral link spend more on average than visitors from a less costly referral link? The only way you'll ever know is to look at this report.

Of course, the report comes with all of the standard tools: Click the double arrow to select more analysis options, use the Graph Column drop-down menu to select other graphic views, and add or remove filters for the data included in the report. All of these tools are labeled in Figure 13-4.

Figure 13-3: The Referring Source report shows where site traffic originates.

Choose analysis options.

Compare date ranges.   Add filter.   Change data view.

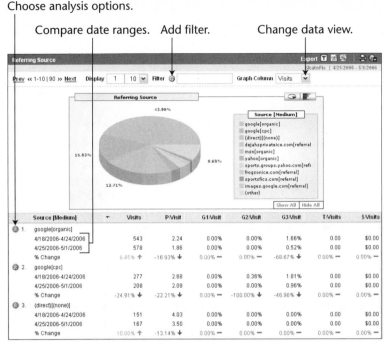

Figure 13-4:   Additional tools are available to dig deeper into report data.

Geo Location

Wouldn't you be surprised if you looked at your site statistics and discovered that instead of the majority of visitors being from your country, they're from another country that it never occurred to you to target? It happens. Many Japanese gaming sites find that U.S. visitors make up a large portion of their traffic, especially right before the release of a new gaming console or device. And they aren't the only sites.

So how are you supposed to know what country the majority of your visitors are from? The Geo Location report, shown in Figure 13-5, is just the tool to give you that information.

Figure 13-5: Learn what geographic location web-site visitors are in.

This report shows you where your visitors are geographically located, but it also shows that information relative to the number of goal conversions and average value of each visit. That information can then be used to target specific segments of your web-site audience according to their location.

Dig deeper into each entry by clicking the double arrow or the plus sign beside each geographic location. Figure 13-6 shows the result of clicking one of the plus signs beside a country — you're taken deeper to view the region or state. From there, you can click a plus sign beside a region or state to view the cities within that region or state.

In addition to these tools, the standard set of tools that you've come to know and love is available: analysis options, filters, and the ability to change views with the Graph Column drop-down menu.

Check the plus (+) sign to see cities within a state or region.

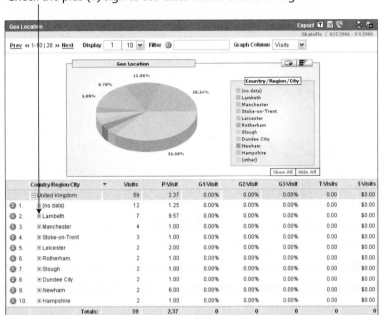

Figure 13-6: Additional information is imbedded within the Geo Location report.

Geo Map Overlay

Remember way back in Chapter 9 (Seems like eons ago, doesn't it?) when we covered the Executive Dashboard? Recall that in the Executive Overview four small graphics gave you a quick look at the state of your web site. Now one of those reports appears again. The Geo Map Overlay report, shown in Figure 13-7, appeared in the Executive Overview, in a much smaller form.

This larger view of the Geo Map Overlay lets you (more clearly) see where visitors to your site are located. Now, remember, you've got to take this information with a little skepticism. The dots that indicate visitor location could be located in the city where the visitor's ISP (Internet Service Provider) is located. Generally, it's pretty close to the same location, but in some instances, where a visitor lives in a rural area, the location could be off just a little.

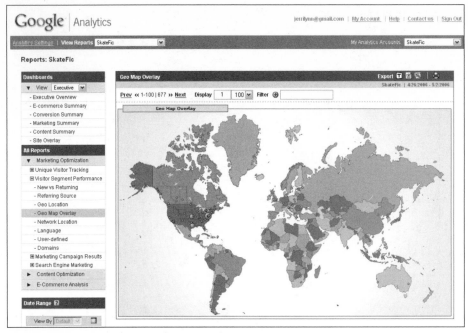

Figure 13-7: Where in the world are your site visitors coming from?

Still, the graphic is valuable in helping you to understand where the majority of your visitors are located. For example, if your web site is very American-centric but the Geo Map Overlay shows that a significant portion of your visitors are from Europe, you could be missing an untapped market. You'll also want to figure out what's drawing those European visitors to your site, but that's best discussed under Navigational Analysis in Chapter 18.

So you have the Geo Map Overlay, and it shows you where in the world your visitors are located. How do you use it? Maybe you have a local computer repair business and your web site offers troubleshooting information designed to lead users to your physical location.

What happens if you look at your Geo Map Overlay and find that the site is getting more visits from a nearby city than from the city where you're located? What you get is a clue that maybe there's an untapped market for your business in another location. So improve your targeting. Expand your marketing. Increase your business. Each task is relative to the location of your visitors.

> **TIP** When you're looking at the Geo Map Overlay, a few clusters of visitors are probably hard to distinguish. When several visitors from one location are counted, the spots that represent those visits can be piled on top of one another. There's good news, though. You can zoom in on the graphic by right clicking it and selecting **Zoom In**. Zoom in multiple times or zoom out using the same method. (And a tip within a tip: Try this for other graphics, too.)

Network Location

Just having looked at the geographic location of your visitors, when you see the term "network location," you might think it refers to the geographic location of our network. In this instance, you'd be wrong. The Network Location report, shown in Figure 13-8, is misleading. It actually tells you to what ISP or corporate network visitors to your site are connected.

What can possibly be gained by knowing the ISP or corporate network to which your users are connected? Here's a good example. In preparing this report, we noticed that among the list of networks in Mary's report is Emporia State University. By itself, that fact really doesn't mean anything. But when you consider that Emporia State University is in Kansas, you're getting a little closer to usable information. According to the report, 45 visitors (or 3.51 percent of the visitors) accessed the site from the Emporia State University network. This is illustrated in Figure 13-9. Now, what can you do with that information?

Figure 13-8:   To what ISP or corporate network are your visitors connected?

Additional information about goal conversions

Click various points for additional information.

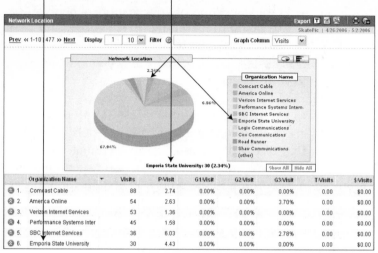

Figure 13-9:   Click a graph segment to see additional information.

Also in Figure 13-9, you can see that additional information about goal conversions is included in the report. So, if you look at the goal conversion information about Emporia State University, you'll see there was none from these visitors. If there had been, however, you would want to pay more attention to that visitor segment and maybe even take advantage of it by placing an advertisement on the University's web site or in the school newsletter. (In this case, the visits may have represented just a class assignment of some kind.)

This is a simple example of how you can use this information. Look at your own statistics over time and think creatively about how you can use them to improve your business or solve a business problem.

Language

The Language report, shown in Figure 13-10, is something you've seen before. Or at least you've seen most of it. Back in Chapter 11, when we were going over the Webmaster Dashboard, we looked at a Languages report that illustrated for you the different languages of visitors to your site. This report takes that segmentation one step further by adding goal conversions and visit values.

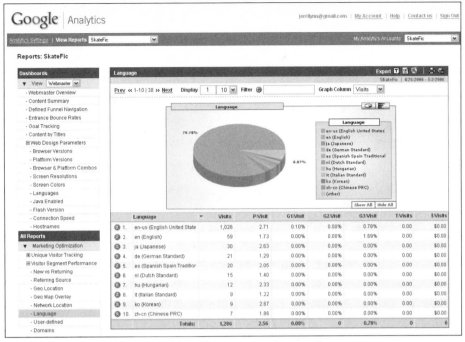

Figure 13-10: What are your visitors' language preferences?

It's a pretty good bet that the majority of your web-site visitors will have language preferences set to your native tongue, but if your figures show that you have a high number of visitors with different language preferences *and* there are a majority of goal conversions within those languages, something on your site is drawing these visitors. You need to find a way to capitalize on that.

User-Defined

Google Analytics gives you a good standard selection for visitor segmentation. The existing reports are fairly standard among analytics programs. There will be some variations, depending on the software you use, but as you saw in the AWStats chapters, the differences aren't dramatic.

As useful as the existing segmentation reports are, you'll probably want (or need) to segment site visitors in a way that's very specific to your business. In Google Analytics, the User Defined report, shown in Figure 13-11, lets you segment your visitors according to measurements that you define, and it shows you how those users measure up in conversions and visit values.

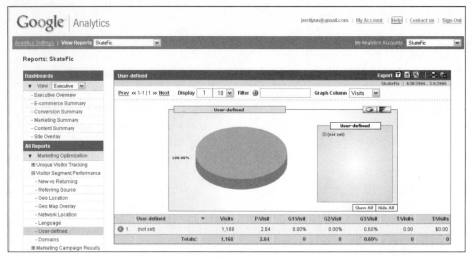

Figure 13-11:   The User Defined report illustrates customizable segmentation data.

When looking at Figure 13-11, you'll notice there's no data there. In that report, a user-defined segmentation measurement hasn't been added. But adding one isn't all that difficult. It requires a snippet of Java-Script code placed on your web page below the tracking code that you've inserted so Google Analytics can collect visitor data from your site.

One measurement that you can use to segment your visitors is information from a form that visitors complete on your site. For example, if you push site visitors through a registration form when they enter a specific point on your site, you could include a drop-down menu in that form that allows the user to select their specific job title. That job title can then be used to track how registrants from each job category navigate through your site.

So, the first thing you need to do to set a user-defined variable is to add the Java-Script code to your web site. The code should include the _utmSetVar command. It looks like this:

```
<script language="text"/javascript>__utmSetVar('Marketing/PR');</script>
```

In this line of code, the script language should be replaced by the script that you're using. There's also a piece that reads ('Marketing/PR'). This is a variable and you should replace this portion of the code with the name of the variable that you want to track. So, in our example of segmenting visitors by job title, your code might look like this:

```
<form onSubmit="__utmSetVar(this.mymenu.options
[this.mymenu.selectedIndex].value);">
<select name=mymenu>
<option value="Technical/Engineering">
```

```
Technical/Engineering</option>
<option value="Marketing/PR">Marketing/PR</option>
<option value="Manufacturing">Manufacturing</option>
<option value="General Management">General Management</option>
```

As you can see, each of the job titles that you have listed in your online form should be given a line in the code. That way, Analytics knows to track each of the separate job functions.

You can also track separately users who click certain links. The code for that segmentation might look like this:

```
<a href="link.html" onClick="__utmSetVar('Marketing /PR');">Click here
</a>
```

One other option you have is to track users according to a specific page that they visit. For example, if you have a visitor who stops by your Marketing/PR page, you can set a segmentation variable that will then track that visitor's movements through your site as a part of the Marketing/PR segment. Your code for this type of tracking might look something like this:

```
<body onLoad="javascript:__utmSetVar('Marketing/PR')">
```

Visitor segmentation is all about figuring out how certain segments of your visitors behave in the context of that segmentation. There's a lot to be gained from segmenting your users. If you're segmenting by information included in a form, such as job titles, you can quickly learn how engineers use your site versus the way that IT managers use it. This is an easy way to learn quickly who your most profitable segments of site visitors are.

Domains

How does a user's domain affect how they use your site? It will be different for each domain, because some domains — or ISPs — are much more effective for driving traffic to your site. And your site performs differently for different domains. A good example of this is a dial-up domain like AOL.com versus a DSL domain like BellSouth.net versus a cable domain like Comcast.net.

Each domain offers varying amounts of bandwidth, which translates into different speeds. So where do most of your visitors come from? If you know this information, you can use it to optimize your web site for visitors who come from the most frequently used domain.

Analytics provides the Domains report, shown in Figure 13-12, to let you know which domain your visitors most frequently use.

Figure 13-12: Use domain information to optimize your site for visitors.

The domain report also shows you the number of goal conversions for each domain and the visit value for each domain. Then you can find the domain with the most goal conversions or the highest visit value and use that information to drive more conversions and/or sales from those visitors.

The information can also be used to learn for which domains you need to improve your service. For example, if you have a domain that has a very high number of conversions and another domain that leads to no conversions at all, you know that you need to improve your site in an effort to draw more conversions or sales from the latter domain.

Moving On

Visitor segmentation is your key to understanding how different groups, or segments, of your visitors react to different aspects of your site. The information you gather by segmenting your visitors lets you improve features of your site that don't work or capitalize on the parts of your site that do work.

Take advantage of your segmentation data, but remember that it's not the only indicator of success or failure on your site. Other factors, like the effect of marketing campaigns, should also be taken into consideration, and as luck would have it, that's exactly what's covered in Chapter 14.

Marketing Campaign Results

Tracking the effectiveness of your marketing campaigns is just half the battle. The other half is understanding how the campaign affects the number of people who reach a defined goal on your web site. This is called goal conversion. And marketing is all about conversions.

The goal could be for a visitor to make a purchase, sign up for a newsletter, or even just link to the page. Whatever your desired marketing campaign results are, the number of conversions can be looked at in a variety of ways, and each conversion view tells you something more about the effectiveness of your marketing campaign.

Campaign Conversion

If you're running only one marketing campaign, keeping up with the results of that campaign won't be too difficult. But it's more likely that you're running multiple paid (and free) campaigns. And keeping up with multiple campaigns might leave you feeling as if you've been chasing your tail — lots of work for very little return.

The Campaign Conversion report, shown in Figure 14-1, is a quick glance at how all your marketing campaigns are performing. You'll recognize this report. You saw it back in Chapter 10 when you were reviewing the Marketer Dashboard.

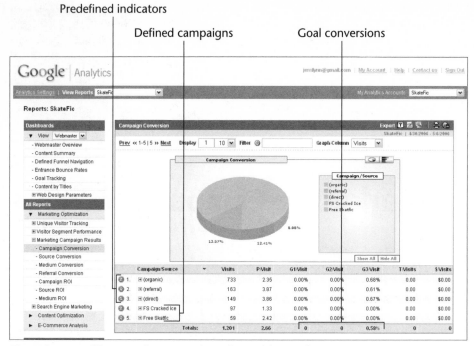

Figure 14-1: This report is an overview of campaign performance.

The Campaign Conversion report shows you your top-performing market-ing campaigns, as long as they have been tagged for tracking by Google Ana-lytics. Each of the lines in the table beneath the graph is dedicated to one marketing campaign that is either auto-tagged or that you have tagged for a specific campaign.

You may remember that Google tracks some special cases. You'll see some of those cases in this report. For example, in Figure 14-1, three general campaign categories are listed as (organic), (referral), and (direct). You may recall that the organic campaign represents visits from an unpaid search engine; referral is the indicator used for visitors who clicked through an untagged marketing link; and direct indicates visitors who typed the URL for your site into the address bar of their web browser.

The tag (not set) may also appear in your list of campaigns, though it's not shown in Figure 14-1. This indicates visitors who came to your site through marketing links that were tagged but for which a campaign variable hasn't been set.

So, in the report shown in Figure 14-1, besides the three general categories, Mary has two campaigns currently active for SkateFic.com. She has those cam-paigns labeled: FS Cracked Ice and Free Skatefic.

Mary can quickly look at all these reports and see how many visits are related to each category and how those visits translate into goal conversions for each of the three goals she has set for the site. With this information, she can then adjust marketing campaigns to improve performance in an area where her campaigns aren't performing as well as she thinks they should.

The information also tells Mary which of her campaigns results in the highest visit value. That information can then be used to expand or shape future marketing campaigns.

Source Conversion

A source is the web site or search engine that led users to your site. If you're using cost-per-click advertising from Yahoo! or Google's AdWords, then when a user clicks through one of your AdWord advertisements, the page (Yahoo! or Google) that refers the user to your site becomes a source of traffic for that site.

The Source Conversion report shows you the top sources driving traffic to your site and how valuable those sources are in terms of conversion and visit value. The report, shown in Figure 14-2, is similar to other reports that you've seen. The source tracking is what sets this report apart.

Goal conversions generated by Yahoo!

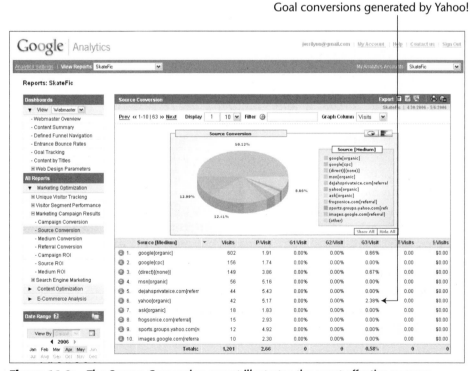

Figure 14-2: The Source Conversion report illustrates the most effective sources.

In Figure 14-2, notice that the SkateFic.com report shows no goal conversions for Goal 1 or Goal 2. This means that none of the visitors from the sources listed in the report completed the task in the goal. In Goal 3, however, there are several goal conversions, with the source Yahoo! having the highest number of goal conversions.

Since the Yahoo! source is organic — meaning that it occurs naturally as potential visitors stumble around the web and doesn't come from paid advertisements of some type — Mary knows that more goal conversions are coming from Yahoo! visitors than from other sources. This might prompt Mary to increase her exposure at Yahoo! by purchasing key-word advertisements.

You may also notice that all of the sources for SkateFic.com have a zero visit value. This is because there is no e-commerce information set up for SkateFic.com, although the site does sell some products. But if you have e-commerce capabilities set in your Google Analytics account and you're still seeing zero visit values, either the application is improperly set up or you just don't have any sales. Refer to Analytics' help files to learn more about setting up e-commerce tracking.

Medium Conversion

You may remember that back in Part I we defined medium as the type of marketing campaign being tracked — e-mail campaigns, banner advertisements, and organic searches are just a few examples of what's considered a medium. The Medium Conversion report shows you which of these types of marketing efforts is performing best according to goal conversions and visit value.

The Medium Conversion report is shown in Figure 14-3 and is another of those reports that's similar in appearance to other reports but different in content. You'll see that all of the same controls — double arrows, pluses in some cases, and drop-down Graph Column menus — are consistent across all these reports.

The key to using the Medium Conversion report effectively is to evaluate each marketing medium according to the number of goal conversions *and* the visit value if you have e-commerce capabilities. It's not enough to have goal conversions if you don't have the sales to support them. Using the report, you can determine where you should increase your marketing investments to capitalize on the user's purchasing trends in relation to goal conversions. If you don't see any success (or only small success) in your goal conversions and visit values, you can tell which marketing mediums are not working, and that investment can be redirected to more successful efforts.

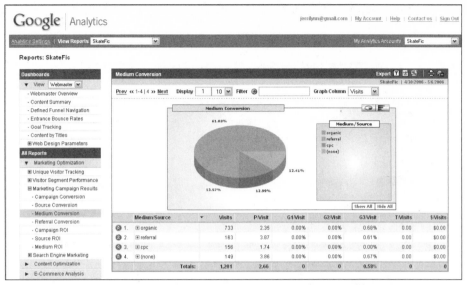

Figure 14-3: Learn which marketing medium performs best with this report.

Referral Conversion

How many links are there to your site from other sites on which you didn't pay to have a link placed? Bet that's a number you can't accurately answer. That's because other people will link to your site without your knowledge and without going through any type of affiliate plan that you might be running. If visitors like your site, they want to share it. And that's a good thing.

If you want a clear picture of the top sites that refer visitors to your web site, the Referral Conversion report, shown in Figure 14-4, is where you can find it.

Remember that these are *unpaid* referrals, so you'll probably see some strange URLs in the report. For example, when you're looking at the report shown in Figure 14-4, you'll see that one of the referring sources is Plover.com.

Just looking at the URL, it's hard to say how this relates to figure skating. So, the next logical step is to dig deeper. What on the Plover.com site relates to figure skating? If you click the plus sign next to Plover.com, you're taken to the referring page from the web site, as shown in Figure 14-5.

Click the plus (+) sign to learn more about the mysterious plover.com.

Figure 14-4: Who is referring visitors to your site?

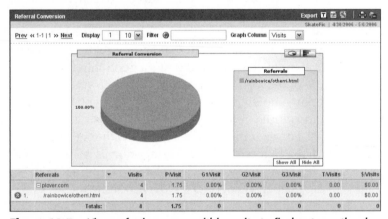

Figure 14-5: View referring pages within a site to find out exactly where a link is.

When you step deeper into the data, you see that the page within the Plover.com site that contains a link to SkateFic.com is /rainbowice/ otherri.html. This page, RainbowIce, is a site for figure skaters.

So, you've learned that this site is linking to SkateFic.com; now how do you use that information? Your first move is to look at the number of visits, conversions, and visit values. In this case, there were four visits that resulted in no conversions and a zero visit value. So for all practical purposes, the link is exposure and nothing else.

Under different circumstances — if there were more visits that resulted in more conversions and a higher visit value — you could use that information to improve a relationship with the referring site. You could increase your success with that link by negotiating a more prominent link or a partnership of some type. In the case of SkateFic.com, maybe the partnership could be a sponsored link for a contest or competition. What you can do to take advantage of the naturally occurring traffic is limited only by your imagination.

Campaign ROI

Return on investment — also called ROI — are three words that can cause tremors for you or any business person in the position of explaining why a company has to spend money, even if the only person you're explaining it to is yourself. So when you invest in a marketing campaign, you need to know how well it performs in relation to the amount of money that you've spent.

The Campaign ROI report, shown in Figure 14-6, shows you just that — how well tagged marketing campaigns perform in the context of visits, cost, revenue, cost per acquisition (CPA), revenue per acquisition (RPA), and ROI.

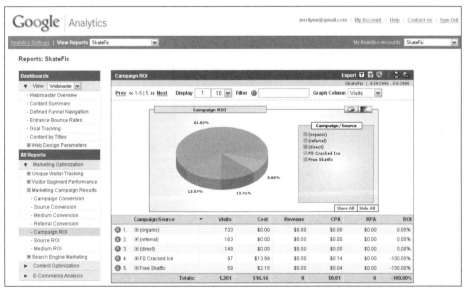

Figure 14-6: Learn your marketing return on investment using this report.

In addition to the main report shown in Figure 14-6, you can click the plus sign next to any entry on the report to drill down further into the data. As Figure 14-7 shows, when you drill down, you are taken to a subreport that shows you what the source for a campaign is. In this case, the main source (from the first report) is FS Cracked Ice, and when you drill down into the next report, the secondary source is Google.

In Figure 14-7, the cost for the marketing campaign, which is a Google AdWords Cost-Per-Click campaign, was $13.99 for the given time period. At 97 visits, that breaks down to a cost per visit of about $0.14. However, because there were no e-commerce sales realized from those visits, the ROI on that particular campaign is a negative 100 percent, because none of the money spent was recaptured in sales.

As you can see, the ROI report quickly gives you an overview of your return on investment for your top campaigns. If your ROI is high for any given source, you should consider expanding your marketing efforts for that source. But if it's low, it's time to consider some different marketing avenues.

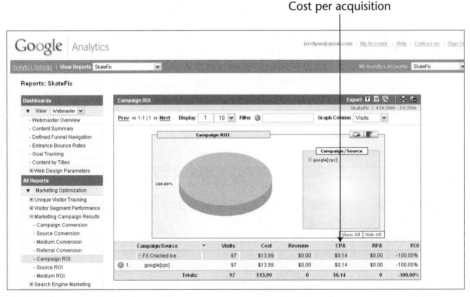

Figure 14-7: Drill down into the ROI report to see specifics about sources and ROI.

Source ROI

We're back to sources — paid and unpaid referrals — again. Only now we're looking at the return on investment for each source. To clearly illustrate the ROI for your marketing efforts, the Source ROI report, shown in Figure 14-8, gives you the scoop on how referrals cash out.

In this particular report, you can see that the organic referrals from Google result in a higher number of visits than the Cost-per-Click referrals. Not only that, but the CPC referrals cost money and aren't pulling in conversions or e-commerce sales, so they result in a negative ROI. Over time this could indicate that the capital being spent on the CPC campaign should be redirected to a marketing method that's more successful.

Top referrals

Analysis options tool

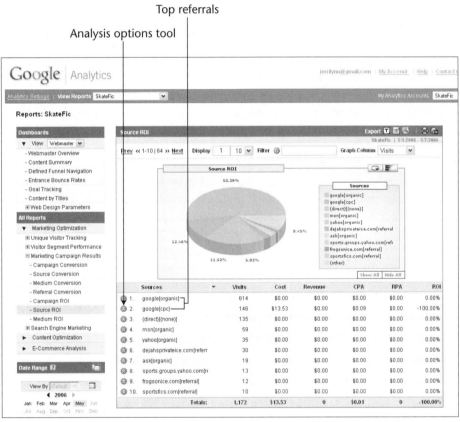

Figure 14-8: Learn what sources generate the best ROI in this report.

In fact, if you use the analysis options tool — the double arrow — to look at the Data Over Time report for Google CPC, and change the date range to April 1 thru May 1, you'll see that the ROI on this marketing campaign has been at negative 100 percent for the entire month, as Figure 14-9 shows. This means that the cost of the CPC campaign has resulted in zero revenues over that one-month period. That should be enough to indicate that it's time to try a different marketing method.

Medium ROI

Do you remember covering medium earlier in this chapter? In the Medium Conversion section, we looked at how different types of marketing campaigns perform for goal conversions. The other part of medium performance is in ROI. How do different types of marketing affect your return on investment?

The Medium ROI report is where you'll find the answer to that question. As you can see in Figure 14-10, this report shows the costs and revenues of your marketing campaigns, based on the type of campaign and the number of visits. This information is then translated into ROI.

You may see the special cases of marketing campaigns in this report again, because this isn't all about paid marketing or unpaid marketing. Both types are included, so you may have categories for referrals and organic visits as well. If you haven't tagged all of your marketing campaigns, you may even have a category labeled (none).

This information should guide you in making decisions about the type of marketing campaigns that you invest in. For example, if you're investing heavily in a banner advertising campaign but you find that the CPC campaign in which you're investing less money results in better sales and a higher ROI, you should consider rebalancing the division of marketing capital for each type of marketing.

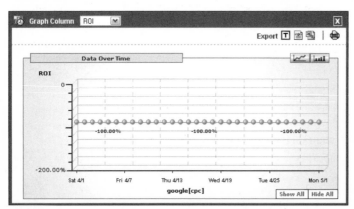

Figure 14-9: This report shows negative ROI for the specified date range.

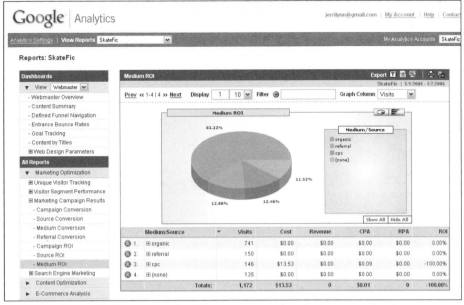

Figure 14-10: What's your ROI for different types of marketing campaigns?

Show Me Your ROI

"Show me the ROI" is a command often heard in corporate America, in much the same way that Cuba Gooding Jr. told Tom Cruise to "Show me the money" in the movie *Jerry Maguire*. Everything is about the bottom line, and if your marketing campaigns aren't contributing to the bottom line, you have to move on or risk losing everything.

The figures in the Marketing Campaign Results area won't solve all of your ROI issues. You still have to do some creative thinking and make some educated guesses about what works and what doesn't, but the reports do help you see ROI trends. And from those trends you can decide what's working and what's not.

Next on your list is a closer look at Search Engine Marketing reports. Once you understand those, you should have a clear picture of your marketing campaign results.

CHAPTER 15

Search-Engine Marketing

If you have a web site, you know it's not all that difficult to get your site listed in search engines like Google or Yahoo! For the most part, especially if your web-site URL and title are the same, all you have to do is put the site up and wait. In many cases, within a few days a potential visitor could type the name of your web site into a search engine and it will appear in the search listings. Give it a little more time and you might even make it to the first page of results.

That's the only easy part of search-engine marketing. If you have a service or product that you want to market by search engine, landing good placement in search-engine results is like catching electric eels by hand — it's slippery and unpredictable and if you do get your hands around it, there's a very good possibility that you're going to get a serious shock.

To help combat the difficulties of creating web pages that actually land on a relevant search-term result, an entire discipline of marketing is targeted at optimizing search-engine results. It's called Search-Engine Optimization. At the heart of this marketing strategy are key words and key-word marketing.

Lumped together, this all adds up to search-engine marketing — the art of gaining prominent placement in search-engine results. And if you're trying to improve your search-engine results, you're probably using some kind of key-word marketing.

Keeping up with the results of that marketing can be a very difficult task that leaves you wishing you had a clone or maybe six of them. It's a difficult, time-consuming process. Or at least it *was*. Now that Google Analytics offers metrics for search-engine marketing, all you really have to do is tag your key-word campaigns properly and Analytics will provide your tracking reports.

CPC Program Analysis

The CPC Program Analysis report is the first of four reports that you've seen once before. These reports made their debut in Chapter 10 in the Marketer Dashboard. They're no different in this chapter, so rather than boring you with all of the same information a second time, we're going to use these reports to illustrate how they can help you improve your key-word marketing efforts.

Okay, back to CPC Program Analysis. Remember that this report, shown in Figure 15-1, illustrates how your key words perform. Included in the analysis are:

- Number of impressions
- Clicks
- Number of transactions
- Cost
- Revenues
- Click-through rate
- Conversion Rate
- Cost-per-click
- Revenue per click
- ROI

These measurements are for both organic (unpaid) and paid key words, which means you can look at the top key words used to locate your site regard-less of whether you're purchasing the placements or not.

One company that uses the Analytics CPC Program Analysis is FT.com, the online arm of the Financial Times. By looking at which keywords perform well, the company makes informed decisions about when to spend more money on key-word advertising.

For example, FT.com can examine a key word with this report to see how much it costs for users to click their advertisement for that key word. Then the company can analyze how much visitors who clicked through the key-word advertisement spent on the site to determine how valuable the key word is.

Figure 15-1: CPC Program Analysis shows the top key words used to find your site.

But don't let the numbers fool you. It's possible to have a key word with a very high number of click-throughs that doesn't generate much in the way of revenue. On the flip side, you can also have a key word that doesn't generate as much traffic but does generate high revenues. It all comes down to ROI. In order to determine which key words perform best, you have to take all of the available information into consideration.

So, once you find a key word or group of key words that seems to work, what do you do? If it's an organic key word, you need to find a way to capitalize on it. If it's a key word that you're already investing in, consider increasing your investment. Be sure, however, that any decision to increase your investment will be met with an equal amount of success in converting the investment into sales.

It's a tough balancing act to perform. And it would be impossible to give you all the information that you need in the small space here. Besides, reams of pages are written on the subject. Why get repetitive now?

> **LEARN MORE ABOUT KEY-WORD MARKETING**
>
> Key-word marketing is a very precise science. There are more nuances than can possibly be covered in a single book. But if you'd like to learn more about key-word marketing and how to use it to enhance your Internet business, here are a few titles that will get you started:
>
> Beginner
>
> - *Pay Per Click Search Engine Marketing For Dummies* by Peter Kent. Wiley. ISBN: 0471754943.
> - *Pay-Per-Click Search Engine Marketing Handbook: Low Cost Strategies to Attracting New Customers Using Google, Yahoo & Other Search Engines* by Boris Mordkovich and Eugene Mordkovich. Lulu Press. ISBN: 1411628179.
>
> Intermediate
>
> - *Search Engine Marketing, Inc.: Driving Search Traffic to Your Company's Web Site* by Mike Moran and Bill Hunt. IBM Press. ISBN: 0131852922.

Overall Keyword Conversion

The Overall Keyword Conversion report is the first of two conversion reports in this chapter. As you may recall from Chapter 10, this report, shown in Figure 15-2, shows you the number of goal conversions for both organic (or unpaid) and paid key words.

But how do you use the information? To start with, use it to find out where the highest number of goal conversions is coming from. To do this, look not only at the key word but also at the search engine visitors used to search for that particular key word. You can find out what search engines were used by clicking the small plus sign next to each key-word entry.

You also should consider not only goal conversions but also the visit value for each key word. A high number of conversions that result in low sales tells you that the visitors drawn by that particular key word may not be as valuable as conversions that come from a different key word that might have a higher visit value.

Don't look just at the most valuable key words; look at the least valuable key words, too. These are key words that indicate you either need to make changes to the advertisement driven by them or eliminate the key words altogether.

Key words are usually purchased through either a flat fee per click. But in the case of very popular key words, you have the opportunity to bid on them within the confines of the daily budget that you've set. If you find that a key word is performing poorly, you can remove the key word from your list and return the cost of that key word to your budget. In turn, that additional budget can be used to purchase higher, more frequently converting key words.

Click plus (+) sign to see which search engine was used.

Monitor goal conversions and visit values.

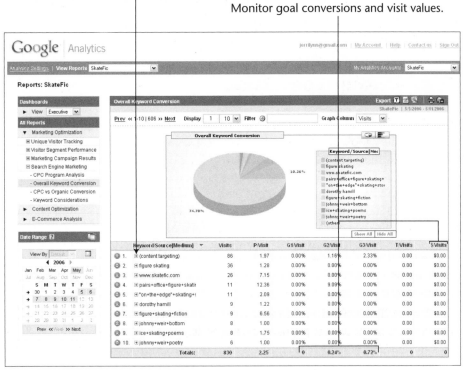

Figure 15-2:   Monitor goal conversions for organic and paid key words.

Another hint you may get from this report is what key words (that you're not already using) you should consider including. If you find that a specific key word or set of key words seems to be performing well, you can test similar key words to see how well they perform.

Finally, if you find that you have a key word or set of key words that has activity but that this activity is lacking either conversions or visit value, you know that something within your site probably needs to change. Maybe you need to modify the pages that users land on when they are clicking a key word.

For example, if you find that the key word "pomegranate" has a lot of hits but the conversion rate is low, you should consider changing the page that this key word leads to. Maybe you have only one product on that page, or maybe that page just happens to have a strange navigational structure that makes it hard for the user to find other items on your site.

Try changing these aspects of your site — improve navigation, feature additional products, or entice visitors to click deeper into your site — and continue to monitor the key-word performance. Sometimes, something as simple as putting a recommendations bar on one side of the page will improve the length of time visitors spend on your site and the amount of money they spend while they're there.

Overall Keyword Conversions is a useful tool for helping you fine-tune your key-word marketing efforts. Use the various aspects of the report to improve high-performing key words and weed out key words that are as worthless as two left shoes.

CPC vs. Organic Conversion

The CPC vs. Organic Conversion report is like one half of a set of twins. They dress alike, they look alike, but when you get down to their hearts, they may be similar, but they are also very different.

The CPC vs. Organic Conversion report, shown in Figure 15-3, looks very much like the Overall Keyword Conversion report. But here's where the difference comes in. This report shows you how paid and organic search engines perform when driving traffic to and conversions at your site.

Where the Overall Keyword Conversion report showed you how specific key words function for driving traffic to your site, this report shows you how search engines (or more precisely, which search engines) drive traffic to your site.

By clicking the small plus sign next to any sources entry (search engine), you can tell which key words were used as search terms for that search engine. This makes it easy for you to determine which search engine you might want to invest your marketing dollar in.

Click plus (+) sign to find out which key words are searched.

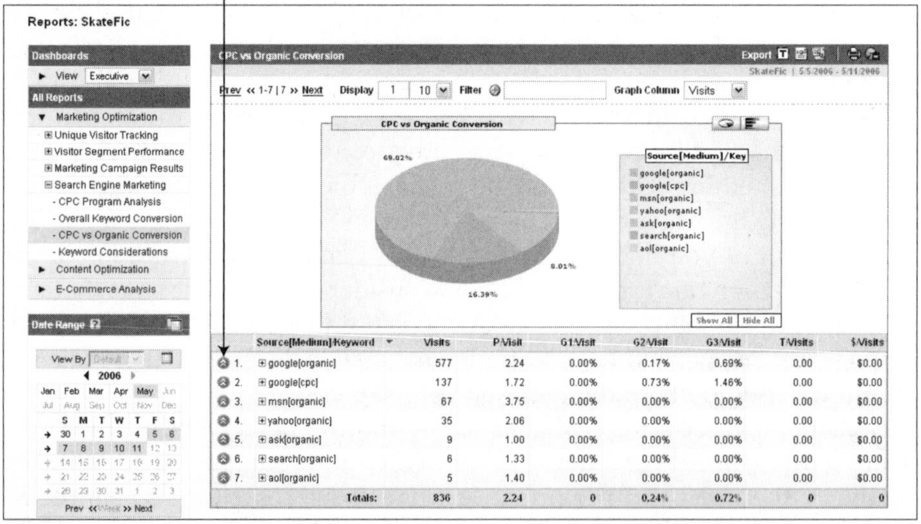

Figure 15-3: This report compares paid and organic search-engine searches.

If you're already investing in Google's AdWords program but this report shows that nearly half of your key-word conversion comes through Yahoo!, you should consider funneling some of your marketing budget to the Yahoo! key-word program. If, on the other hand, you're using both Google and Yahoo! but your report shows that the organic searches at Google are performing better than your AdWords campaign, you know it's time to readdress that campaign and test new key words — perhaps even the same key words that seem to be performing well at Yahoo!

Keyword Considerations

How could you use information about organic key words that are generating conversions and high visit values on your site? Do you even know what those key words are? If not, don't worry too much about it, because you always have this Keyword Considerations report. It's shown in Figure 15-4, but you saw it back in Chapter 10.

What you didn't see in Chapter 10 was what to do with the report. It's not enough to know that some key words organically funnel visitors to your web site. You also have to know what they are. Then you need to find a way to use them.

The most obvious way to use these key words is to convert them to paid key words using a CPC program like AdWords. But you don't necessarily have to spend money to get mileage from these key words.

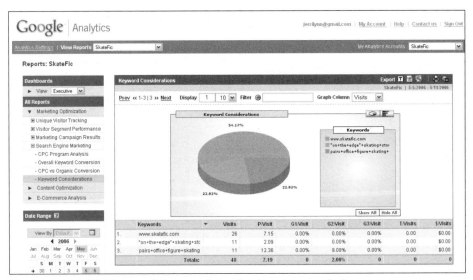

Figure 15-4: Which organic key words lead visitors to your site?

One of the ways to use this report is called Search Engine Optimization (SEO). SEO is the concept and strategies used to optimize your web site for search engines. Remember how bots, spiders, and crawlers probe your site? Those programs are looking for key words and metadata tags (which are like key words on steroids) that can be used to classify your web site when users search for specific key words.

If your Keyword Considerations report shows organic key words that are frequently used to find your site and that seem to result in a high number of goal conversions or a high-value visit, you should consider using those key words in prominent places on your web site.

For example, in the report shown in Figure 15-4, there are three organic key words for the selected time period. These key words can be "planted" in a web site to help draw users to the site. However, this is a bit of a tricky situation.

One of these key-word combinations, *pairs+office+figure+skating*, might be hard to work into the body of a web site. But if you can't work them into the web-site text, you can't take advantage of the traffic they are naturally generating. If, on the other hand you can logically work them into the site, the chances are good that you'll be able to build on the traffic that your site is already generating.

So, key-word optimization, when done right, can be a low-cost way to generate traffic — traffic that leads to goal conversions and increased visit values.

Getting Past Key Words

Now that you've got a clear understanding of key words, how to optimize them, and when to let nature take its course, it's time to move on. And now we're making the break from marketing optimization to content optimization. That's where things get interesting. Or at least, that's where we hope you'll find ways to make your web-site content more interesting and more valuable in terms of leading your customers to your site to make purchases or reach other goals that you set for them.

Content Optimization

One of the most important elements of any web site is the content on that site. And content optimization is no easy task. It requires knowing everything from how traffic comes to your site to how your site performs when visitors are navigating through it.

To truly understand all of these facets of content optimization, however, you need some metrics to tell you how each aspect of the content performs. Google provides some of the most commonly used metrics, such as Content Performance and Navigational Analysis.

This section of the book contains reports that illustrate those metrics. In the pages that follow, we'll walk you through each of the reports in Part V and tell you how to use them to improve your web site.

CHAPTER 16

Ad Version Testing

SurePoint Lending, a subsidiary of First Residential Mortgage Network, is designed to excel in the very competitive market of online financial services. SurePoint is one of the top-rated financial services sites on the web, but it didn't get there by sheer luck.

Agency.com is the company in charge of ensuring that SurePoint ranks high in online financial services, and the company does that with Google Analytics. More specifically, the company does that by using Google Analytics to test ad versions for the key-word marketing campaign that drives traffic to the site.

Testing consists of comparing the results from hundreds of key words, key-word landing pages, and content to learn which elements are most effective in driving qualified traffic to the site, leading in turn to high levels of conversions.

It's not a tool available only to companies like First Residential Mortgage Network or Agency.com. You can use these same tools to create very similar results with your site. All you need to do is test your marketing efforts to learn which are most effective and then put that information to use increasing traffic and conversions. And it's really not all that difficult.

Overall Ad A/B Testing

The first step in testing any marketing campaign, or group of marketing campaigns, is to compare one against another. (The A/B in the preceding title simply means comparing one thing with another.) This type of comparison has been going on for as long as there have been advertisements. Heck, you may have even started studying advertising way back in grade school when you were scrawling "Roses are red/Violets are blue/If I looked like Susie/I'd join the zoo" in a note, passing it around and waiting for results.

It wasn't nice, but it does illustrate the point. If it was a note not too many people saw, you were safe. If everybody saw it, Susie would be checking out handwriting and heading your way, fire in eye, brick in hand. Different ads perform at different levels in different places. And your online ads work in very much the same way. That's why you'll find the report, Overall Ad A/B Testing, shown in Figure 16-1, the first among the Ad Version Testing reports available to you.

This is not a report that you've seen before, so you need a little more information about it. In Figure 16-1, two separate ads are listed: Figure Skating Scandal and Free Skating Fiction. At a glance, you can compare the number of visits, the pages per visit, the goal-conversion rate for each ad, and transactions and value per visit. If one ad is performing better than another, it's all right there in clearly defined detail.

On the other hand, you may be running only one ad. Or maybe you don't have any ads running. In that case, when you pull up your report, it's going to look like the one shown in Figure 16-2. To change this, you either need to begin running ads (like key-word ads from AdWords or other types of ads that are properly tagged), or you need to tag your own ads properly.

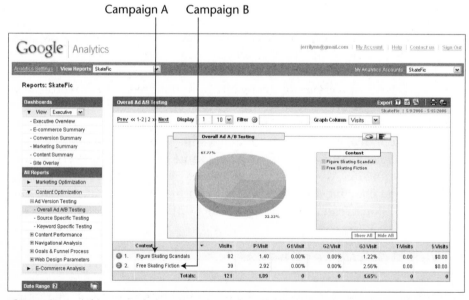

Figure 16-1: This report lets you compare the effectiveness of two ad campaigns.

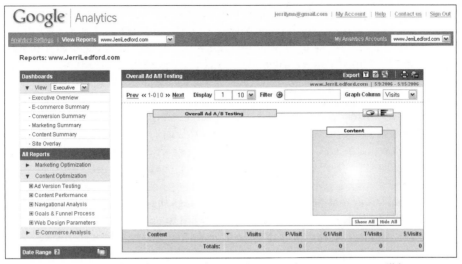

Figure 16-2: If you don't have tagged campaigns running, your report will be empty.

Back in Chapter 8 we discussed tagging and gave you a little preview of how to go about doing it. You can flip back now if you need to. It's okay. Really. We'll wait.

Finished? Good. If you need more information on tagging your campaigns, you can find it in the Help section of Google Analytics by searching for "tagging."

So, exactly how do you use this report? Well, it starts with tagging your advertising campaigns (which is why you just flipped back for a refresher). For the comparison to work, you have to tag two different ad campaigns in different ways to distinguish them.

Specifically, what will change for each campaign are the tag elements: `utm_source`, `utm_medium`, `utm_term`, `utm campaign`, and `utm_content`. Some but not all of these were mentioned in Chapter 8. And you don't have to use all of them — use only what applies to your specific needs. If you were tagging, say, to track your newsletter name, you might change `utm source` to `utm source=MyNewsletter`. If you wanted to tag key words for a specific ad, you might make it `utm term=running+shoes`.

You might also need to use the `utm_campaign` tag to compare different marketing campaigns. For example, if you're using a 15-percent-off coupon in e-mail to drive traffic to your site and you also have a link in an industry newsletter, you can use the `utm_campaign` tag to compare the effectiveness of each of those campaigns. That information can then be used to determine which campaign should have more capital investment based on the return on that investment.

Before you start muttering to yourself about the complexities of tagging, we have good news. Google Analytics provides a URL Builder tool, shown in Figure 16-3, that makes it easy to create the tagging URLs. To find the URL Builder tool, search Help once you've logged in to your Analytics account.

Once you have the tag, all you have to do is insert it in your campaign. For example, if you're using two different types of links, you would generate a URL for each link and replace the direct URL (in a form such as `http://www.example.com`) with the tagged URL:

(`http://www.JerriLedford.com/?utm_source=Newsletter&utm_ medium=link&utm_content=textlink&utm_campaign=example_ad`).

NOTE Remember that AdWords automatically tags the source and medium of your key-word campaigns. However, you may want to add an utm_term addition to your key words to track specific, paid key words. This also can be done in the URL Builder tool.

One more note about tagging your ads. Remember that these tags are very sensitive. They translate EXACTLY what you tell them to translate, so if you are inconsistent in naming your campaigns (Spring-Sale versus Spring_Sale), Analytics will read that as two different campaigns.

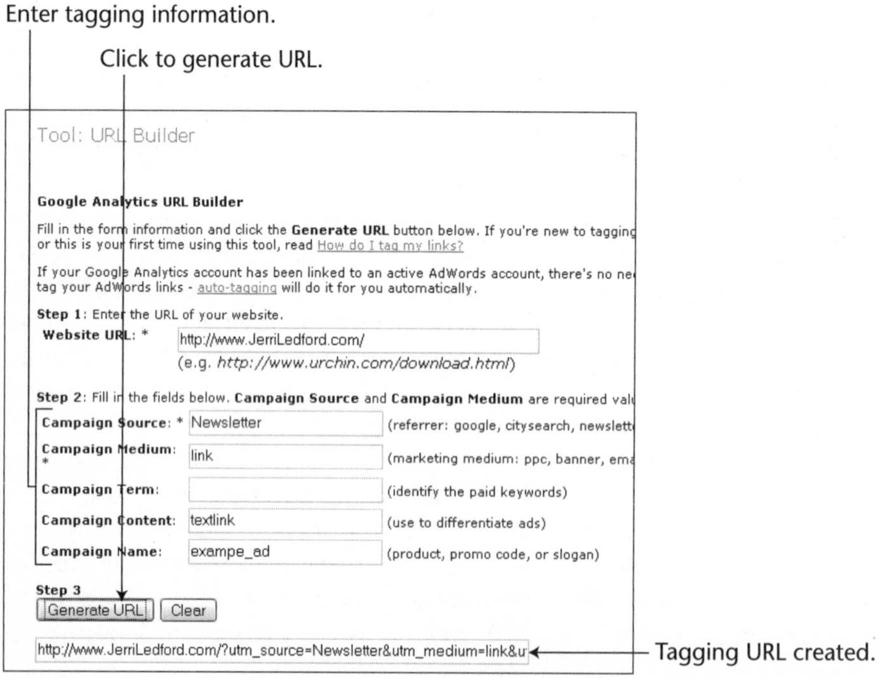

Figure 16-3: The URL Builder tool creates your tagging URLs for you.

With the information that you garner from comparing one ad campaign to another (or from comparing different ads within the same campaign), you can analyze the performance of those campaigns or ads. That information, in turn, lets you know where to invest more or less of your advertising dollars, based on the results those campaigns generate.

Source Specific Testing

It's unusual for any professional web site to have a single version of a single advertising campaign. It's more likely that you'll have several versions of the same campaign running in different locations. It's like those ads you see on television during the Super Bowl. You may see a similar ad 127 times after the Super Bowl, but it's not likely that you'll see exactly the same ad. For that matter, you might even see several versions of that ad, each on a different station.

But you'd better believe that the advertising company wants to know how each version of the ad is doing in addition to its overall performance. Just as those companies that spent millions of dollars on an ad want to know, you probably also want to know how different versions of your online ads are performing. The Source Specific Testing report, shown in Figure 16-4, is the place to find your answer.

In Figure 16-4, you'll notice that only one campaign is listed. That's because the Google CPC (AdWords) campaign is the only one running for this site right now. If other campaigns were running, you'd see those campaigns listed here as well.

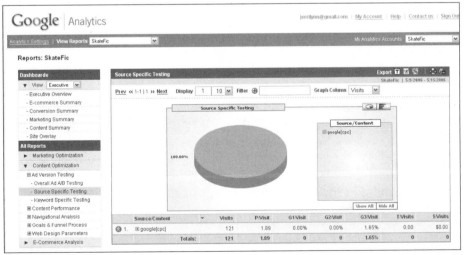

Figure 16-4: Track different versions of your ads with this report.

Using the information in this report, you can compare how different campaigns are performing for the number of visits, pages per visit, goal conversions, transactions per visit, and the value of the visit.

If you happen to be running key-word ads with both AdWords and Yahoo!, you can quickly tell which source generated the most visits, conversions, or the highest dollar value. That information can then be used to redirect marketing dollars to the most valuable source. Need an excuse to switch from Yahoo! to Google? This report will give you one if your AdWords are performing better than your Yahoo! key words.

Keyword Specific Testing

If you're like many first-time CPC users, the first thing you did when you set your CPC account up was select every key word even remotely related to your site in the hope that something good would come of it.

It won't take long for you to see that's not going to work well. What you end up with are a handful of key words that perform well and a whole bunch that don't. For the ones that perform well, or even close to well, you have some decisions to make.

There's no sense in spreading your marketing budget too thin, but you could if you tried to rely on all of those key words (not to mention all of the gray hair you'd cause). Instead, some Keyword Specific Testing will help you decide where your dollars are best invested.

The Keyword Specific Testing report, shown in Figure 16-5, is your tool to find out just what works best on your CPC program.

If you haven't done any specific tagging for your key words, what you'll notice first about this report is that it's a comparison for all of the key-word campaigns you have running. Without special tagging, that's really all it is, a comparison.

However, using some of the tagging methods mentioned earlier in this chapter, you can use the Keyword Specific Testing report to show how well a key-word ad performs (the actual ad part), how the key-word landing page affects your site, and how the content on that site affects your key-word performance.

The thing is, key words drive traffic to your site. However, if your site doesn't have what users are looking for or expecting when they click your key-word ad, they are going to "bounce" right off your page. Using this report, you can find out where the bounces are happening and then compare factors to learn how to improve your bounce rate.

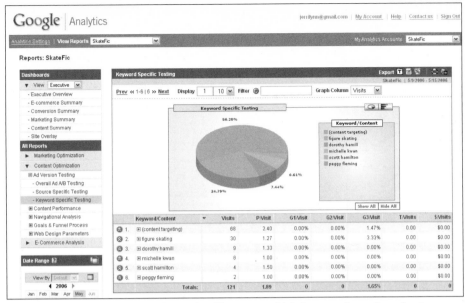

Figure 16-5: Keyword Specific Testing illustrates which key words perform best.

The catch is that you have to use the `utm_content` tag to find the results you're looking for. Again, this tag can be generated in the URL Builder tool, but without this kind of tagging, all you have is a comparison of your key words by number of visits, goal conversions, transaction values, and visit values.

Remember the example of SurePoint Lending back in the beginning of this chapter? One of the steps that SurePoint's ad agency (Agency.com) did was to use Keyword Specific Testing to track changes such as changing the wording in advertisements, changing landing pages, and even changing the content on the page. By testing various configurations, the company learned what worked well and what stank. Then they could improve their marketing investment by capitalizing on the key words the company chose to buy.

Keyword Specific Testing has many different uses. It's more than just comparing one key word against another. Many other factors affect keyword ads, and testing each of those factors leads you closer to the best key words and key-word ads.

Big companies don't blindly put out advertisements without testing and monitoring them. Why should you? Google Analytics offers great tools for testing and monitoring your ad campaigns. Use them, and you'll have the tools you need to make informed decisions about how and where your advertising dollars are best invested.

CHAPTER 17

Content Performance

How does the content on your web site affect your traffic patterns? Does it lead users to the site? Does it drive users to make a purchase, sign up for a newsletter, or fill out a form that you have on the site? And is there content on your site that performs better than you expect it to?

These are all questions that the reports in this section can answer. The content on your site — the content users land on when they come to your site — plays a big role in how long users stay and how much deeper into the site they go.

If you have an e-commerce site, there might be a natural driver that pushes users deeper into your site. Maybe users come to your site because you have a great price on laptop computers. But how is the content on your site going to direct users once they land there? If done well, you might be able to drive additional sales or create return users.

The only way you're going to know if your content is done well is to analyze the metrics associated with how users *use* your site. The reports in this section will show you exactly that. And what you do with that information determines just how useful it is for you.

Top Content

In many cases, the top content on your site will be your front page — also called your index page. This is the first page that users who type your URL directly into the address bar on their web browsers will usually see. But that's not so in every case. If you're running a marketing campaign that pushes users to a page that's deeper in the site, that could be your top content. The only way to know for sure is to look at the Top Content report shown in Figure 17-1.

In this report, content pages are listed by the most frequent visits. You'll also find measurements for the number of page views for each page, the average time users spent on that page, and the percentage of exits that occurred from that page.

Percentage of visitors who exit from page listed

Average time users spend on page

Pages that drive high-value conversions

Number of pages shown and number of pages tracked. See attached pages by clicking Next.

Figure 17-1: The Top Content report ranks your site content by visits.

There's also a measurement, indicated on Figure 17-1, that shows the most commonly visited pages that led to a high-value goal conversion. This helps you see what content is leading visitors to goal conversions and will come in handy later when you're tracking your funnel-navigation process.

Another measurement on this report that you want to pay special attention to is the percentage of exits for each page. If you have a page that seems to have an unusually high number of exits, the content on that page could be the reason for visitors leaving. If you can use this report to locate the pages where you're losing visitors, you can change or update the pages in an effort to improve "stickiness."

You may also want to make note of the average time users spend on each page. There's no guideline that says users should spend X amount of time on each page. You have to figure a baseline for your site using the measurements you have available you. Then, if you decide that on average users should spend a minute and a half to two minutes on each page and you find you have a page (or pages) on which users spend less than a minute, you know you should analyze the page to find out why users are clicking through (or worse, exiting) at that page.

Of course, each of these measurements alone is only valuable for that measurement; however, when you look at them as a whole, you begin to see a larger picture — such as how many users are exiting a page where they only spend 15 seconds or how many users are clicking through a page after two minutes to make a large purchase or complete some other goal you've established.

These traffic patterns give you insight into the minds of your users. Use them to improve goal conversions and sales through your site.

Content Drilldown

How is your web site designed? Do you have pages that have subpages? For example, maybe you have a page on your site that includes articles about issues related to the products on your site. And from that page, there are links to past articles. Those past articles are probably located on subpages. So how do you know if those pages are of any value to your site at all?

You can find the answer by reviewing the Content Drilldown report, shown in Figure 17-2.

These folders contain sub-pages
with additional metrics.

Use menu to change metrics view.

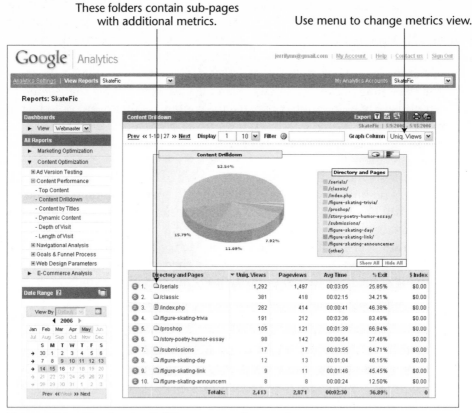

Figure 17-2: The Content Drilldown report shows subpage measurements.

The Content Drilldown report is built differently from any of the reports that you've seen so far. This report shows rankings for every page on your site, including subpages related to that page. For example, when you click the folder indicated in Figure 17-2, you're taken deeper into the content results to see the numbers for subpages related to that page. The report that's returned when you click one of those folders might look something like what's shown in Figure 17-3.

For every page that you're shown in this report, there is a set of measurements that includes the unique views and pages, the average time spent on the page, the percent of visitors who exited from that page, and the value of pages that are commonly visited before a high-value conversion during that visit. The conversion could be a sale or another type of goal conversion, depending on how you have your conversion goals set up.

The purpose of this information is much the same as the purpose of the Top Content report — use the information to determine which sites need to be changed or updated and which sites work well as indicated by visits, goal conversions, and the value of those conversions.

Dig even deeper by clicking another folder.

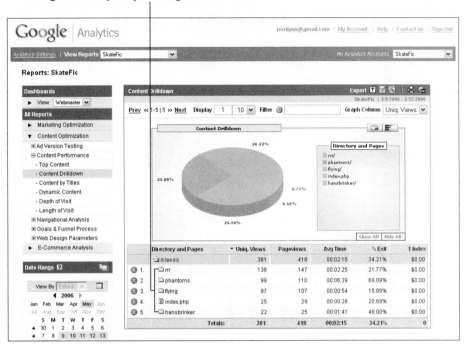

Figure 17-3:   A view of subpages is the result of clicking one of the content folders.

Content by Titles

Another way to view the traffic to your site is with the Content by Titles report. This report, shown in Figure 17-4, shows the value of your web pages by page title, using the same measurements as before: unique views, page views, average time spent on the page, percentage of exits that occur on that page, and the value of goal conversions that result from that page.

For example, if you're looking at the report in Figure 17-4, you'll find that not only does the first page, *Figure Skating Fiction, Short S*, have the highest number of unique visitors, but it also has the highest percentage of exits.

This isn't a unique phenomenon. Usually, the page with the highest number of visits will have the highest number of exits. However, if you happen to notice that a page with a low number of visits has the highest percentage of exits, you know that there's likely some kind of problem with that page and it needs to be changed or updated in some way.

Figure 17-4: View content metrics by page title.

The most important factor for you to know about this report is that page titles are determined by HTML titles. In the design of your page, there was probably some titling algorithm that set the HTML tagging and titling for the page. It's also possible that you set it manually. Either way, that's what's used to classify the page for this report. Here's the catch: If you happen to have multiple pages with the same HTML titles, those pages are going to be counted as a single page for measurement purposes. (It's possible to tinker with the HTMLs to separate them, but your skills have to be pretty high.)

So, while these measurements are useful, they can be a little deceiving in their presentation. However, as long as you remember that each of these measurements could feature more than one page, you should be able to adequately use the information to determine where you need to change or improve your content.

Dynamic Content

When you think of dynamic content, you probably think of things like articles or blogs — content that changes frequently. But that has nothing to do with dynamic content here. Most blogs are actually static pages — pages prebuilt and stored in final form on the web server — that were created on submission of individual entries.

Dynamic content refers to pages where one file may be associated with multiple pages of content. Dynamic pages are built on the fly with a technology such as PHP, ASP, or Java Server Pages. These technologies use variables in the URL, called page query terms, to dictate what content goes together to form the finished page. In fact, this section of Google Analytics' reports was originally called "Page Query Terms." Site-search and catalogue functions are generally dynamic pages. Other sites implement dynamic pages for various other reasons.

Dynamic pages have unique challenges as far as tracking because what differentiates one dynamic page from another is not the file name. It's the query term or combination of terms. The Dynamic Content reports break out views for dynamic pages by individual query term.

The Dynamic Content report, shown in Figure 17-5, shows the most popular dynamic base pages on the web site. It shows everything before the ? in the URL of the dynamic page.

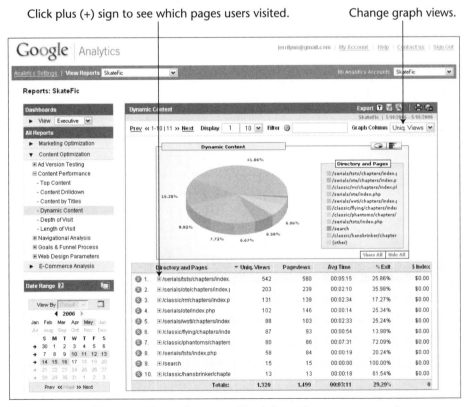

Figure 17-5: This report shows the most visited dynamic pages on your site.

Each of these dynamic URLs represents multiple pages of content, so you'll also see a small plus sign next to each entry, as indicated in Figure 17-5. If you click on one of these plus signs, you're taken deeper in the results, as shown in Figure 17-6.

What you see in Figure 17-6 depends on how your site dynamic content works. In the SkateFic example, the page that serves individual serial chapters takes a single query term, the chapter number. So now, rather than seeing how many times visitors viewed the base page, you can see what chapter they actually read.

Here, the even distribution of visits has a couple possible meanings. First, it's possible that a small number of individuals are visiting the site and reading each chapter in turn. Second, it could mean that even though there are no new chapters, old ones remain about equally popular. If one chapter got the majority of the views and it was newly posted, it's reasonable to believe that the number of unique views says something about how many readers follow the serial closely, reading new chapters as they come out.

How does this help you?

Imagine that rather than serving serial chapters, you're selling items in a catalogue. If your catalogue is implemented with dynamic scripts and you just looked at the base-page metrics, you'd be tearing out your hair and screaming, "But what products are people looking at?"

Click minus (-) sign to return to previous view.

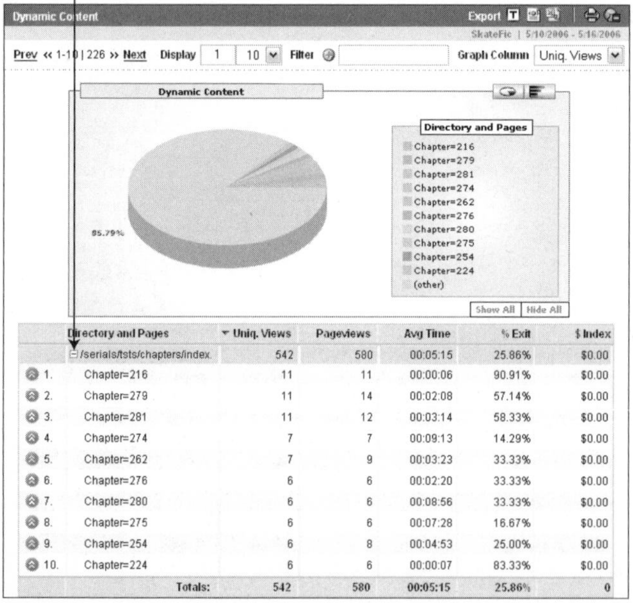

	Directory and Pages	Uniq. Views	Pageviews	Avg Time	% Exit	$ Index
	/serials/tsts/chapters/index	542	580	00:05:15	25.86%	$0.00
1.	Chapter=216	11	11	00:00:06	90.91%	$0.00
2.	Chapter=279	11	14	00:02:08	57.14%	$0.00
3.	Chapter=281	11	12	00:03:14	58.33%	$0.00
4.	Chapter=274	7	7	00:09:13	14.29%	$0.00
5.	Chapter=262	7	9	00:03:23	33.33%	$0.00
6.	Chapter=276	6	6	00:02:20	33.33%	$0.00
7.	Chapter=280	6	6	00:08:56	33.33%	$0.00
8.	Chapter=275	6	6	00:07:28	16.67%	$0.00
9.	Chapter=254	6	8	00:04:53	25.00%	$0.00
10.	Chapter=224	6	6	00:00:07	83.33%	$0.00
	Totals:	542	580	00:05:15	25.86%	0

Figure 17-6: Dig deeper into the results to find out the content that users saw.

With the Dynamic Content report, you can see for each product how many unique views and page views occurred, the average time spent on that product page, and the percent of users that exited your site from that page. There's also a listing for the value of the visit that shows you if that page was visited before a major goal conversion. That's a great way to track the value of the dynamic content on the site.

Depth of Visit

Depth of Visit is a quick little report designed to show you one thing — how many pages users visited during their brief stop on your web site. It's like travelers who stop at a roadside store during a journey. One traveler might make a pit stop in the restroom, then swing by the soda cooler, stop at the chip display, and finally end up at the register to make a purchase. A different traveler might dash into the restroom and then leave without making a purchase. A third could come in only to purchase a soda and never even approach the restroom.

There's a lot to be learned about people's habits by studying their stops along a journey, even if their journey is a virtual one through your web site.

The Depth of Visit report, shown in Figure 17-7, shows you just how many stops your visitors make as they pass through your site.

Functionally, this information might seem a little obscure. Why in the world would you want to know how many pages your visitors viewed? Well, in short, the more pages viewed, the better. But if you look at this information and you find that your visitors are more the "get in and get out" types, you know that there's nothing compelling those readers to dig deeper into your content. So how can you change that?

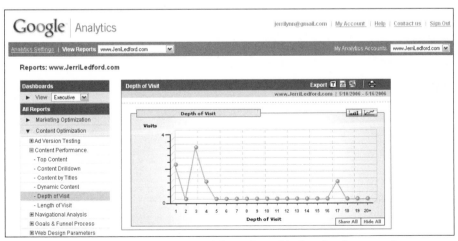

Figure 17-7: Learn how many pages visitors viewed before leaving your site.

It will take some experimentation. What drives your visitors? What would catch their attention and make them spend longer on the site? As an example, let's consider the (completely fictional) site BusyMommy.com. A visitor coming to this site is obviously very busy. The visitor is likely female, and she has children — probably young children — vying for her attention. So when she stops by your site, she's looking for something specific. And she doesn't want to spend too much time looking for it.

But if Busy Mommy finds what she wants and it leads her to something else that she didn't know she needed, she might spend a few extra seconds on your site or visit an additional page or two. Your content, of course, has to be very compelling and has to entice her to dig deeper into your site.

Now, this report won't tell you how to create that content, but it will tell you if you're reaching your audience in the way you want. If visitors are hitting one page and leaving and your site consists of hundreds of pages, there's some problem you should be worrying over. If your site is only a few dozen pages long, and visitors are hitting most of them, you know that you're appealing to those users. All you need to do is figure out how to capitalize on that.

Length of Visit

A report similar in design and use to the Depth of Visit report is the Length of Visit report, shown in Figure 17-8. Instead of showing you how many pages your visitors stopped on, this report shows you how long they spent on your site.

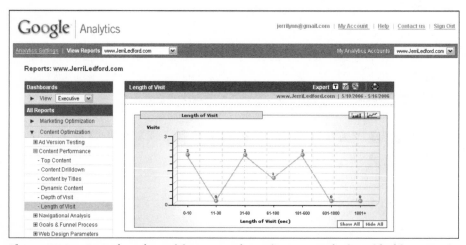

Figure 17-8: Learn how long visitors spent browsing your web site with this report.

I hear you already: "Why does it matter how long a visitor spends on my site?" Because if they aren't on your site, they're probably spending their time on a different site. Since you want them to spend as much of their available Internet time as possible on your site, you need to have content that draws them in and keeps them busy for a while.

How long is "a while"? That's a question for which there is no right answer. The time that a person spends on each of your web-site pages depends on numerous things: what the user is looking for, what your page has to offer, how quickly users read/scan pages and find additional information to navigate to, and how often the phone rings while they're on the page. Really.

Here's a situation for you. On Monday, a visitor comes to your site, spends about 10 minutes surfing through the various pages, and then leaves. On Tuesday, that same user returns but spends only eight minutes, because on Monday he saw all of the pages and his return visit today is to hit some of the dynamic content on your site (think blog, podcast, or new articles).

Then on Wednesday, he returns again. This time he's in the middle of surfing through the same dynamic content, but the phone rings. Rather than closing out of the page, he takes the call, which just happens to be his mother-in-law, and he spends 20 miserable minutes listening to her tell him how he's not good enough for her daughter before she asks him to come trim her shrubs before it rains.

When the call is over, he shakes it off (it's an old routine by now) and goes back to your site to finish reading the blog post he'd started when the phone rang.

Now you have this strange blip on your length-of-visit graph. It shows that one user spent more than half an hour on your site. Woohoo!

Just don't get too excited, because unless multiple users are spending that long, or it happens on a consistent basis, chances are that it's just a blip. On the other hand, if something is consistently drawing multiple users to your site who spend an unusually high amount of time surfing your pages, you may have a factor upon which you can capitalize.

If the number shows the opposite, you know that you need to add something to your pages to keep users there longer. What you add should be determined by what your users need. And that's a topic best left for a web-design book.

CHAPTER 18

Navigational Analysis

Knowing how many visitors come and go or knowing what they see while they're there is useful information without a doubt. What it doesn't tell you is how visitors are moving through your site. Remember back in the AWStats chapters that we talked about how people entering and people leaving had no connection between them? It would be useful to know just how people move through your site, wouldn't it?

Entrance Bounce Rates

As we've discussed before, a bounce is when a visitor arrives on a page and immediately leaves. It differs from an exit, which refers just to the page from which the visitor left the site, possibly after visiting other pages. A bounce means "Did not visit another page. Did not collect $200." For the purposes of this report (and only this report), a visit, a visitor, and a page view are pretty much all the same thing (subject to the caveats about counting unique visitors and length-of-visit limitation discussed in Chapters 2 and 3).

Bounce rates can show how effective a particular page is. For example, in Figure 18-1, the single most visited page on the site, the skating trivia page, also has the most bounces.

The bad news is that nearly 90 percent of the visitors who arrive on this page also leave immediately. The goods news is at least some of those people were looking for figure-skating trivia. Having found what they wanted, they left. That's not a bad thing. Giving visitors what they are looking for is what a content site wants to do.

However, the trivia page also has another specific goal — to lure visitors deeper into the site. In the grand scheme of things, as promotions go, having more than 10 percent of those who respond to the promotion take the next step is pretty darn good. Almost 800 visits that started on the trivia page delved deeper into the site to see what SkateFic is. As a content site, new readers are life blood and hard money. As a gateway page to the rest of the site, the trivia page does a pretty good job.

On another note, the third-ranked page on this report is a sales page. Lots of visitors are coming in. Lots of visitors are leaving immediately. Coupled with information about sales of this item during this period (which were abnormally low), it would be reasonable to believe that either this particular page is not effective or that the ad bringing in those visits is not bringing in the right kind of visitors. Both those observations require action from a business standpoint.

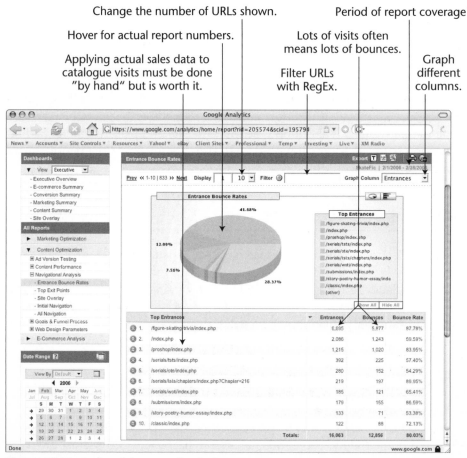

Figure 18-1: Is the trivia page effective?

If we haven't made this point enough, it's important to remember that you can't look at Google Analytics' metrics in isolation from other information about your business. As capable as Google Analytics is, it's still a medium-tier product. It won't function like a high-end (read "expensive") analytics package. You're going to have to use your head when applying outside data — such as actual sales — to Analytics' metrics. Analytics won't do everything for you.

Top Exit Points

While knowing where visitors arrive is important, knowing where they are leaving from is also important. You'll note that it's fairly common that your busiest pages overall will also be busiest from the entrances and exits standpoint. In Figure 18-2, you can see this effect.

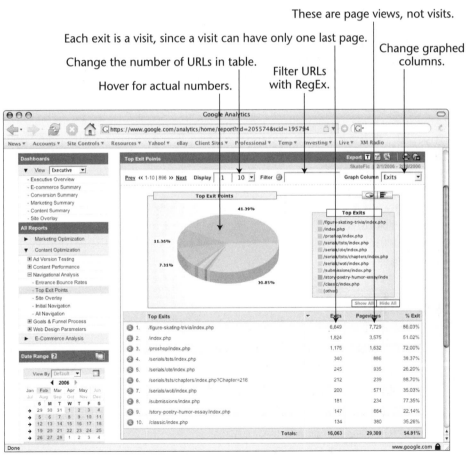

Figure 18-2: Busy pages tend to dominate both entrances and exits.

Unlike the Entrance Bounce Rates, you can't assume that each page view on the Exits report is a visitor. A visitor could load the page, then wander off deeper into the site and eventually wander back. However, because you can assume each page view is a visit in the Bounce report, you can do interesting things with the Exits report. You can isolate how many visits ended on a particular page when it's not the first and last page visited.

For example, SkateFic's index page is ranked number two in exits and in bounces. Each entrance is a page view, so subtract Entrances from Pageviews for that line.

```
3575 - 2086 = 1489
```

What this tells us is how many page views came from visitors who had come in from other parts of the site.

Bounces are exits, so subtract Bounces from Exits for that line.

```
1824 - 1243 = 581
```

This indicates how many of the visits entering from other parts of the site left once they hit this page. That in itself is an interesting metric, but it means more if you translate the two new figures to a percentage.

```
581/1489 * 100% = 39%
```

So overall, while 51 percent of page views mark the end of a visit and 60 percent of new visitors leave from here immediately, only 39 percent of visits that include other pages leave from here.

In English?

Once visitors get into the site, they are much less likely to leave from this page. For the home page (which this is), it may not mean much, but this kind of additional analysis can be helpful for other pages such as those involved in the sales process.

Site Overlay

Sometimes it's easier to make heads or tails of a complex set of metrics if you draw a picture. That's exactly what the Site Overlay is. Each page of your web site has an overlay. On the overlay are small bar graphs for each link on the page. If you click the graphs, you get an overview of information for that link. But the point is that you can see at a glance how the various links on a single page are performing compared to one another.

Figure 18-3 shows the Site Overlay for SkateFic's home page. As you can see, a fair number of people click the link directly back to the home page. Don't ask us why. It's a laughably stupid thing to do, but people do it all the time, perhaps because, due to SEO concerns (that's search-engine optimization), the link to the home page isn't labeled "home."

The blue upper bar on each graph is the number of clicks to the specified link relative to the total number of clicks on the page viewed. The green lower bar is a measure of the quality of those clicks — the value of the link based on average revenue generated per click. It will appear in all conditions where a click from the designated link led to goal or e-commerce conversion for the time range selected. The rates of conversion for the three goals are fairly low. So as you might expect, the quality rating for the clicks is pretty much nonexistent, too.

Different links to same URL have aggregate number.

This graph goes with main logo, even though it overlaps others.

Blue bar

Change address here.

Green bar

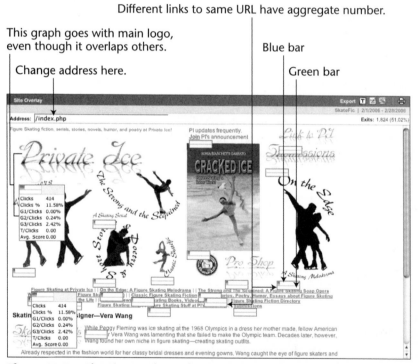

Figure 18-3:   The Site Overlay makes it easy to see which links carry the most traffic.

CAVEAT WEBMASTER: SITE OVERLAY IS ITCHY GLITCHY

At the present time, the Site Overlay has some glitches. Sometimes the small graphs overlap each other — and the all-important links you need to navigate the Site Overlay! The graphs also appear somewhat below and to the left of the link. If the link is a graphic, the graph for that link may overlap another graphic, making it somewhat tricky to see which link owns the graph.

Site Overlay doesn't always work the way you'd expect. An editable text box for the address should indicate that you can change the address in the address bar and have the Site Overlay navigate to that page on the site. Alas! It doesn't work that way. Perhaps in the next version.

The Site Overlay does not work with a variety of page technologies including:

♦ Javascript links

♦ CSS content

♦ Flash navigation

♦ downloadable files (.pdf)

♦ outbound links

♦ frames

♦ auto redirects

♦ Links using the deprecated `target= "_blank"` attribute

We also noticed some problems with the particular PHP templating scheme that SkateFic.com uses. It took about an hour to kludge in code to accommodate the Site Overlay, because instead of requesting `/index.php`, it was cURLing, or repeating, `/index.php/index.php`, and instead of requesting `/serials/tsts/index.php`, it wanted `/index.php/serials/tsts/index.php`. This caused all kinds of PHP warnings because a part of the page could not be found in the file structure.

Also, if two or more links go to the same URL, the information from those links will be aggregated. There are separate graphs for each link, but they all show the same aggregated information. This is because, short of tagging each link, there's no way to say which link on a page the user clicked.

At any rate, there are 414 clicks from this page on that link and the one to the same URL in the text menu at the bottom. About 11 percent of the traffic that comes to this page clicks that link, and during the visit some small percentage of those visitors completes goals 2 and 3. There are no transactions from these clicks during this period.

The Average Score is zero as well. When a click results in a high-value conversion, such as a purchase, a lead, or a contact, the links in the chain to that conversion get points. Over the time period, those points add up and are averaged out to get the score. The higher the average score, the better the link is working toward achieving your conversion goals.

Initial Navigation

The Initial Navigation report gives you an even more detailed view of how people move through your site — at least for the first three clicks. Often as not, for e-commerce sites, three clicks are all you get. It's a relatively old (in web time) rule of thumb that your content should be no more than three-clicks deep. For some content sites, it's quite possible that a visitor might hang out for more than three clicks, but don't count on it.

In Figure 18-4, you can see the top ten entry URLs. These are the first click in a multitude of three-click paths. For each click along the path, you can customize the graph and table. By choosing from the drop-down menu, you can make the list show the top 10, 25, 50, 100, or 500 URLs or filter the URLs shown with Regular Expressions (check Chapter 6 for more information on RegEx). You can also set the graph to show values from any of the different columns of metrics, but you'll only get bars for the top 10. There are totals for each column at the bottom of the table.

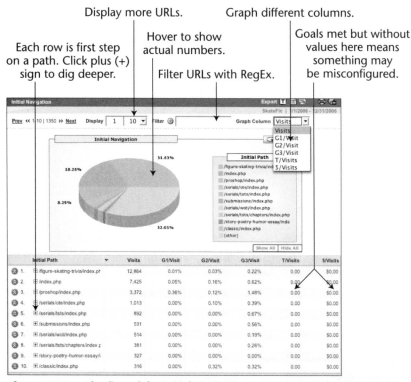

Figure 18-4: The first of the Initial Navigation report's three levels.

Each of the URLs listed has a plus (+) sign to the left that drills down to the next level of URLs. Clicking the plus (+) sign next to /proshop/index.php gives us Figure 18-5. Note that the URL we expanded in the first screen is now the first shaded line in the new table. There's a minus (-) sign next to it that you can use to collapse the report back to the previous level.

At this level, there are a few things worth noticing. First, a whole lot of people are leaving. Of the 3,372 visits, 2,785 of them exit here. That's about two thirds — not great, not bad.

Some of the paths are yielding conversions at various relatively low rates. None of those conversions seems to be worth anything, since the $/Visits metric is zero across the board. This is an indication that somewhere in the SkateFic profile, something is misconfigured; goals being met and each of those goals has a monetary value attached, but it's obviously not being counted.

Finally, you'll note that there's a 100 percent in the G3/Visit column. That's because this is the goal-landing page for G3. If you make it to that page, you've met G3. Clicking the plus (+) sign in that row yields Figure 18-6.

This was Step 1 on the path.

Users often detour to this page since it offers discounts at the Proshop.

Goal 3 is getting to this page, so percentage is 100.

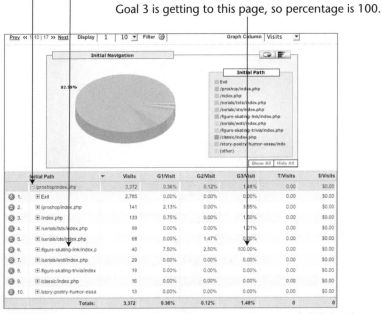

Figure 18-5: Goals are starting to be met on the second click level.

Second step

First step

Each row here
is a third step.

Completed sales meet Goal 1.

All clicks have met Goal 3.

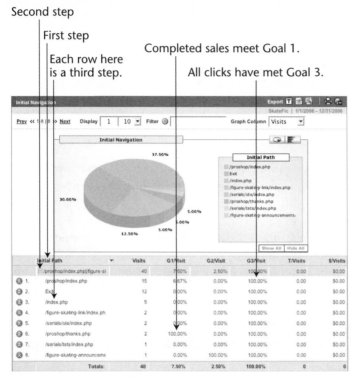

Figure 18-6: At the third level of clicks, multiple goals are being met.

At this level, a couple things are happening. First off, G3 is met for all the clicks in this path no matter where the users go next, so the G3 column reads 100 percent all the way down. One person (in Row 8) wandered over to the announcements page, which met G2, so there's a 100 percent in that row for G2. Two people (in Row 6) went to the `proshop/thanks.php` page, which means they purchased the book that's for sale on the `/proshop` page.

However, Row 2 is of more interest. Of the 15 people who came to the figure-skating-links page from the proshop, one of them subsequently made a purchase to meet G1. This is not bad in itself, but add a little information about the business (the links page offers a way to get a discount on the purchase by linking to the site) and put that with the fact that 14 of 15 people who were interested in the discount went on *not* to make a purchase . . . . Doesn't look so good now, does it?

There are a couple points here. For e-commerce sites, you can see how people are moving through your sales process. If they are taking too many clicks to get to the sale, you may be losing potential customers. You can get an idea of how well your promotions and inducements are working. For content sites, you want to see readers get to the meat of your content by that third click — especially if they are going in the direction of content to begin with (rather than any e-commerce you may have). Even if your goals are content related rather than e-commerce related, you can follow people through the initial clicks and see where they are going and what goals they are meeting along the way.

All Navigation

If you thought the Initial Navigation report was confusing, strap yourself in for a very cluttered view of your site's complete navigation that is a whole lot simpler than it looks.

Gotcha goin' there, didn't we?

Depending on how busy your site is, how much search-engine traffic it gets, and how long a time period you're looking at, you may have a whole lot of garbage in the left-hand frame of the report, or you may not. You'll see some folders that may not actually be on your site, like the /search/ folder in Figure 18-7.

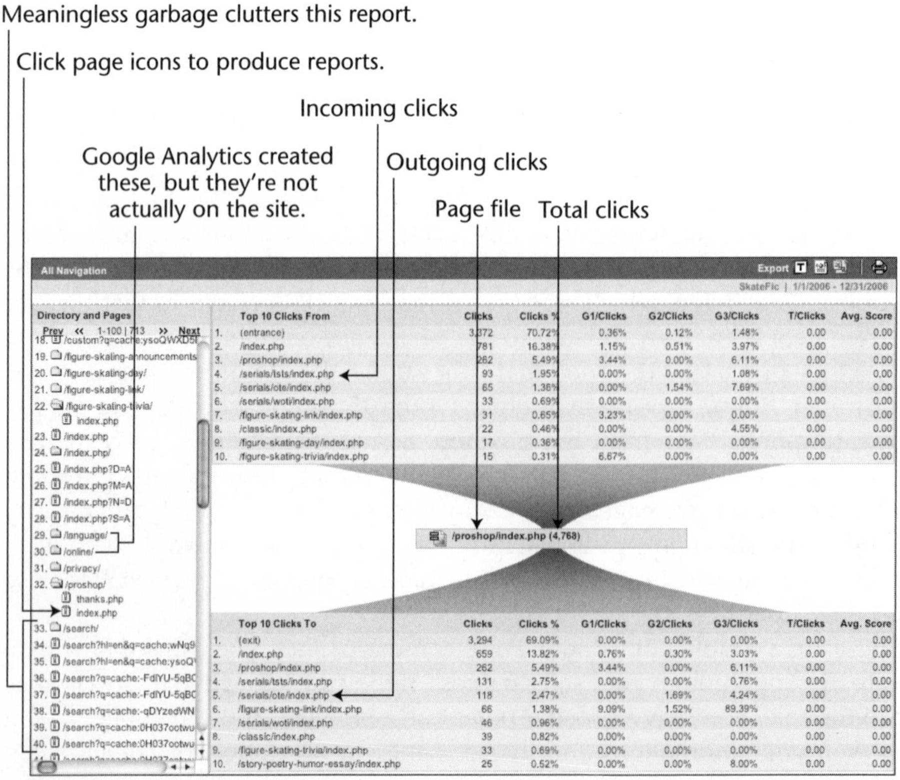

Figure 18-7: The All Navigation Report is confusing because of extraneous garbage.

There's no physical folder named /search/ on SkateFic.com; this is just Analytics' created place to keep cached search results that, as far as we can tell, don't actually lead to any pages. It's pretty safe to ignore folders that don't actually exist on your site.

You may also see a bunch of pages that look something like this: /search?query=cache:blah blah blah blah blah. Depending on the age of the cached (meaning stored) query, some of these will load and produce meaningful output in the right-hand frame. A great many of them will not. Either they won't load at all, because they're too old, or they will load a "from" click and a "to" click with only the cached query term and no further information. Neither is very useful or helpful. These pages are also safe to ignore.

Now, we click the /proshop/ folder and then click the index.php file to produce the information in the right-hand frame of Figure 18-7. The list at the top of the page represents pages *from which* users came to the proshop. The list at the bottom is where they went *to* after they left the proshop page. In the middle is the page entered and exited with the total number of clicks the page received.

Each row in the tables shows the source/destination URL, the number of clicks from/to, the percentage of the total clicks (that is, the percentage of visits where a goal was later met for each goal), a value for any transactions completed during that visit, and the average score for that URL.

The point here is that for any given page on your site, you can see where people are coming from and where they are going. If you're trying to funnel people in from a particular page using a promotion strategy, you should be able to see, by looking at the reports for the two pages, how well it's working.

For example, say SkateFic is using the trivia page to drive traffic to the proshop page. You can see from Figure 18-8 that it's not working awfully well.

Only 15 people out of almost 15,000 total clicks went from the trivia page to the proshop — about one-tenth of one percent. Not good. Embarrassingly not good.

However, thankfully, the real purpose of the trivia page is not to funnel people to the proshop. It's actually a content lure rather than an e-commerce hook. And not quite 1,950 clicks are flowing from the trivia page to other content pages. Considering that some 1,600 of those clicks are entrances that didn't bounce (from the Entrance Bounce Rate report for that time period), this means that there were some 1,600 new visitors to the site who were induced by the trivia page to explore the site.

Not too shabby. Not too shabby at all.

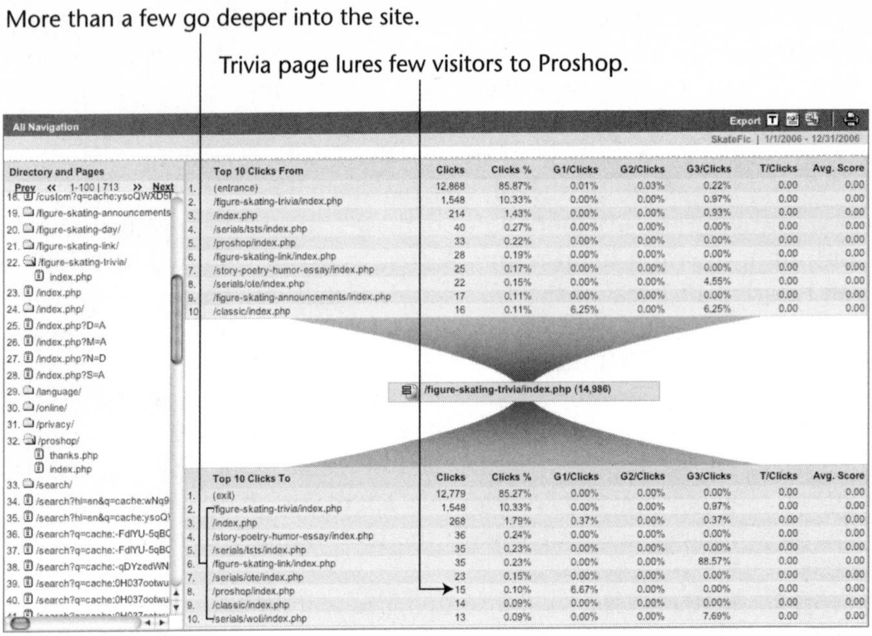

More than a few go deeper into the site.

Trivia page lures few visitors to Proshop.

Figure 18-8: The trivia page isn't funneling potential customers to the proshop.

Things That Sound Easy, Aren't

Navigational Analysis is one of the more powerful functions of Google Analytics. Expect to do a lot of digging and a lot of thinking: "What does this mean to my business?" and "How do I use the information to make my site better?" A great deal of the meaning of these metrics depends on the structure of your site, the function of its pages, and what you're trying to achieve. Once you figure out which means what, though, you have a wealth of information about the efficacy of your pages that you can use to improve your site and better meet your goals.

CHAPTER 19

Goals & Funnel Process

Creating goals. Goal tracking. Goal conversions. Goals, Goals, Goals. You think you've heard enough about them already. But you haven't. There's more yet to add to the larger picture.

Goals and all of the activities that go along with them are important to the success of your web site. It all comes down to what you want from that site. So in this chapter, we're going to look a little more at goals and what you can accomplish by using them. You'll see a few things that you saw back in Chapter 7. And you'll see terms that have been used repeatedly through the book. But there's some new stuff here, too, so don't skip ahead. This is important information, and if you miss it you may find that your site doesn't work the way you want it to work.

Goal Tracking

Chapter 11 is where you first saw the Goal Tracking report. The report is the same here as it was there, as you can see in Figure 19-1.

Figure 19-1: Track all your goals for a single site using this report.

As you may remember, this is an overview of the goals that you have set for your web-site profile. You can have up to four goals, although only three are shown in Figure 19-1. And those goals can be anything that you want them to be, whether they have a monetary value or not.

So what's the purpose of this graphic?

It's nothing more than a quick glance at the number of conversions that you had for each goal during a given time period.

And why is it important?

If you're not getting goal conversions, there's a problem somewhere. Or if you're getting goal conversions but they're low, you can see this at a glance and then dig deeper into the information in later reports to find out why you aren't getting these conversions.

If you happen to be getting a very high number of goal conversions or an unbalanced number of goal conversions across all your goals, that's important information, too. Either of these cases should lead you to investigate what's working and, if necessary, what's not.

So, let's look separately at each of the goals included in Figure 19-1. The first, or Goal 1, is Mary's goal: *Bought Cracked Ice*, shown in Figure 19-2.

As you can see, there's no indication that any of the visitors to the SkateFic.com site bought a copy of *Cracked Ice*. Now, this is not entirely accurate. There have been some sales for the book, but they aren't showing up in this report, because the sales go through PayPal. Google Analytics isn't designed to track PayPal accounts; it's designed to track the sales on your site, using e-commerce systems that work through your site.

However, assume that you didn't know that. Then, looking at this report, you can see there are no sales, and you have to ask yourself why. This report shows you that the goal conversion page hasn't been reached. But it doesn't tell you why. You have to find that out on your own.

That's where testing comes in. You can test various key words that would lead visitors to this page; you can test page content to see how users are using the page, and, as you'll learn later in this chapter, you can test different funnel-navigation schemes that will lead users to this page.

Leading visitors to the page won't guarantee that they'll purchase, but at least you'll know they've seen your product.

The second graphic, shown in Figure 19-3, is for *Goal 2: Signed up for PI announcement*. This is a goal for users to reach the conversion page — which happens to be a "Thank you" page — for signing up for the Private Ice newsletter/announcement list. As you can see in the graphic, there are some conversions taking place for this goal.

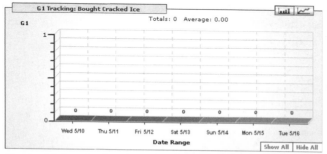

Figure 19-2: Analyze how 'Goal 1: Bought Cracked Ice' performs.

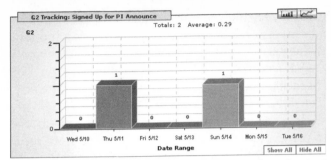

Figure 19-3: How many goal conversions are there for Goal 2?

So, a few people are signing up for the PI newsletter/announcement list. The question now becomes, "Is that a good number?" And if it's not, how do you increase those conversions?

There may not be an easy answer to those questions. How many conversions is enough? Obviously, you'd like every visitor who comes to your site to reach a conversion goal. But 100 percent conversion is probably unrealistic. So you have to decide what your target goal is; if your numbers aren't showing that goal being met, it's time to try something different. Maybe users aren't finding the link to sign up. Or maybe the newsletter/announcement list isn't portrayed in such a way that users think will interest them. This is where you need to decide what's enough and what needs to be done if what you have doesn't reach that criterion.

Finally, there's Goal 3, shown in Figure 19-4. This goal actually has the highest number of conversions. Why? Why do users want to link back to this page? You can probably only speculate, but you have to say that some of them link back because your site meets their needs and they want to pass that on to others who share their interests. It could also be that your site offers something of value for creating the link back. Whatever is driving these folks to meet this conversion goal is a source that you want to identify and try to use in other goals that don't seem to be converting as well.

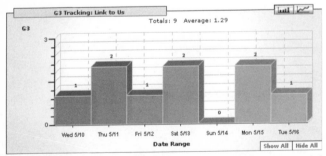

Figure 19-4: More visitors convert on the "link to us" goal than on any other.

The problem with establishing goals (as you may remember from earlier goal discussions) is that knowing which is the right goal isn't always easy. If you're looking at the three reports that we've just covered, you can see that not every goal is created equal. Some will naturally be more successful than others. However, if you find that you've created a goal that does not result in conversions, you know something is fundamentally wrong with that goal. Something needs to be changed. You're challenged with figuring out just what it is. Fortunately, some of the other reports in this section may help on that front.

Goal Conversion

Bet you recognize the report shown in Figure 19-5. You should. You learned about the Goal Conversion report back in Chapter 12.

Figure 19-5: This report shows a percentage of increase in goal conversions.

You may notice that this report is very similar in appearance to the Goal Tracking report. In fact, it contains much the same information, just presented differently. Where the Goal Tracking report showed you the number of conversions for each goal, this report shows you the percentage of change in goals over the designated time frame.

The information is presented differently so you can see whether the number of goal conversions is increasing or decreasing without having to flip back and forth between different reports.

You even use the information in much the same way as the information from the Goal Tracking report. However, here you can also use the information to see whether goal conversion for one of your goals is increasing or decreasing. If you can correlate that information with any changes that you've made during the specific time period shown, you can attribute those changes to the difference and either repair the damage you've done or use what you've learned to improve other goal conversions.

Defined Funnel Navigation

Here's where things start to get a little bit interesting. Throughout these pages, you've seen information about defining a navigational funnel to lead users to a goal page. If you've been scratching your head and thinking, "How do I do this?" you're about to have your question answered.

First, though, let's recap a bit. A funnel is a page or group of pages that lead users to the page that you have established as a goal. So, if one of your goals is for users to sign up for your newsletter, the pages that lead users to that goal would be the funnel.

There's a bit of philosophy to remember here. Water poured into a funnel has no choice where to go. But visitors in your navigational funnel do have a choice, even if it's only to get irritated and leave your site. So the purpose of your funnel usually isn't to force visitors anywhere. Rather, it's to see in a more sophisticated way how they're moving around on your site and how you can make them more comfortable and ease their travel. And in the process maybe steer them a little toward your goals. Think of college-campus planners watching where students wear out the grass and then building sidewalks there.

When you first set up a goal for your site, you probably saw a page similar to the one in Figure 19-6. This is where you enter your goal information. But you may also notice that there's a segment of this page (it's indicated in Figure 19-6) titled Define Funnel. This is where you'll enter the navigational path for your funnel.

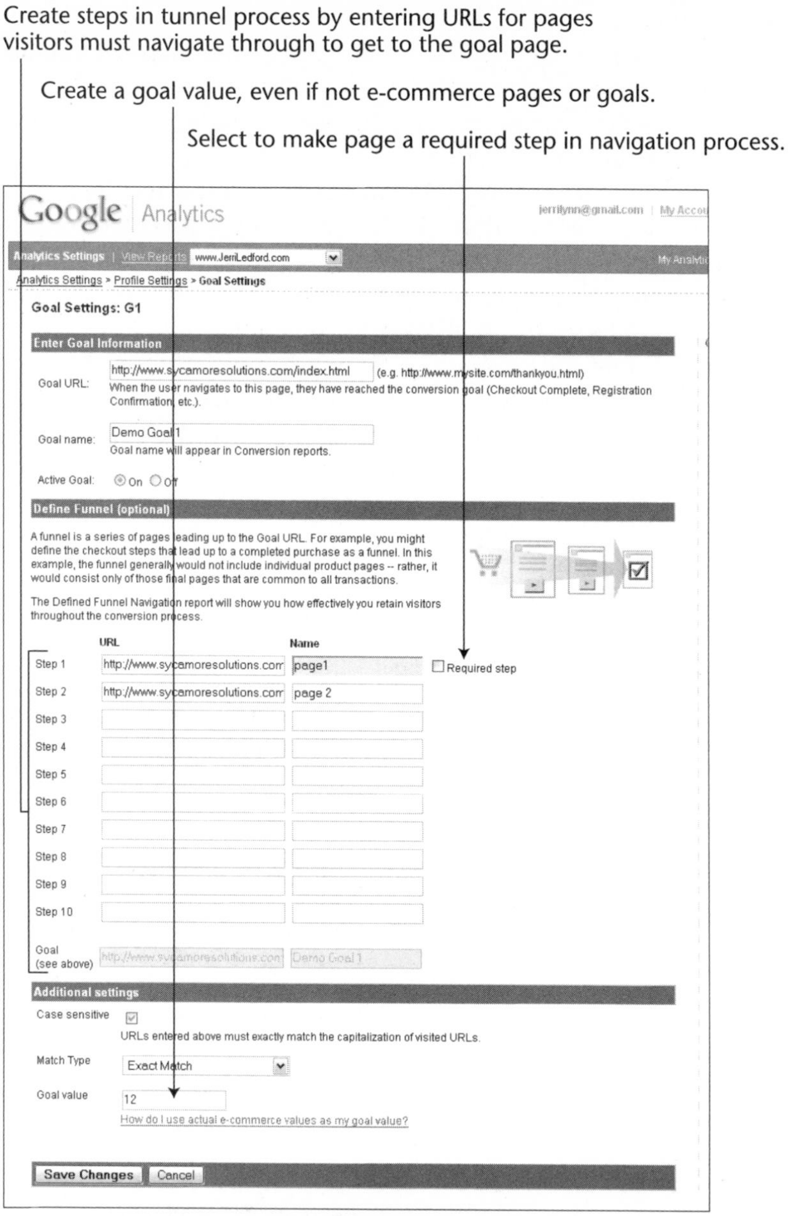

Create steps in tunnel process by entering URLs for pages
visitors must navigate through to get to the goal page.

Create a goal value, even if not e-commerce pages or goals.

Select to make page a required step in navigation process.

Figure 19-6:   Establish goals and funnel navigation on the Goal Settings page.

As you're entering this information, you have the option to make pages in
the funnel navigation path required for the goal to be considered a conversion.
Use these pages sparingly; otherwise, you'll end up with goal conversions that
don't appear to be conversions, because users didn't hit the required pages.
However, if the user *must* go through a specific page to reach a goal conversion, you should include that as a required page.

Also, toward the bottom of the page where you're defining your funnel navigation, you'll see there is a text box for a goal value. If you have an e-commerce site, including this goal value is easy. What's the value of your product (or the product the user needs to purchase to reach a goal conversion)? That's your goal value.

But what if you don't operate an e-commerce site? Then can you enter a goal value? Of course you can. The fact that you're not selling a product doesn't mean your goals have no monetary value. If, for example, you're a consultant and your newsletter brings in new clients, the value of your newsletter goal conversion might be the value of one hour of your consulting time. You'll have to determine how much that goal conversion is worth, but once you do, you can place a specific monetary value on your goal conversions.

Now, back to this Defined Funnel Navigation report. Once you've defined the funnel navigation for one (or all) of your goals, within a few days you can begin to generate the report. It might look something like the Defined Funnel Navigation report shown in Figure 19-7.

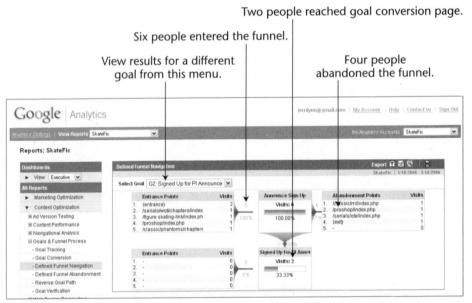

Figure 19-7:   This report shows how users navigate through the defined funnel.

The report illustrates where users enter the navigation process and how they follow the funnel until they either leave the funnel and eventually drop off the page or reach the goal conversion. In the report shown in Figure 19-7, six visitors entered the funnel, four navigated out of it, and two went on to reach the goal conversion. If you're looking at the number of conversions versus the number of visitors, that's a small percentage. However, if you're looking at the number of conversions versus the number of people who entered the funnel, the numbers paint a different picture. So, using this same report as an example, how would you go about getting more people into the funnel? That's the kind of question that these reports lead you to ask, and if you can answer them, you can improve your goal conversions.

In some cases, you'll see pages in the report that aren't part of your defined funnel navigation. This might mean you need to reevaluate your funnel navigation. The same is true if you tend to lose users along a specific portion of the funnel navigation, but that's covered more in the next section.

Defined Funnel Abandonment

In the previous section, I briefly mentioned the people who abandon the funnel navigation process. The Defined Funnel Abandonment report shows you exactly what percentage of people who start in a funnel navigation process abandon it. The report, shown in Figure 19-8, gives you a clear picture of how often your funnel process is ineffective.

When you view this report, keep two things in mind. First, if you have not defined a funnel navigation for a goal, the graphic for that goal will look like what's shown in Figure 19-9. In this example, there is no funnel navigation defined for Goal 3 for the SkateFic.com site.

The other thing you need to remember is that a funnel is simply an indicator of how *you* think your visitors will navigate through your site to reach a specific goal. You can require that users hit certain pages, but even then not everyone thinks the same, so you could be missing out on conversions because you think differently than your users.

In short, this is a tool, nothing more. Use it to figure out where you're losing users along their journey to goal conversions. If you think that your users should hit a specific page as they make their way through purchasing a specific item, but they don't hit that page, view the pages they do hit and learn why their behavior is different from what you would expect it to be. That information will help you better understand your site users, and then you can create pages and content that specifically meet those users' needs.

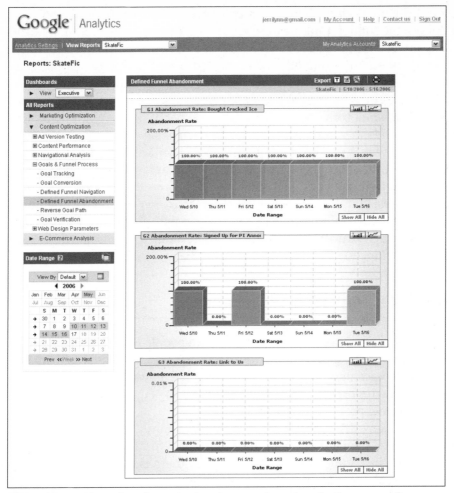

Figure 19-8: How often do users abandon your funnel navigation process?

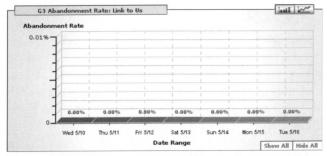

Figure 19-9: If there's no funnel defined, the report will be empty.

Reverse Goal Path

We've already established that not every visitor is going to use the same path that you've designated as a funnel to reach a goal conversion. And the path those users take can hold valuable clues as to how they navigate through your site. This is especially helpful if all users, even those who don't navigate through your funnel, reach a goal conversion through a specific page.

The Reverse Goal Path report, shown in Figure 19-10, shows you exactly how users reach your goal conversion pages.

You can also use this report to find out exactly what pages are required for a user to feel comfortable making a conversion. For example, in the report shown in Figure 19-10, four navigational paths are shown. Each navigational path ends with the page `/figure-skating-link/index.php`. So each goal conversion went through that page. This means that any users you want to convert will likely need to go through that page before they are comfortable meeting the conversion goal, which in this case is linking back to the SkateFic site.

Differing paths users take to reach a goal conversion.   Change goal view.

Figure 19-10: Learn what route users actually do take to your goal conversion pages.

Reverse funnel navigation is not limited to the defined funnel navigation that you laid out when you created your goals. That makes this report valuable for learning the movement patterns of your users and for further refining your funnel navigation.

Goal Verification

When you set a goal for your site, it's possible to set a directory as the goal page. If you've ever done that, have you wondered how many goal conversions from that group of pages are actually attributable to each page? The Goal Verification report, shown in Figure 19-11, illustrates exactly which of those pages is responsible for goal conversions. It gives you a measurement for the goal pages viewed by users.

So how is this report useful? Well, in truth, it's not all that useful if your goal is a single page. However, if you have a directory of pages as your goal (for example, you want people to reach a specific category of products, each with its own page), you will eventually want to know which of those pages within the directory led to the goal conversion. This is where you'll find that information.

Once you have the information, you can use it to determine which pages within a directory are the most useful or most valuable. That information can, in turn, be used to gain more conversions from those pages or to improve conversions on other pages.

Figure 19-11: How many people viewed your goal conversion page?

Goals and funnels and conversions and verification and tracking. It's confusing. There is a lot of value to be derived from creating and properly using goals and the processes surrounding goals. However, it might take you some time to learn how each of these reports is useful to you and how each helps you do business better.

Now that you've been through every aspect of goals and goal tracking at least once (and sometimes twice), you should have a clearer understanding of how it all fits together. The most important point to remember is that goals and goal tracking are about learning the habits of your users and how their habits affect them in reaching your goals, which should be meaningful in the context of your business. If you keep that in mind, as you work your way through the reports, you'll see more value in them and begin to understand them much more.

CHAPTER 20

Web Design Parameters

By now, you've seen a lot of technical stuff, but you're almost to the top of Everest. Keep slogging. This will be short, but it's important if you really want to understand why paying attention to technical stuff matters to the sales success of your web business.

Back in Chapter 11, we touched briefly on something called Web Design Parameters. But we were just telling you then that such things existed. The following few pages are designed to *show*, graphically, what they mean to you.

Little Things Mean a Lot

Your web site looks beautiful to you, on your web browser. But there are people out there — your potential customers — who have different browsers, and to them your beautiful child may look like a deformed troll. Oh, sure, you can still recognize it, sort of, but would you buy anything from it?

On the next pages you'll see screenshots taken from the sites of co-authors Jerri and Mary. Jerri isn't selling things, so she hasn't worried much about how her site might come up on different browsers. Mary's SkateFic.com site is a business, so she worries — and does something about it. Each screenshot was taken with a different browser and OS combination by a service called Browsercam (http://www.browsercam.com).

CAVEAT WEBMASTER: BROWSERCAM

Browsercam maintains machines running various browsers and various OS versions. Members can take screenshots of sites through a web-based interface. Browsercam is an expensive service, really meant for big-time design professionals.

You're not a big-time design professional? Keep reading.

If you're purchasing a web site, ask your designers if they test in Browsercam. Make sure they test each page in a variety of browsers (not just Internet Explorer). If you're doing your own site or if you own a small design shop, Browsercam allows (or at least tolerates) the purchase by co-operatives of memberships on behalf of multiple people, each of whom receives an account.

It's a smart thing to do and makes cross-platform design a whole lot easier. Just a few screenshots will give you a good idea of what your site looks like to people who aren't running exactly the same software you are, without the hassle of installing and maintaining different operating systems and browsers.

We'll start (Figure 20-1) with a look at Jerri's web site in IE 6 under Windows XP — a reference shot for what the site should look like. On average, about 70 percent of visitors to a web site (Jerri's, Mary's, and yours) will be using this browser/platform combination.

Figure 20-1: Jerri's web site in IE 6 under Windows XP — the ideal look

When you get more into using Google Analytics, you'll be able to see what your dominant browser/platform combination is. If you run a niche site, it's quite possible your readers will be running Konqueror/Linux, Safari/Mac OS X, or even iBrowse/Amiga. At the very least, you probably want to support the last two versions of IE (three if Microsoft has just released a new major version) and the most recent versions of Firefox and Safari.

Analytics can help your business in this area. Most designers (and even design programs) try to create sites that are compatible with the most common browsers: IE, Firefox, Safari — sometimes only IE. But your business may not be like everyone else's. You may attract a different demographic — people who don't run IE 6 on Windows XP. With the browser information from Analytics, you can decide how much money and resources you want to put into compatibility.

The next series of screenshots is representative of errors we saw across the board.

The first shot (Figure 20-2) shows Jerri's page in Safari 1.3 on Mac OS X 10.3 (Panther). This is an older version of Safari on the previous version of OS X. You won't find huge numbers of people visiting your site with this browser unless you're a Mac-specific site. However, the screenshot demonstrates minor font and layout differences and what they can do to your pages.

CAVEAT WEBMASTER: TOOLS MATTER

Jerri is not a professional designer, so she uses MS Publisher 2003 for Windows to design and maintain her site. Publisher does not produce tight, compatible code. It's 1500 lines of spaghetti — modern, CSS-based spaghetti but spaghetti nonetheless. Publisher took 85,000-plus characters — that's about 85K sans images — for a three-screen page, with very little text and lots of white space. This is not tight code.

Over the next several pages, you'll see how incompatible it is. We took 30 screenshots in various different browser/platform combinations. We won't show you all the screenshots here, but you can see every one on our blog.

Eleven out of 30 showed the page pretty much as it should appear — at least readable with only minor errors. Thirteen had major but not critical rendering errors, where significant parts of the page didn't appear at all. Five had critical errors where the page did not function in any meaningful way — didn't load, wasn't readable, and so on. One shot didn't come out.

Just under two-thirds of the browsers tested showed errors. Decide for yourself if having 19 errors out of 30 tested browsers is a good indication of compatibility. Then ask yourself, "How much less compatible could this page be?"

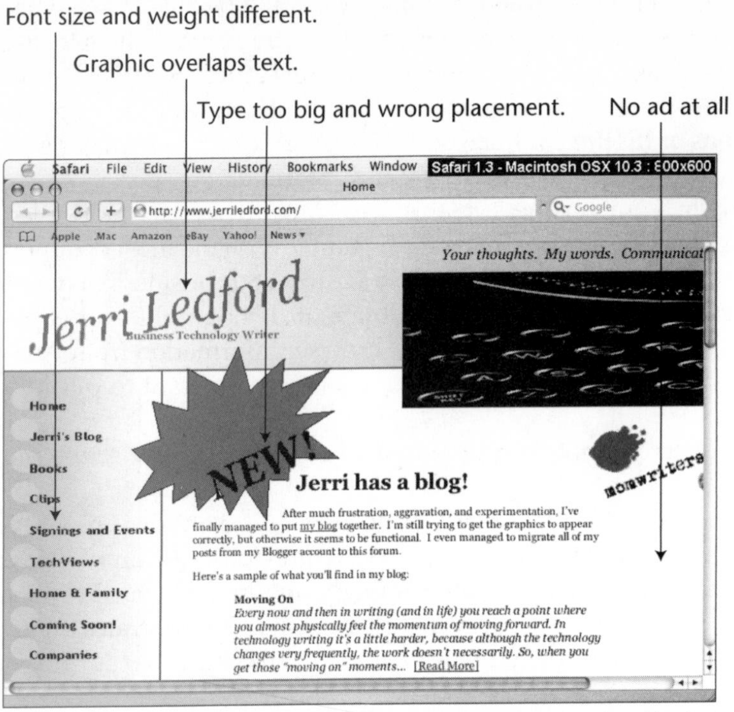

Font size and weight different.

Graphic overlaps text.

Type too big and wrong placement.   No ad at all

Figure 20-2:   Jerri's page in Safari 1.3 on Mac OS X 10.3 (Panther)

Figure 20-3 shows Jerri's page in IE 5.2 on Mac OS X 10.4 (Tiger). Though it dates to 2001, IE 5.2 is the most recent version of IE available for Mac. Some sites require IE. This screenshot shows why that's not a great idea. Netscape 6.2 on Windows 2000 and XP also refused to render the page, producing the same sort of gobbledygook.

Below is the page yet again (Figure 20-4), this time in Opera 8.5.0 on Mac OS X 10.4 (Tiger). Opera's in the bottom of the top 10 browsers, so you may not have more than a few hundred visitors using it even if your site is busy. Because the code is such spaghetti, there's no way of telling at a glance if the anomalies here are the browser's fault or are due to problems in the code. All the user will know is that the site obviously doesn't look the way one would expect a professional's site to look. These are just minor rendering errors, but they add up to a poor corporate image.

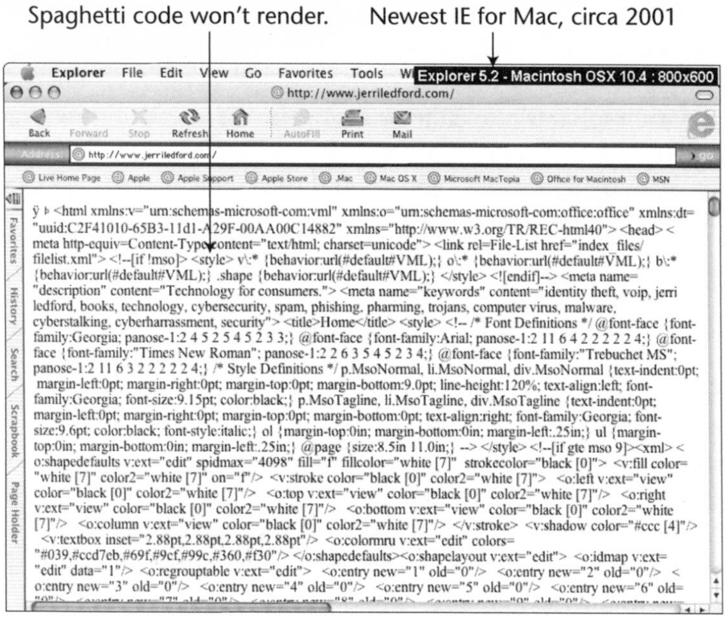
Spaghetti code won't render.
Newest IE for Mac, circa 2001
Explorer 5.2 - Macintosh OSX 10.4 : 800x600
http://www.jerriledford.com/

Figure 20-3: Jerri's page in IE 5.2 on Mac OS X (Tiger)

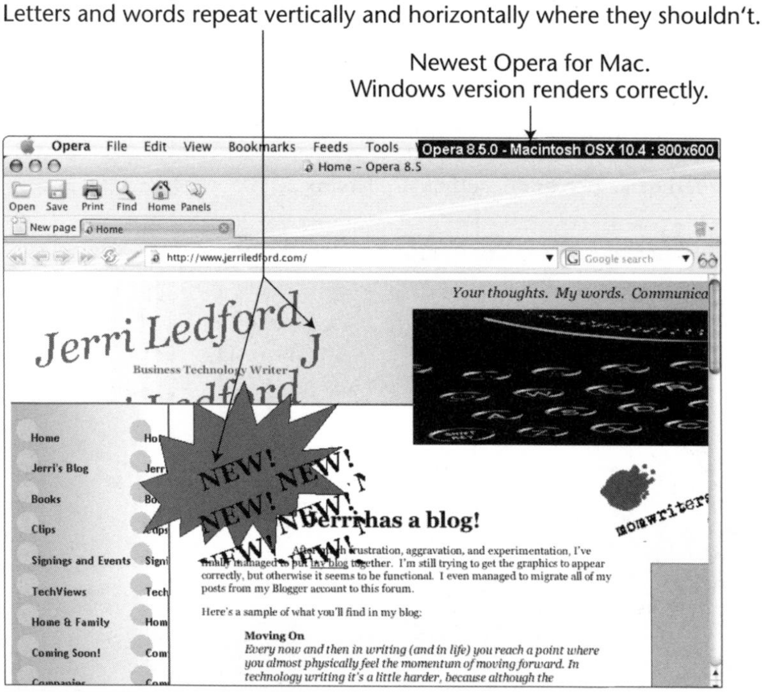
Letters and words repeat vertically and horizontally where they shouldn't.
Newest Opera for Mac.
Windows version renders correctly.
Opera 8.5.0 - Macintosh OSX 10.4 : 800x600
Home - Opera 8.5
http://www.jerriledford.com/

Figure 20-4: Jerri's site in Opera 8.5.0 on Mac OS X 10.4 (Tiger).

Here's a final look at Jerri's site, in Firefox (Figure 20-5). One thing's for sure: While the error's not critical — the web page still loads — Firefox does not render Jerri's site properly. This is true no matter which version of Firefox (1.0.x, 1.5.x), and no matter what platform it's running on (Linux, Windows, or Mac). The home page loses a lot of the impact — and all of the branding. With 10 to 12 percent of surfers using Firefox, and even though this is not a critical problem, it's not something that should be allowed to persist. Camino 1.0 for Mac OS X 10.3, Mozilla 1.7.12 on Mac OS X 10.4, and Netscape 7.2 on Windows 2000 and XP all exhibited this same behavior.

Now let's look at SkateFic.com (Figure 20-6). Check the blog for the complete 30-shot gallery, because we're only going to show you one screenshot here. They all look basically the same, with small variances in fonts due to cross-platform issues.

Why is this page so compatible?

Part of it is experience. Mary has been doing web design and development since 1997. She rolls her own code in HTML and CSS 2.0, and this results in clean, tight, compatible code. In addition, SkateFic pages are tested in every browser that Browsercam offers, ensuring as far as is reasonably possible that the site will render the same way no matter what.

NOTE You can also get good results with a variety of professional-grade tools. Even FrontPage, which has an infamous but rather outdated reputation, isn't all that bad these days.

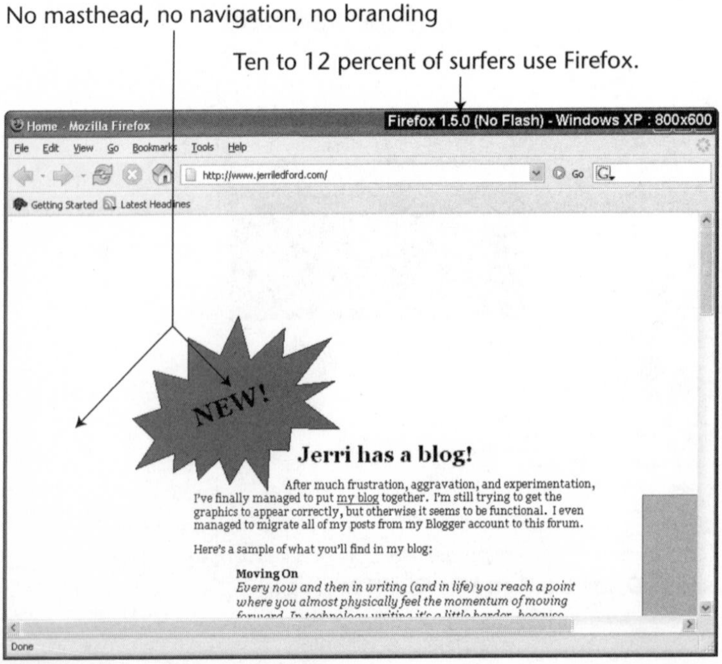

No masthead, no navigation, no branding

Ten to 12 percent of surfers use Firefox.

Figure 20-5: Jerri's site in Firefox

Designed a bit narrower than 800 pixels

Small layout error in the CSS code

Figure 20-6: Mary's SkateFic site loads well for anybody. Good design pays off.

SkateFic has grown over the years. Developing the pages costs time rather than money. Taking money out of the equation makes this kind of compatibility an achievable goal instead of a laudatory principle — as long as time is no object. Since the development "budget" was not an issue, and since the site has developed over time, Mary has been able to emphasize cross-platform, cross-browser compatibility. This is part principle: Mary's a Mac user and Mac people can be fanatical about compatibility for *everyone* — not just Windows users.

Even so, only the first few levels of pages have been checked thoroughly. No one knows everything, nor is anyone perfect, so there are likely to be errors here and there. And of course, there are pages still sporting table-based code from 1999. The site is moving only slowly — very slowly — from 4.1 Transitional to XHTML.

One more thing, though, about both sites, and this will affect pretty much everyone as far as we can tell. After adding the Google Analytics tracking code, neither site worked in IE 4 anymore. Jerri's site loaded partially and then threw an error and didn't finish loading. Skatefic.com threw an error before loading any content at all, possibly due to where the script is located in the code. The Analytics script is the only common code between the two pages and the only script on the SkateFic.com home page.

Figure 20-7 illustrates that the ancient IE 4 doesn't like either page because of the Analytics script. It's a small price to pay for this kind of information and tracking ability provided by Analytics. If you absolutely have to support an ancient browser like IE 4, there are a variety of tactics you can use to mitigate the scripting problems, but these strategies are beyond the scope of this book.

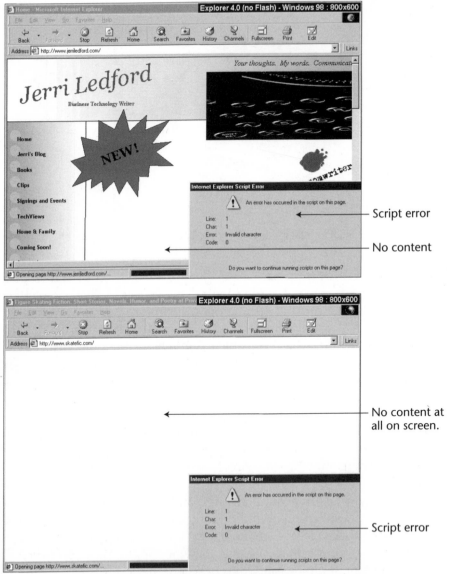

Figure 20-7: Internet Explorer 4 isn't a good match for Google Analytics.

Digging Deeper

Chapter 11 gave you quick looks at a number of other web-site factors besides browser versions. These included platform versions, browser and platform combos, different screen resolutions, screen colors, languages, Java, Flash, connection speed, and host names.

You don't want to see all that again — or if you do, it's all there in Chapter 11. The next paragraphs give a few additional thoughts, for those curious about the finer points. Not curious? Go on to Chapter 21.

Bottom feeders on the browser list: In Chapter 11, we looked only at the top six browsers. If you go deeper, to the top 10 (see Figure 20-8), an interesting thing or two emerges.

SkateFic gets a substantial amount of traffic from Firefox users. There's definitely a case to be made for providing full support for Firefox's various versions. Even Safari, Netscape, Opera, and Mozilla bring in reasonable numbers of visits that it's worth making some effort to support them.

But is gzip a browser? It's not. It's actually a compression utility (http://www.gzip.org/). So this may be a bit of geek-surgery gone wrong, or it could indicate that someone is using gzip to compress files on their site. It's important to know what information is valuable in these reports and what information isn't. That last tidbit in the report? It's probably not valuable.

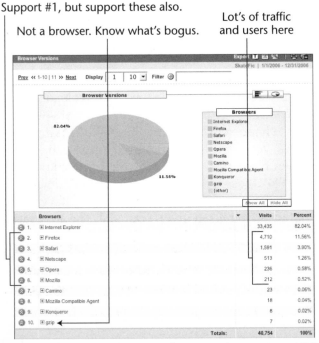

Figure 20-8: SkateFic's top 10 browsers show some oddities.

Platform versions: Is there something about a Mac? More often than not, web sites support only the dominant operating system. As we discussed in Chapter 3, that may not be good business. Now let's dig a bit deeper. Figure 20-9 shows the To-date Lifetime Values . . . and maybe something important about Mac and Windows visitors. At least in this case, Mac-based visitors were twice as likely as others to buy (that is, complete Goal 1) and also seemed significantly more likely to complete other goals. These are the kind of customers you want, even if their numbers are not all that great.

Browser and platform combos: Just a caution or two. There are strange things out there in the real world. Ancient browsers like IE 5 on Windows 98, or Firefox 1.0.7 on Windows XP, or whizzy new browsers on ancient PCs like IE 6 on Windows 98. It never ends! Be aware. And because fonts and screen resolutions differ from OS to OS and because layout can vary slightly from browser to browser, you can't count on Firefox being Firefox being Firefox on all OSs and versions. Different versions and different OSs can produce totally different results.

Screen resolutions and colors: It's nice to be able to say that some things don't matter as much as they once did. Remember when you had to scroll sideways to see some sites in full? No more. There are (we think) still people out there using 8-bit color; somewhere, someone also may be hunting game with flint-tipped arrows. But neither is vital to your business. Analytics will tell you just what resolutions and colors your visitors are arriving with — but this would be a good time to go out for an El Grande Super Latte.

Languages: Think creatively. If lots of people are coming to your site from Mongolia, maybe you should think of offering a catalog in Mongolian or starting a splinter site in it or adding instructions in Mongolian to your top-selling widget.

Java-enabled: Another caution. Remember that only a small percentage of your customers is Java-enabled and that few people love to download special programs. You want to feature technology that a high percentage of your customers can use easily. And if you happen to be in something like banking, government, or emergency services, you want 100 percent of them able to.

And finally: We hate it when Flash crashes our browser, but we know it's here to stay. And we even like those Flash-based anime and other cartoonesque figures. Analytics will tell you how many visitors have Flash installed, but be careful about throwing Flash up on your site. The annoyance factor can be high.

Analytics will also tell you how fast visitors can download your pages. But it's enough to know you have about two seconds to capture most surfers. Write tight pages that are beautiful and download fast — like a butterfly breaking the sound barrier.

Lower response rates make individual visitors less valuable.

To-date Lifetime Value - Platform Versions			
		Export T	
Windows	**First Time**	**Prior**	**Total**
Absolute Unique Visitors	33,475	449	33,924
Goal 1 (Bought Cracked Ice)	0.04%	0.22%	0.05%
Goal 2 (Signed Up for PI Announce)	0.09%	0.67%	0.10%
Goal 3 (Link to Us)	1.06%	2.23%	1.10%
Average Visitor Value	$0.00	$0.00	$0.00
Total Ecommerce Revenue	$0.00	$0.00	$0.00
Total # Transactions	0	0	0
Average Order Value	$0.00	$0.00	$0.00

Are Mac users more likely to meet goals?

To-date Lifetime Value - Platform Versions			
		Export T	
Macintosh	**First Time**	**Prior**	**Total**
Absolute Unique Visitors	2,235	50	2,285
Goal 1 (Bought Cracked Ice)	0.13%	0.00%	0.13%
Goal 2 (Signed Up for PI Announce)	0.13%	0.00%	0.13%
Goal 3 (Link to Us)	1.25%	0.00%	1.23%
Average Visitor Value	$0.00	$0.00	$0.00
Total Ecommerce Revenue	$0.00	$0.00	$0.00
Total # Transactions	0	0	0
Average Order Value	$0.00	$0.00	$0.00

Figure 20-9: Mac-based visitors seem more than twice as likely to buy as others.

The Analytics hostnames report can tell you if someone is copying your web site's source code to build their own or to create a spoofed copy of your site. There are evildoers out there.

To summarize, small changes can make a huge difference in traffic. Learning to read your parameter metrics can help you decide which changes are good and which aren't. Depending on what you want to do with your site, Web Design Parameters can tell if you can, if you should, and if you must. Use your powers wisely.

E-commerce Analysis

Transactions, revenue, conversions, loyalty — all these are elements or factors in an e-commerce business. They're also measurements of how successful your e-commerce business is at driving sales.

These measurements are important in helping you track and monitor what works and what doesn't in your e-commerce infrastructure. Do your page contents make sense to customers? Is the way those pages are laid out intuitive, or do you lose users because they can't find what they are looking for?

Your e-commerce measurements can tell you. This section gives you a detailed look at the E-commerce Analysis reports included in Google Analytics. Each chapter explains different reports, how those reports function, and how you can use those reports to improve your web site and increase sales.

CHAPTER 21

Commerce Tracking

Commerce is defined as the buying and selling of goods. On a macroeconomic level, commerce could represent all of the sales within a city, state, or region, but we're not concerned with macroeconomics. We're concerned with microeconomics — the buying and selling of goods on a specific web site: your web site.

Even more specific, you're probably concerned with how much you're selling from your web site. It's not enough just to know what you're selling, though. You also need to know how those sales happen, because when you know, you can duplicate the process.

Google Analytics provides reports that help you understand the circumstances under which your products are sold. For example, do you sell more products on Monday than on any other day of the week? You can know for sure using the reports in this section.

Revenue & Transactions

Revenue and transactions are the basis of any commerce reporting. What are your sales, and how many transactions did it take to reach that sales level? The Revenue & Transactions report, shown in Figure 21-1, illustrates that information.

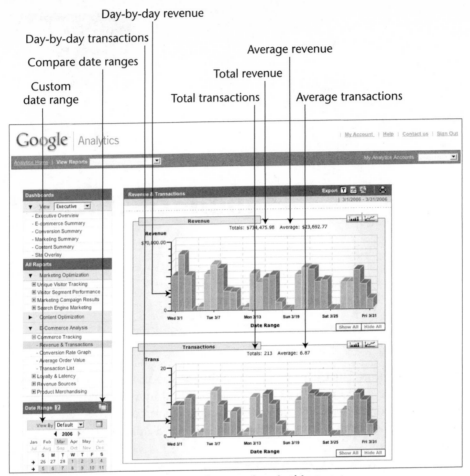

Figure 21-1: Learn your revenue and transactions in this report.

The top graph in this report shows your total revenue, day-by-day revenue, and average daily revenue. And the second graph shows your transactions by day, the total number of transactions, and the average number of transactions.

So, how do you use this information? Aside from the obvious "quick-glance" format, which you can use to tell quickly where your revenue and transactions stand for the given time period, you can also use this information to determine which day of the week the most revenue and transactions are generated.

Use this information over time to find patterns in user purchases and spending, or combine this information with other reports (such as the marketing reports) to learn what's driving customers to your site on a given day.

For example, if you send out a weekly newsletter, compare your revenue and transactions to the Marketing Campaign Results for that particular time frame to find out if the newsletter is driving revenue and transactions on your site.

You can also define a custom date range for your Revenue & Transactions report, or you can compare date ranges using the calendaring tools on the left side of the page. This allows you to see how one date range compares to another.

Conversion Rate Graph

Conversion is the measure of how well you do at driving users to complete a transaction on your site. And transactions per visit is the name of this game. The Conversion Rate Graph, shown in Figure 21-2, illustrates how transactions per visit are displayed in this report.

Transactions can be defined in a number of ways. There is, of course, the exchange of money for goods. But you can also consider a visitor's signing up for a newsletter, downloading a file, or completing a form as a transaction. It requires that you set that specific action as a transaction and give it a monetary value. That information was addressed in Chapter 19, and you can flip back now if you need to review it.

Finished? Good. One last aspect of these reports: You also have the same capabilities that you had with the previous report, to change date ranges and compare by date ranges.

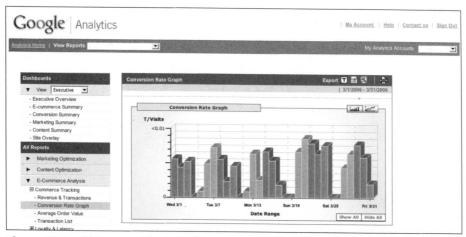

Figure 21-2: This report illustrates how many transactions each site visitor completes.

Average Order Value

Companies like McDonald's completely understand the importance of average order value. Higher average order values translate into higher revenue. And even e-commerce sites need to keep track of this metric, especially if that site happens to be the type that changes products or layout on a regular basis.

The Average Order Value report, shown in Figure 21-3, shows you what the average value of transactions are on your site. Whether you have 50 sales or 500, the high-value transactions are interesting, the low-value transactions are depressing, but the average value tells the tale.

With this information, you can watch, over time, as changes in your site affect your revenue. The information is also useful for learning when you need to boost sales programs or increase resources and capabilities (if your average order values are consistently rising).

In this report, you also have the time range and comparison features that you have in previous reports.

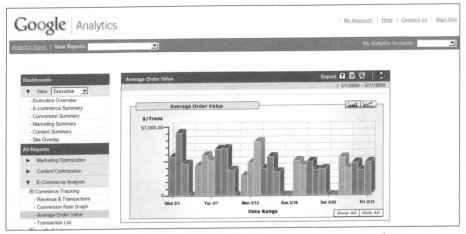

Figure 21-3: The Average Order Value report shows your average over time.

Transaction List

The last report in this section is the Transaction List report. This report is exactly what it says, a transaction list. As shown in Figure 21-4, the report lists all of the transactions for your site within in a given time frame.

This information is most commonly used for auditing purposes, to ensure that actual transactions are represented properly in records and reports. It's a useful report if you want to see more details about the transactions that generate revenue.

There are also columns in this report for tax, shipping, and the number of items in a transaction. This additional information gives you a method for monitoring changes in these categories. So if you find that the number of items in the average transaction is only two, you know you might need to recommend additional products using recommendation software or incentives to customers.

All the reports in this section seem minor when taken by themselves; however, when you combine these reports with additional information, you begin to put together a clear picture of how your site is performing and how that performance leads to conversions, transactions, and revenue. Then, if you need to follow up, having a complete list of transactions makes auditing easier and provides additional information on the transactions.

Figure 21-4: The Transaction List report shows all of the transactions in a given time frame.

CHAPTER 22

Loyalty & Latency

Two words that have been used consistently since the Internet started to draw both businesses and consumers are loyalty and latency. Loyalty is the measurement of how many visitors you can persuade to return to your site on a regular basis. It's also one of the most elusive elements of e-commerce. It's so easy for users to click to another site that many companies have to work hard to build a loyal group of users.

Latency is also a pretty common term, and you might think of it as the time it takes for you to get off the couch and answer the door when the bell rings. The time period from the time you get the request (the ringing bell, which signifies that someone wants your attention) until you answer that request (opening the door) is called latency. Another word for it is delay.

Loyalty and latency are linked at the hip like conjoined twins, because latency has a direct bearing on loyalty. For example, in trying to access a well-known web site today, every other page I requested timed out. This is very frustrating, and with so many other web sites that offer the same information and products as this site, I finally gave up and went off to the other site.

Now, the delay that caused the pages to time out is latency. My loyalty with this site has been tested. I might go back one more time, but, being the busy professional that I am, if I do return to the site and experience the same problem, the chances that I'll try a third time are almost nil — why waste time with latency issues when I can go to a site that I know will provide what I need and will do it immediately? This is how loyalty and latency work.

Put all of this together, and what you have are a couple of reasons to monitor loyalty and latency. First, you need to keep up with how often users are returning to your site and how your site responds to them. And the second reason is more like troubleshooting. If you're not getting return visitors, why? And if those visitors are experiencing delay issues, again why?

This information can be used to improve user experience and increase customer loyalty. That's why Google Analytics offers this short section of reports. Each report illustrates how loyalty and latency affect your revenues.

New vs. Returning

The New vs. Returning report was first discussed back in Chapter 13. This report, as shown in Figure 22-1, illustrates the percentage of new versus returning visitors and how those visitors perform in metrics such as overall transactions, overall revenue, and revenue per visitor and transaction.

This is where you'll find evidence of the importance of building a loyal community of users. Dozens of books have been written on building customer loyalty, both online and offline, so we won't go into detail about all of the strategies that go into building loyalty. However, you'll have proof of just how important it is if you view these reports. In most cases, you'll find that returning customers spend more than first-time customers. They also tend to do business with you often, so there's an additional increase there.

Analysis options

Calendaring options

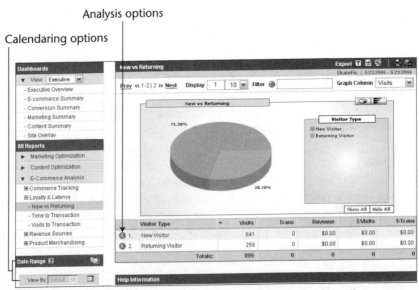

Figure 22-1: New vs. Returning shows how each type of visitor affects revenue.

What's more, these reports let you know if your marketing campaigns are working. Have you been trying to draw customers back to your site with sales or specials? If it's working, you'll see an increase over the previous time period (or the same time period the previous year) in your returning visitors. Generally, the increase in revenue follows as a natural progression of the relationship that you've developed with your user.

You do have the option to analyze this information over time and to compare date ranges using the calendaring options. Analysis options are also available in this report. Click the red double arrow next to any entry to view Data Over Time, To Date Lifetime Value, or Cross Segment Performance reports.

Time to Transaction

I know a person who spends a lot of time thinking about a shopping decision. He compares prices at all of the web sites that carry the product he seeks, he visits a page multiple times before making the decision to purchase, and he may even start the purchase several times and never complete it because he's indecisive about spending money, especially if he's looking for a high-ticket item.

This describes a large number of people in today's world. Money is tight for almost everyone, so we agonize over making purchases of all sizes. That's why you've designed your site to help your users make those purchasing decisions. If you have a good site, there might be reviews of the product included on the product page, or maybe there are articles about how the product could improve the user's life or workflow. It's even possible that you've included video testimonials from other users who have purchased the product and were happy with it.

The point here is that very often, users don't make a decision about buying a product on the first day. It's more likely they'll take several days to make the decision, but once it's made, the purchase is usually completed fairly quickly. Are your customers the instant-gratification types who want it right now, or are they more like the Thinking Man, stuck for a time in indecision?

The Time to Transaction report, shown in Figure 22-2, should answer that question for you. If you find that the majority of your users make purchases on their first day, you know that whatever is drawing them to your site (it could be newsletter coupons, advertisements, or word of mouth) is working to complete the sale.

On the other hand, if your users seem to take several days to make a purchase, how could you improve that? What information could you provide to the user to close the sale? This graph shows you which area you should concentrate on: driving more traffic or decreasing the time-to-purchase ratio.

Calendaring options

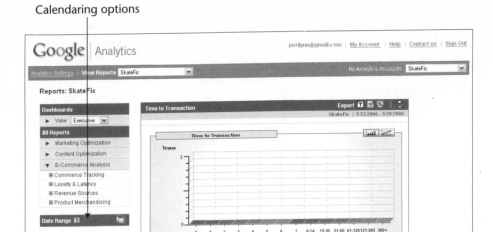

Figure 22-2: Using this report, learn how quickly users make a purchase on your site.

NOTE In the Time to Transaction report, the number zero represents users who make a purchase from your site on the first day they visit it. If users make a purchase more than one year from the date of their first visit to your site, they are shown to the right of the graph.

In addition to the illustrative graphic of this report, the time analysis options — for measuring different time periods or comparing time periods — are available to you near the calendar on the left side of the page.

Visits to Transaction

A complement to the Time to Transaction report is this Visits to Transaction report, shown in Figure 22-3.

The difference between the Time report and the Visits report is the measurement of time used. In the Visits report, the measurement is the number of visits a user made to the site before making a purchase. Rather than measuring how long it took a user to make a purchase, you're monitoring how many times they came to the site before making a purchase.

This report might seem a little redundant, but it's not. How many of your visitors make a purchase the first time they visit your site? How many visitors come to your site five or more times before they make a purchase?

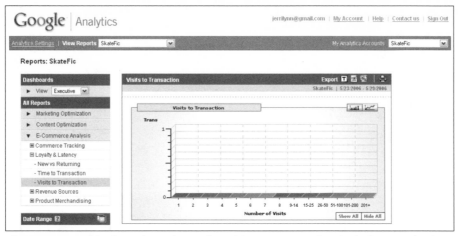

Figure 22-3: This chart shows how often visitors came to the site before purchasing.

These measurements help you learn whether the content on your site is doing its job — making it easy for the visitor to make a decision. If your users have to return to your site numerous times before making a purchase, that probably means they were out comparing prices, reading reviews, or learning more about the product.

Is there any amount of that information that you can provide for the user so they don't have to leave your site to find it? If you can provide it, you have a greater chance that the visitor will make a purchase with you. It's all about convenience. And he who provides the most convenience wins.

Use this report to build more convenience into your site. It tells you how often visitors have to leave and come back; now all you have to do is change that.

Visitor loyalty and latency are timeless measurements. In the same way that bricks-and-mortar stores provide customer loyalty programs (as Office Depot has the Office Depot Advantage program), web sites should have customer loyalty programs. And web-site designers should take into consideration all of the information that consumers need to make a decision. Put that information at the customer's fingertips, and you're likely to decrease latency and increase loyalty, which in turn increases revenue. It's timeless economics. What's new now is the medium.

CHAPTER 23

Revenue Sources

If you've ever put on a coat or a pair of jeans during the early months of winter and found a $20 bill in the pocket, you know that found money leaves you feeling lucky. Those days make the coming winter seem a little more welcome. As nice as it is, though, there are some instances where you don't want to just happen upon an amount of money without knowing where it came from.

Your organizational revenue is one of those places. Finding revenue with no specific category can leave you in a bit of a lurch. How do you explain that revenue if you're audited? Furthermore, if you had known about the revenue all along, it could have been put to good use — upgrading equipment, investing in software, or hiring a marketing consultant.

Understanding where your revenue comes from is also essential to maximizing it. After all, if you don't know that a product on a page buried in your site is generating more sales than a product featured on your front page, how are you to maximize the sales from that product that users have to search for?

The reports covered in this section are designed to shed a little light on the problem. By looking at everything from the referring sources to the affiliations that result in revenue, you have a complete picture of your revenue and a glimpse at the unique factors driving it.

Referring Sources

You may remember that back in Chapter 13 we covered a report called Referring Source. That report is very different from this source because it illustrated the source from which visitors came to your web site. Using the report, you could tell at a glance if users were coming directly to your site or from some search engine or link.

The Referring Sources report that we're looking at in this report is specific to revenue generated. The report, shown in Figure 23-1, illustrates which referral sources — search engines, marketing campaigns, newsletters, and so on — are responsible for the most revenue on your site.

As previously mentioned, you can use this report to help build on the potential that you might be missing, but even more important, the report also makes it obvious where something is not right. If you expect that products featured on your front page should generate more revenue than they actually do, you can easily see there's a problem that needs to be addressed.

Using this report, you can also clearly see how well your marketing and advertising efforts are generating revenue. You do need to tag the marketing links to persuade the report to track them, but by now you should be pretty comfortable with the process of tagging these links.

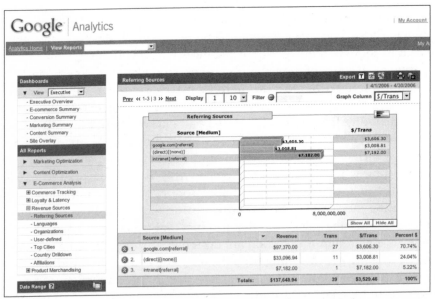

Figure 23-1: This report shows which referring sources generate the most revenue.

Languages

If you're operating a U.S.-based e-commerce site, would you be surprised to find that a sizable chunk of your revenue comes from Japanese-speaking customers? I'll bet you would.

Like the Language report in Chapter 13, this report provides information about visitor languages. However, the report in Chapter 13 is in reference to visitors generally, while the Languages report in this section, shown in Figure 23-2, shows you what languages are spoken by the visitors who generate the most revenue on your site.

When you view this report, if you find that the language that seems to generate the most revenue is not your native language, you can use that information to capitalize on revenue by providing additional language support on your site. It also helps you understand the users who come to your site.

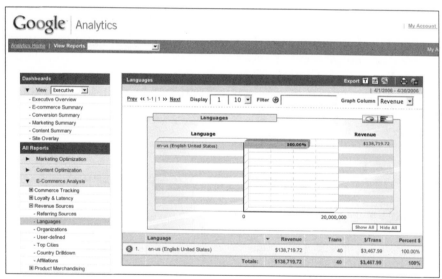

Figure 23-2:   What language is spoken by visitors who generate revenue on your site?

Organizations

The company or host that visitors are using to access the Internet often has a bearing on how they view the site and what they do during the visit. For example, if a visitor comes to you from a corporate network, you may notice that this visitor's revenue is less than that of others.

Any number of factors could determine this, but the most likely is that the visitor is in a hurry because it's during the work day. On the other hand, the same visitor might come to you from a broadband ISP when not at work, and the revenue generated could be much higher. This is because the visitor is more relaxed, doesn't have the boss standing by, and can take time to browse through the site and therefore might find more to purchase or might reach more goal conversions.

No matter what the circumstances, knowing what host or ISP your visitors are coming from when they generate revenue for the site gives you more insight into the visitors' habits and behaviors. The Organizations report, shown in Figure 23-3, gives you a graphical illustration of that information.

If you find that a specific host or ISP is generating the bulk of your revenue, you can use that information to target those users specifically. For example, if the majority of your users come from AOL, you can target marketing campaigns to AOL users or maybe even create a partnership with AOL that could generate additional revenue for your site.

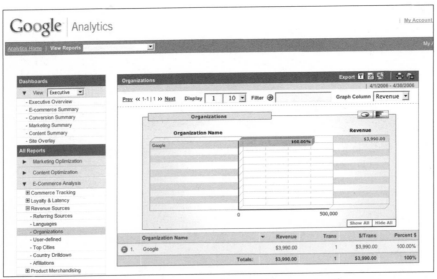

Figure 23-3: This report illustrates what host or ISP generates the most revenue.

User-Defined

Every organization has some measurement that's specific to the business. If you're a recruiting company, knowing what education your visitors have can have a bearing on how you design the site. Or if you're a product company, knowing whether your visitors are male or female will help you provide products that appeal to those people.

These specifics are measurements that can be user-defined and have meaning for your organization. User-defined measurements were first addressed in Chapter 13, but they reappear here in the User-defined report to illustrate how those measurements translate into revenue. The report is shown in Figure 23-4.

These user-defined measurements are the same measurements that you set previously. The difference is that now you can see how those measurements relate to the revenue that your site generates.

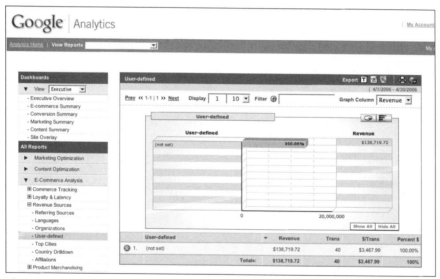

Figure 23-4: Learn how user-defined measurements perform in relation to revenue.

Top Cities

An interesting measurement in Google Analytics is what city site visitors live in. As we discussed in Chapter 13, learning what city or country your visitors live in can give you advantages in advertising and other areas. For example, the owners of the Japanese gaming site www.Kotaku.com might have been surprised to learn that many visitors to their site come from the United States.

But once the site owners have this information, they can then change or add to the site to appeal to those users and thereby generate additional revenue.

The Top Cities report, shown in Figure 23-5, defines what cities have the most revenue and transactions during a given time period.

In addition to seeing the cities listed in this report, if you click the plus sign (+) beside any city, additional geographic information such as region or country information is displayed. This information can then be used to determine where advertising and marketing efforts should be focused or what areas need additional efforts to improve revenue generation.

Figure 23-5: The Top Cities report shows revenue-producing localities.

Country Drilldown

Much like the Top Cities report, this report — the Country Drilldown — illustrates what geographic region customers who generate the most revenue live in. The report, shown in Figure 23-6, aggregates transactions and revenue by country, but clicking the plus sign next to each country will lead you to additional information about cities within the country. This information can then be used to make comparisons by revenue.

Like previous versions of this report, which you saw as the Geo Map overlay in Chapter 13, this report is about geographic location. However, rather than just telling you the number of visits or transactions, there's also a revenue measurement included in this report. And as with previous reports, you have the ability to drill deeper into the report by clicking the plus sign (+) located next to each country.

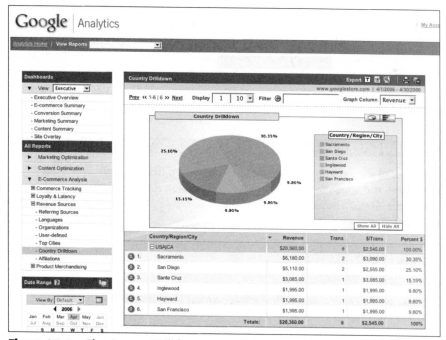

Figure 23-6: The Country Drilldown report lists revenue by country.

Affiliations

Affiliate marketing is highly effective (so effective, in fact, that even Google and Amazon have affiliate marketing programs). The idea behind these programs is that users who are happy with a product or service will recommend it to their friends and family members. It works very well.

If you're like the majority of other businesses on the web, you probably have an affiliate marketing program of some kind. Wouldn't it be nice to know exactly how much revenue those programs generate? With the Affiliations report, shown in Figure 23-7, that's exactly what you can expect.

To use this report, you must provide an affiliation in the transaction line of your e-commerce transactions. You have the option to do this when you set up your e-commerce tracking.

Once the tags for tracking affiliates are in place, this report provides information on which affiliations provide the highest number of transactions and the most revenue.

When you know which affiliate programs are most effective, you can adjust your affiliate marketing efforts to capitalize on those efforts. For example, if you're running two affiliate programs, you can use this report to track both programs. If one proves to be clearly better than the other, you know you should move the investment in the low-performing program to the program that generates the most revenue.

MORE ABOUT AFFILIATE MARKETNG

The specifics of affiliate marketing programs can be a little complicated, and we don't have the space to cover them here. However, if you're interested in learning more about affiliate marketing, the following books might be useful.

Beginners

◆ *Building Your Business with Google For Dummies,* by Brad Hill. Wiley, ISBN: 0764571435

Intermediate

◆ *Successful Affiliate Marketing for Merchants,* by Shawn Collins and Frank Fiore. Que, ISBN: 0789725258

◆ *Affiliate Selling: Building Revenue on the Web,* by Greg Helmstetter and Pamela Metivier. Wiley, ISBN: 0471381861

There are also affiliate program-specific books such as those for Google, Amazon, and Yahoo! if those programs are of interest to you.

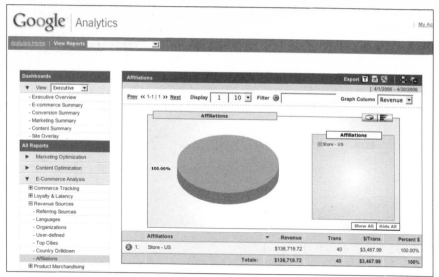

Figure 23-7: Track revenue generated by affiliate programs with this report.

The report also provides another outlet to track additional affiliate programs that you might be interested in testing.

Understanding the source of your web site's revenues — what works and what doesn't — makes it easier for you to capitalize on those that do work. And that, of course, leads to additional revenues.

CHAPTER 24

Product Merchandising

Every item in every store you've ever been in has been strategically placed right where it is so that you'll see the item in a certain light or at a certain time in your visit. It's called product merchandising, and companies spend millions of dollars each year ensuring that product placement is just perfect, because it really does matter when it comes to sales and revenue.

Several years ago there was a large craft company with several dozen sizable stores scattered around the Southern U.S. The company generated several billion dollars in revenue each year and spent millions on ensuring that products were placed within the store in a way that was intuitive for customers. A large part of every employee's job was to make sure each department conformed to company standards for product placement.

Then a new CEO took over. One of his first orders of business was to change the layout of every store within the company. The problem was that the CEO didn't understand how customers shopped in the store, and customers were not happy with the new layout. They began shopping elsewhere, and within three years the company went belly-up. It probably wasn't only because the merchandising in the store was off, but that played a part in the overall demise of the stores.

If that CEO had looked at some of the measurements indicating how product merchandising affects revenue, he might have corrected his mistake before it was too late. Measurements like the ones in this chapter are essential to tracking the health of your product merchandising and how it affects revenue.

Google Analytics understands that it's all about the placement and supplies the tools you need to monitor the important merchandising metrics for your e-commerce business.

Product Performance

Product performance measurements give you insight into how well the product is placed, priced, and displayed. In bricks-and-mortar stores, this is the measurement to end all measurements. In e-commerce stores, it's a little trickier. You may need to play with your page placement to find the best place to display your products.

The Product Performance report, shown in Figure 24-1, is designed to help you see how well (or poorly) your products sell. The report shows the number of items sold, the total revenue, the average price, and the average order quantity for each product you sell online.

Additionally, you can click the plus sign (+) next to each product category to drill down to specific SKUs (Stock-Keeping Units) for more detailed information about sales.

These numbers are important because poorly performing products could indicate poor placement. If you find that an item that *should* perform well does not, consider moving the item to a different page on your web site or featuring the product more prominently on the front page of the site.

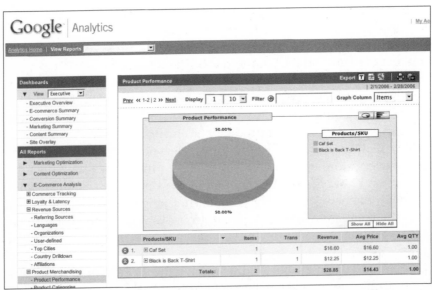

Figure 24-1: View sales by product in the Product Performance report.

These measurements are also a good indicator of product-specific marketing that you may be conducting. If the marketing is driving sales, you should see an increase in sales for that specific product. If you do not, the marketing may not be performing effectively.

Product Categories

Product categories are another helpful indicator of web-site performance and product merchandising. For example, if you have two categories of products on your site — racing memorabilia and sports memorabilia — knowing which of the categories performs the best is essential to understanding how you should display those products.

If the racing memorabilia are selling better, you may decide to feature those products more prominently and increase articles about race car drivers or racing teams. If you really wanted to increase visitor interaction with the site, you could add a quiz or game related to racing.

The Products Categories report, shown in Figure 24-2, gives you the measurements that show which category of products on your site is generating the most revenue.

The report shows the number of items sold, the total revenue, the average price, and the average order quantity for each product you sell online. You can also drill down into the categories to find specific SKUs by clicking the plus sign next to each category of products.

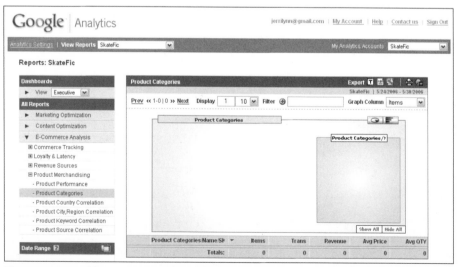

Figure 24-2: This report measures which categories of products perform best.

Product Country Correlation

One of the most interesting aspects of e-commerce is that it truly makes it possible for your business to reach customers globally. In a bricks-and-mortar business, if you want to sell to customers who live in another country, you have to have a presence in that country. In e-commerce, it doesn't matter where you're located.

A good example of this concept is www.ThaiGem.com. The company, which is located in Chanthaburi, Thailand, sells gemstones and jewelry around the world. But that's only possible because it's an e-commerce company. If the company had to have a physical facility in every country in order to sell its products there, it would not be nearly as widespread as it is.

E-commerce gives you capabilities that were never possible in the past. It's entirely possible that no matter what your product, you're selling it in some other country. The Product Country Correlation report, shown in Figure 24-3, breaks your sales down by country. Are you selling more widgets in Japan, the United States, or the UK? This is where you can find that information.

The report shows you the number of items sold, the total revenue, the average price, and the average order quantity for each product you sell on line, and you can click the plus sign (+) next to any entry to drill deeper into the collected data.

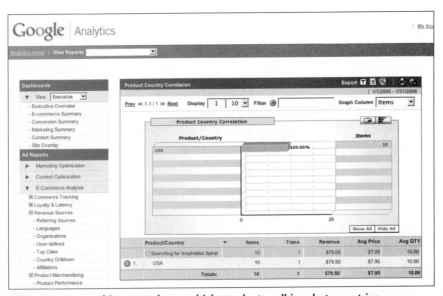

Figure 24-3: In this report, learn which products sell in what countries.

What do you do if you find that a different country seems to be responsible for the majority of sales in a product category? Well, appeal to the customers from that country, of course. Maybe you should consider revamping your shipping program to make it more affordable for customers in that country. Customers who spend less on shipping are likely to spend more on products.

You may even want to provide country-specific information about product uses, if it's appropriate. Use the information to improve customer experience. Increased sales volume and revenue are sure to follow.

Product City, Region Correlation

Like the Country Correlation report, the Product City, Region Correlation report shows geographical data related to sales. In which cities do your customers live, and which of those cities is responsible for the highest percentage of sales.

The report, shown in Figure 24-4, shows the number of items sold, the total revenue, the average price, and the average order quantity for each product you sell online.

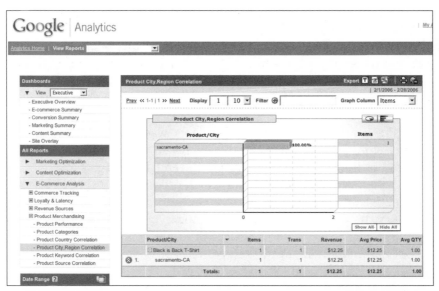

Figure 24-4: This report indicates what cities purchasing customers reside in.

Once gathered, this information can be used to improve marketing efforts or to introduce new product categories that appeal to the specific locations responsible for the highest sales volume. For example, if you find that the majority of your customers live in Chicago, you could add a product category to your offering that would appeal specifically to those Chicago residents. Alternatively, you could add content to your site that would appeal to those visitors. Coupons for local attractions are one option; creating a partnership with a local merchant is another. Knowing where your customers reside gives you additional options for expanding that customer base.

Product Key-Word Correlation

Customers who buy online usually know what they want, at least in general terms, before they begin shopping. For the customer, it's just a matter of finding the best deal online. And that search usually starts in a search engine or a product-specific search service like Froogle.com.

If you want your potential customers to be able to find your products, you need to have access to the key-word marketing capabilities available in today's marketing world. Programs like Google's AdWords and Yahoo's key-word marketing program make it possible for you to use key words to drive customers to your products.

Key-word marketing has been covered throughout this book, but now is where you get to see the payoff from all of your previous efforts with key words and key-word reports. The Product Keyword Correlation report, shown in Figure 24-5, links product purchases to the key-word search used to find the product.

For example, if a user searching for widgets was directed to your site through a key-word ad and consequently purchased widgets from your site, that sale would be linked to the user's original search for widgets.

This information provides insight into which products you should be promoting in creative ad content and landing pages to drive the most business through the site. It can then be used to maximize your key-word marketing efforts.

Additional information about the key-words search can be found by clicking the plus sign (+) next to any key-word entry.

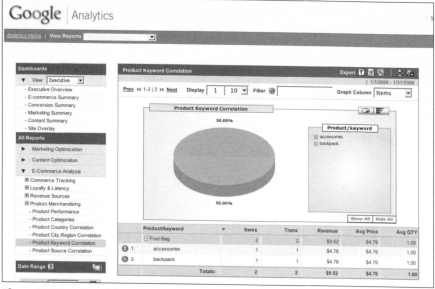

Figure 24-5: Use this report to tell which key words drive the most sales, by product.

Product Source Correlation

In previous chapters, we've defined *source* as the link or advertisement that leads visitors to your site. Now it's time to look at the purchases those users make once they come to your site. But linking the source to the sales provides additional information on how your marketing and advertising efforts are working.

The Product Source Correlation report, shown in Figure 24-6, illustrates how sources relate to sales.

Say you're running a small ad in a newsletter targeted to working mothers and when the visitors who click through that ad come to your site, they consistently purchase an organizational book that you sell through your site. This report would link the sales of that book to the number of times users who clicked that ad made purchases. You can then use that information to target those users more effectively.

One way to do that would be to offer a discount coupon, available only to readers of that newsletter, for the organizational book. Another way might be to develop an article that features organization tips and recommends the book. You could then offer the article to the newsletter, free of charge. The result should be increased sales from that specific audience.

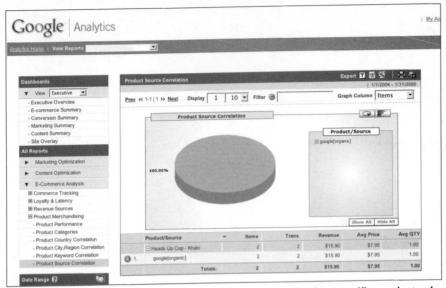

Figure 24-6: This report shows which referral sources lead to specific product sales.

Linking your product sales to the sources that referred those visitors to your site opens marketing doors and makes it possible to reach out to customers you might otherwise never be able to reach. In fact, that's the purpose of all of the reports in the Product Merchandising section — to provide information about how your products and services sell when ad placements, page placements, and geographic regions are taken into consideration.

With this information, as with much of the information supplied by Google Analytics, you can improve your marketing techniques and increase your sales. And just as with the other capabilities in Analytics, you don't necessarily have to have an e-commerce site to take advantage of these measurements. You just need to assign a value to the various goals you have in place. Then, when it all comes together, you still have access to all of the capabilities that Google Analytics has to offer.

Index